Resilience

Books by Eric Greitens

STRENGTH AND COMPASSION:
Photographs and Essays

THE HEART AND THE FIST:
The Education of a Humanitarian, the Making of a Navy SEAL

THE WARRIOR'S HEART:
Becoming a Man of Compassion and Courage

RESILIENCE:
Hard-Won Wisdom for Living a Better Life

Resilience

HARD-WON
WISDOM FOR LIVING
A BETTER LIFE

Eric Greitens

HOUGHTON MIFFLIN HARCOURT
Boston · New York 2015

For information about permission to reproduce selections from this
book, write to Permissions, Houghton Mifflin Harcourt Publishing
Company, 215 Park Avenue South, New York, New York 10003.

www.hmhco.com

Library of Congress Cataloging-in-Publication Data
Greitens, Eric, date.
Resilience : hard-won wisdom for living a better life / Eric Greitens.
p. cm.
ISBN 978-0-544-32398-8 (hardback) — ISBN 978-0-544-32399-5 (ebook)
1. Resilience (Personality trait) 2. Life skills. 3. Self-help techniques.
I. Title.
BF698.35.R47G743 2015
155.2'4 — dc23
2014035279

Book design by Patrick Barry

ILLUSTRATION CREDITS
Page 127: *The Veteran in a New Field,* 1865, by Winslow Homer.
Photo by DeAgostini/Getty Images. Page 174: *Dempsey and Firpo,* 1924,
by George Wesley Bellows. Photo by Universal Images Group/
Getty Images. Used with permission of the Bellows Trust.

Printed in the United States of America
DOC 10 9 8 7 6 5 4 3 2 1

To Sheena

Contents

Note to the Reader

When I saw Zach Walker's number come up on my phone, my heart sank a little. It was late and dark and I was flying down the highway in the middle of Missouri, and I assumed that he was calling to tell me that another of our friends—a classmate from our Basic Underwater Demolition/SEAL training class, BUD/S 237—had been killed.

Walker and I were in the same training class in 2001 and 2002 in Southern California. We'd shared a lot together, served together, and suffered together.

After graduation, he went to the East Coast and I stayed on the West Coast. I saw him for a few minutes in 2004. Walker was back from Afghanistan, working in the training cadre, and I ran into him when he came to San Diego for a few days of maritime operations training. It was a busy day—we were both running in different directions—and except for those few minutes, I hadn't seen Walker in eleven years.

It wasn't bad news about one of our friends, and for that I was grateful. But Walker was calling me for help. And that wasn't what I was expecting.

In a class of tough guys, Walker was one of the toughest. A kid from a Northern California logging family, he was the kind of guy who— even standing in formation, clean-shaven, in a pressed uniform and spit-shined boots—still seemed as if he was wearing a beard and had just run out of the woods covered in mud and blood after wrestling a mountain lion. It's not that he was dirty in any way—just that you couldn't shine the tough out of him.

Walker was also the kind of guy who would do anything for someone he loved. People like to say that a lot: "He'd give you the shirt off his back" or "He'd run through a brick wall for you." Walker wasn't quite like that. If you really needed a shirt, he'd climb over a brick wall, rip a shirt off of some pompous ass, climb back over the wall, and give you the shirt you deserved and, he had decided, the other poor bastard didn't. He was motivated by a deep sense of justice. He wanted to know what was fair, what was right. And he was willing to fight for it.

What was also true of Walker — and was true of most of the guys in my class — was that he could have lived quite happily two hundred or even two thousand years ago. He had a truck, but didn't need it. He had boots, but could have gotten on fine in bare feet. And it's not just that he was capable of living without modern luxuries, it was also that, even for a guy in his twenties, he had a moral sensibility with an air of the ancient. He believed in courage. He believed in action. He believed in loyalty.

If you've ever thought, "If I was ever in a really tight spot, I could call . . . ," I hope you have someone in your life like Zach Walker.

He told me how bad things had gotten for him.

After six years in the SEAL teams, he went home to Northern California. By then he had a wife and a son. He bought a concrete pumper and started a business. He helped people out around town. He raised his boy. He looked, to all outward appearances, to be fine.

One day he pulled into his driveway. He stepped out of his truck and dropped to the ground. A sniper had an eye on his position, or so he thought, and Walker lay prone next to his truck, breathing slowly in, slowly out. He moved not at all, but for the blink of his eyelids. Hours later, as the sun began to set, he sprang to his feet and bolted into the house.

Walker is a guy who shouldn't drink. He almost never could stop at one beer, and even after one, you might find him on the pub patio, standing on a chair and making a speech. Later you'd hear a thrown bottle crash on the concrete as he emphasized a point. He was a guy who almost always listened intently — maybe too intently — to what was going on around him. But you put one beer in him and he went deaf.

A few weeks after he landed back home a hero, his brother Ed drove his truck into a tree. Ed was drunk when he killed himself. Walker, a guy who always made connections, began to wonder: *Did Ed die as punishment for what I did in Afghanistan?*

Home now, and his brother dead, he started to drink more. True to form, Walker did little in moderation. Sitting in his backyard on the weekend, he'd go through not a case but a cooler full of beer.

Then he told me about the night he got arrested. You know how when a good friend starts a story and, five words in, you can tell where it's going? This wouldn't be good. He was downtown. He'd been drinking in a restaurant. He sees his wife pull up and he walks out to get some money from her. A police officer asks him to hold on a second. Walker says he's just going to get some money from his wife to pay his bill. He points at her in the car. The officer grabs Walker by the shoulder. And here it gets messy.

They get the cuffs on Walker. Blood is trickling down his face, and he asks in drunken clarity, "Can we talk for a minute about what's going on here?" No. They put him in the patrol car. They charge him with a felony: resisting arrest. Walker is confused. He's been drinking, sure. But what has he done wrong?

His docs at the VA diagnose him with post-traumatic stress disorder. But they don't prescribe exercise or community service. They do prescribe a raft of pills.

What's going to happen in court? Walker was in the wrong. He's apologetic. But that's not worth a lot. And the truth is, if it wasn't this incident with the cops, it would have been something else. Maybe drinking and driving. Maybe he would have killed himself behind the wheel like his brother. Or worse, maybe he would have killed someone else. All things considered, there's only one man at fault here, and it's Walker. Now the war-hero dad is an unemployed alcoholic on disability who looks as if he's on his way to jail.

We talk.

For a few years I'd had a bunch of thoughts — based on my humanitarian work overseas, my time in the military, and my work with veterans — about how people move through hardship to happiness, through pain to wisdom, through suffering to strength. Our phone call brought them to the surface.

It was late when I got home, but when I did, I put some of those thoughts in a letter to Walker. He wrote back. One letter followed another. We talked a lot. We kept writing.

This book is an edited set of those letters. They are letters to my friend. But while his story is unique, what he's up against — loss, fear, a search for purpose — is not. In fact, what he's up against is universal. So, with my friend's blessing — but with his name changed to protect his privacy — I've collected these letters on resilience in the hope that they might benefit you too.

Your Frontline

Walker,

You told me you cleared your house last week. You got up around 0300, grabbed a pistol, and went from room to room, closet to closet, crevice to crevice, checking . . . for what, you weren't sure.

Nobody was in the house, of course.

You've been doing that a couple of times a month. You've been waking up in puddles of sweat. It would be tempting — very tempting — to imagine that you're just having bad dreams. It would be even more tempting to slap a medical diagnosis on what's going on and to let some doctor pump you full of pills.

But you are my friend, and it's not some nightmare memory of war that's really the problem, and you know it.

The problems at night may have a little to do with the past, but they have a lot more to do with what you are choosing to do in the present.

You're home now, and for the first time in your life, you don't know what you're aiming at. You tried the concrete business. It went well for a while and then blew up.

Before, you'd been a Navy SEAL. You were one of the world's elite commandos. You rolled out of bed every day with a sense of purpose, a meaningful mission in front of you, and a team around you. You could walk with your head held high. Now you've been diagnosed with a disorder, you're unemployed, you're surrounded by friends like the marine who is talking about "painting the ceiling with his brains," and all the while you're passing the weekends with your cooler full of beer. You didn't call me until you'd been arrested, and now you're looking at the prospect of having your kids come visit you in jail.

So what do you do?

As a Navy SEAL, you understood the word "frontline" to mean the place where you met the enemy.

The frontline was where battles were fought and fates decided. The frontline was a place of fear, struggle, and suffering. It was also a place where victories were won, where friendships of a lifetime were forged in hardship. It was a place where we lived with a sense of purpose.

But "frontline" isn't just a military term. You have a frontline in your life now. In fact, everyone has a place where they encounter fear, where they struggle, suffer, and face hardship. We all have battles to fight.

And it's often in those battles that we are most alive: it's on the frontlines of our lives that we earn wisdom, create joy, forge friendships, discover happiness, find love, and do purposeful work. If you want to win any meaningful kind of victory, you'll have to fight for it.

We did a lot of hard stuff together. We also had a lot of fun. This'll be the same. You have a lot more to do than read a letter: you have to raise two children (with a third on the way), find direction in your life, support your family. You have some day-after-day, hard-sweating work in front of you. My hope is that if I put some of these thoughts on paper, they'll help you on this new frontline.

And before we start, I want you to know that you are one of the best people I've ever known. I'm not telling you that to blow smoke or to puff you up if you're reading this late at night and are feeling down. I'm telling you because I love you, and if somebody has a better heart or a deeper devotion to friends and family than you, I haven't met him. You inspired me when we were in training, and you've motivated me to write down these thoughts. Your wife is lucky to have you as a husband, your kids are lucky to have you as a father, and I am lucky to have you as a friend.

I'm disappointed that you aren't living as fully as you can. I'm disappointed that all of your gifts — your tough energy, your street-smart, solid intelligence, your kind heart, your vision, your belief in the power of other people — have been lying fallow for too long. The world is a poorer place because you aren't fully in it.

The world needs what you have to offer. But because you've been wrestling with these demons and have been churned and turned and knocked around by your own pain—by the resistance that you've put in your own path—we're all weaker for it. And that, my friend, is bull. You're capable of more than you're living right now.

I'm hoping that as we knock these letters back and forth, they'll help you turn the pain you experience into the strength, wisdom, and joy you deserve.

It's all about resilience.

Resilience is the virtue that enables people to move through hardship and become better. No one escapes pain, fear, and suffering. Yet from pain can come wisdom, from fear can come courage, from suffering can come strength—if we have the virtue of resilience.

People have known this for thousands of years. But today a lot of this ancient wisdom goes unheeded.

In my work with other veterans who have overcome injuries and loss—the loss of limbs, the loss of comrades, the loss of purpose—I have heard one thing over and over again: their moments of darkness often led, in time, to their days of greatest growth.

You can be tough on civilians, on people who "don't understand" what you've been through. But the battlefield isn't the only place where people suffer. Hardship hits in a million places. And lots of people, including your neighbors, have suffered more than any soldier, and they've done so with none of your training, with no unit around them, with no hospital to care for them, and sometimes with no community to support them.

And when those people reflect on their suffering, they often uncover a similar truth: that struggle helped them to build deep reservoirs of strength.

Not all growth happens this way. But a great deal of our growth does come when we put our shoulder into what's painful. We choose to, or have to, step beyond the margins of our past experience and do something hard and new.

Of course fear does not automatically lead to courage. Injury does not necessarily lead to insight. Hardship will not automatically make us better.

Pain can break us or make us wiser. Suffering can destroy us or make us stronger. Fear can cripple us, or it can make us more courageous.

It is resilience that makes the difference.

When people try to help other people, they often promise that they have "new secrets" based on some revolutionary trick or the "latest scientific research." It's true that current science has confirmed centuries-old insights into resilience. But I don't have any such promises. In fact, the only thing I can promise you is that these letters will be imperfect.

Some of what I'll share with you are old insights, often from people who lived in another time altogether. I'll also share a few stories from my own battles and from the great teachers and role models I met along the way. The insights are often old because resilience is a virtue as old as human existence. Since the beginning of recorded history, people have recognized it as essential to human flourishing. For at least three thousand years, people have been thinking and learning about how we become resilient — how we make ourselves, our children, our families, our units, and our communities stronger and wiser as we move through pain and hardship.

A lot of this, then, will strike you as common sense. But that's the nature of common sense: it's built from ideas that have stood time's test. These ideas are accessible to all of us, and they live from one generation to the next.

What worked for us in the SEAL teams, what works for Olympic athletes, what worked for the Greeks two thousand five hundred years ago — much of it is the same stuff, directed at the same human questions. How do you focus your mind, control your stress, and excel under pressure? How do you work through fear and build courage? How do you overcome defeat and rise above obstacles? How do you adapt to adversity?

These are universal questions. Everyone has to answer them. We answer them with practical wisdom, and that wisdom surrounds us. It is embedded in our language, our art, our literature, our philosophy, our history, our religion. But in an age of distraction, we've lost touch with practical wisdom. Our wealth of common sense fails to become common practice.

* * *

Two thousand five hundred years ago, a soldier-poet wrote this:

> Even in our sleep, pain that cannot forget
> falls drop by drop upon the heart,
> and in our own despite, against our will,
> comes wisdom to us by the awful grace of God.

— AESCHYLUS

Aeschylus was an Athenian soldier who fought at the battle of Marathon. At Marathon, he and his fellow citizens — the elite troops of their day — repelled the greatest foreign invasion that Greece had ever seen. When Aeschylus wrote about pain — the hard life of a soldier, or the anguish of those he leaves behind — he wrote from experience. Listen to these words he put into the mouth of a Greek soldier just returned from ten years of war:

> Our beds right up against the enemy walls.
> Rain from the sky, dew from the ground soaking us perpetually,
> rotting our clothes, filling our hair with vermin.
> I could tell you stories of winter so cold it killed the birds in the air.

Hard beds, soaked clothing, hair full of vermin — Aeschylus did not have to learn about them from a book. He lived them. He did not romanticize what it meant to go to war because he had been to war. Aeschylus knew what it meant to live on the frontline.

He knew, in other words, that life is not easy and never has been. And just as he was unwilling to glorify war, he was unwilling to romanticize what it means to grow in wisdom. He knew how much it cost. And he believed the cost worth paying.

Aeschylus knew — and you and I have to remind ourselves and teach our children — that human beings can turn hardship into wisdom because we are born with the capacity for resilience, and we can make ourselves more resilient through practice.

To be resilient — to build a full and meaningful life of strength, wisdom, and joy — is not easy. But it's not complicated. We can all do it. To get there, it's not enough to want to be resilient or to think about being resilient. We have to choose to live a resilient life.

* * *

When we're struggling, we don't need a book in our hands. We need the right words in our minds. When things are tough, a mantra does more good than a manifesto.

I'm going to try to divide each letter into brief thoughts. And I'm going to try to divide each thought further still until we get to some tightly wound common sense that can be easily carried.

And on that note, if you find anything of value here, make it yours. The value isn't that a particular person said it or wrote it, but that you can *use* it.

So scribble notes in the margins. Underline. Highlight. Write down where you disagree and write me back. Think about your own life as you read.

The point, after all, is not just to read. The point is to read in a way that leads to better thinking, and to think in a way that leads to better living.

And because you're my friend, there's one thing I want to share with you before we start down this path. It's relevant to our friendship, and relevant also to what we are trying to do now.

You know that when we were going through BUD/S, the most grueling part of SEAL training, I was married. You may not know that by the time you saw me in San Diego I was divorced.

Things weren't going well when I was in BUD/S, and after a brutal day of training, I often tried to race home and set things straight. I still feel guilty about that. I think I could have been a better officer in BUD/S if I hadn't felt the panicked pull of home the way I did then. Sometimes my mind just wasn't right. I'm sorry about that.

I won't bore you with all the unhappy details here, but on Christmas, 2002, I came home to an empty house and just collapsed. Thank God for work. I'd get out of bed, get a uniform on, and get in on time. When I came home, I'd often fall straight into bed, and for the life of me I couldn't get out of it until the next morning.

Trash piled up in the kitchen. The dishes went unwashed. I never seriously thought about killing myself, but I was so ashamed. When I look back on that year of my life . . . there's almost nothing there.

In time, I found some good in that experience. In a very practical way, it made me a better officer and a better leader. When I had a guy wake me up in the middle of the night in the Philippines because his wife said she was leaving him, or when one of my guys in Iraq had a kid diagnosed with autism back home — well, I think I understood better what they were facing, and I hope that helped me to be of more help to them.

Now a husband and a father, I think I'm more solid and more grateful in ways I might not have been had I never been hurt so badly.

On a deeper, maybe you'd call it a more spiritual, level, the whole experience made me more empathetic. I'd seen a lot of tragedy before that time. I'd worked with refugees in Bosnia and Rwanda, with slum dwellers in India, with children of the street in Bolivia, with kids who'd been hit by land mines in Cambodia. I think I was compassionate before, and I'd always tried to be understanding. Yet even after being so close to misery in so many different places, on some level I still thought of most people's struggles as man against the world, rather than man against the self. But when you're in bed and not tired and it's bright outside and you can't seem to get your feet on the floor, you start to see that a lot of our most important battles are the ones we fight for self-mastery.

Now, in comparison with what so many other people have suffered, I find it a little embarrassing that something like this knocked me down so hard and kept me on my ass for so long. But there it is.

Other things have been hard. I've lost fights, some of them physical. Like you, I've lost friends. I've failed dozens of times to be the leader, friend, husband, son, cousin, boss, and brother that I know I can be. But for all of that, I don't know that I've ever been knocked down as hard as the day I walked into that empty apartment and collapsed on the floor.

I wouldn't wish that on anyone. But in retrospect, I can see some good in it. It's made me stronger and better in a dozen ways.

I've been fortunate in other ways as well. I've been able to learn from great examples of resilience: refugees who survived genocide, other Navy SEALs who endured the hardest military training in the world, wounded veterans who have rebuilt purposeful lives in the face of devastating wounds. The things I talk about in these letters are strategies I've used in my own life, strategies I've seen others use, and I know how much they can help.

We all need resilience to live a fulfilling life. With resilience, you'll be more prepared to take on challenges, to develop your talents, skills, and abilities so that you can live with more purpose and more joy.

I hope something here can help you to become stronger. I look forward to walking with you on this path.

Why Resilience?

*Of all the virtues we can learn, no trait is more useful,
more essential for survival, and more likely to improve the
quality of life than the ability to transform adversity into an
enjoyable challenge.*

— MIHALY CSIKSZENTMIHALYI

Walker,

Resilience is the key to a well-lived life. If you want to be happy, you need resilience. If you want to be successful, you need resilience. You need resilience because you can't have happiness, success, or anything else worth having without meeting hardship along the way.

To master a skill, to build an enterprise, to pursue any worthy endeavor — simply to live a good life — requires that we confront pain, hardship, and fear. What is the difference between those who are defeated by hardship and those who are sharpened by it? Between those who are broken by pain and those who are made wiser by it?

To move through pain to wisdom, through fear to courage, through suffering to strength, requires resilience.

The benefits of struggling — of being challenged, afraid, pained, confused — are so precious that if they could be bottled, people would pay dearly for them.

But they can't be bottled. And if you want the wisdom, the strength, the clarity, the courage that can come from struggle, the price is clear: you have to endure the struggle first.

— 2 —

You bear your struggles. And because they are borne by you, they can feel pressing and heavy to you in a way that they are for no one else.

But you have to remember that while they are *yours,* they are not unique. Your struggles are very much like the struggles of those who went before you, and they are very much like the struggles of those who will come after you. Every human being from the beginning of time has suffered pain and hardship, difficulty and doubt.

And in the record of mankind's struggles our forebears have left clues in stories and philosophies and poems and plays and paintings and songs.

I like the way Nietzsche put it: look at those works "as experimental laboratories in which ... recipes for the art of living have been thoroughly practiced and lived to the hilt. The results of all their experiments belong to us, as our legitimate property."

All of this wisdom belongs to us. It doesn't belong to experts or professional scholars or people who spend their days reading books. It belongs to any one of us who is willing to go out and get it.

This wisdom comes from Aeschylus and Aristotle and Homer and Confucius and Montaigne and many more. It's in the Psalms and in ancient Greek tragic plays. I'm drawing on them not because wisdom becomes wiser when it has a famous name attached to it, but because these people came by their wisdom the way the rest of us do: by acting in the world, by struggling, and by reflecting on their struggles.

They fought, worried, prayed, got involved in politics, scraped to find work, lost people they loved, got sick, got injured, tried not to fear death. If the wisdom they brought back from their struggles was extraordinary, the struggles themselves were ordinary — your basic rubber-meets-the-road stuff of life. It's not too different from what you've been through, Walker.

I can't speak for Aeschylus or Epictetus or Aristotle. But I am convinced of this: they would have hated having their wisdom confined to classrooms and textbooks. This is wisdom about how to *live.* And it's your property as much as anyone's. It is yours. Take it. Use it.

* * *

"Culture" was originally a word for the tilling and tending of the land. Later, people made an analogy and suggested that you could *cultivate yourself.* So culture also came to mean the things that you could see, listen to, read, learn, try, and practice in order to make yourself better and to live a fuller life. A great scholar wrote that "the desire for culture is innate." We all want to touch and taste and hear and see the things that can make our lives richer.

One of the things that was most striking to me in the military was how many very smart people had been made to feel dumb as they became adults. At some point in their lives they'd tried to cultivate their minds and found a giant stop sign reading *You're Not Smart Enough to Enter Here.* Their response was, "Well, then screw you." And the absurd result was that they walked around mouthing abstract grudges against "professors" or "book learning" or "colleges," and all the while they've got a book of Seamus Heaney's poems next to their rack, stashed under a stack of porn.

We can do better. Everyone can learn. We can all cultivate our character. People of action require a sound mind and a strong will as much as a healthy body. "Any nation that draws too great a distinction between its scholars and its warriors will have its thinking done by cowards and its fighting done by fools."

We all need courage *and* wisdom. Compassion *and* strength. We don't look back because life was better in the time of Aeschylus. In fact, in almost every way, life is better today. But to realize the potential of the present, we need to heed the wisdom of the past.

Whatever struggle we have gone through remains, at heart, a human struggle. When we see our struggles in the stories of those who have gone before us, we feel less alone. We begin to see that there are sources of wisdom all around us.

When we first talked, I told you to get a copy of Homer's *Odyssey.* Along with the *Iliad,* it's the first piece of literature in the Western world. It tells of the journey of a man coming home from war: the beasts that threaten him, the women who tempt him, the gods who curse him, the suitors who plague his house, the friends he meets along the way.

I've never seen anyone more moved by the *Odyssey* than my friend Mike, who served with me in Iraq. When Mike came home to a life without purpose and without direction, one of his friends committed suicide. Mike picked up Homer, and he discovered that, as long as there has been war, warriors have found the journey home, the journey back to normal, as trying as battle itself.

People have walked this path for thousands of years. They've earned wisdom, and it's waiting for you.

— 3 —

At the same time, we have to be clear about what you can and can't expect from a guy like Homer. Homer wrote the *Odyssey* about Odysseus's struggle. There's a lot you can learn from it, but you aren't a Greek soldier coming home from Troy on a wooden warship. Homer can offer you insight, perspective, reflection. But you are going to have to live your answer to your own life.

You know how, at the end of a book or a magazine article about training, the author sometimes lays out a sample training plan that tells you how many miles to run each day and what kinds of exercises to perform? Well, there's no training program at the end of the *Odyssey.* And there'll be no training program here.

Sometimes I'll suggest and even insist on specific exercises that we might do. But since I've been home, I've learned from working with hundreds of veterans that no one can build your resilience for you. I can point you in a certain direction, maybe draw you a map and give you some ideas. I can't carry you where you need to go.

For this to work, you're going to have to take what you learn and build your own program for your own life. No one can do that for you.

When Aristotle gave his great talks on the nature of the good life, which were collected as the *Nicomachean Ethics,* he began by making one thing clear: there is no simple equation for the good life. The discussion can only be as precise as the subject matter allows.

Aristotle's students were asking for rules, formulas, guarantees. He told them there was no such thing: "We shall be satisfied to indicate the truth roughly and in outline, since our subject and our premises are things that hold good *usually* . . . The educated person seeks exactness in each area to the extent that the nature of the subject allows."

Math is a subject that allows for precision. If I ask you "What's seven times seven?" you know the exact answer: forty-nine.

But what if I ask you "How do you deal with fear?"

Life — and the subject of resilience — rarely allows for perfect precision. Real life is messy. Attacking your fear can lead to courage, but there is no equation for courage, no recipe for courage. It gets mixed up with anger and anxiety, with love and panic.

This isn't an excuse for sloppy thinking: the virtues have been the subject of rigorous, disciplined thought from before Aristotle to today. But when the question is "How do we live a resilient life?" we also have to be ready to accept ambiguity and uncertainty.

There are strategies for dealing with fear and pain. There are strategies for building a life rooted in purposeful work. There are strategies for building a home that is happy even when things are hard. But the strategies won't reach into your life and resolve *your* fear or *your* pain. You have to live your answer.

And look, Walker, nobody's ever going to hand you a prize for resilience. There is no certificate. No T-shirt. (And don't even think about a tattoo.) There will be no line to mark the point in your life at which you "got" resilience.

With resilience, you and I are not in search of an achievement, but a way of being.

Remember all of this when you go to live your own answer. You demand a lot from yourself. In this case, you're going to need to be patient, even kind to yourself.

You won't be able to judge most of what you do by a standard of imperfect or perfect. Usually our standard will simply be worse or better.

But better sounds good, doesn't it?

— 4 —

A masterful warrior carries everything she needs and no more, just as a masterful painter uses all of the paint that she needs and no more, and a master chef uses all of the ingredients that she needs and no more. In the same way, a masterful philosopher will use all of the words that she needs and no more.

I am not a mountain climber, but a few years ago I had the idea that I might want to climb seriously, so I started to read and to train. I've climbed a few glacier-covered mountains in the northwestern United States with professionals. One of the things that you learn from professional climbers is the discipline of packing well.

Tools are helpful when you climb. Your sleeping bag provides warmth, your lantern provides light, and your gloves provide protection. Lose your footing and your ax can save your life. Every tool has a purpose, and almost any tool can be helpful.

Every tool also has weight.

Standing at sea level, an ax in your hand feels like a feather. At twelve thousand feet, hours from the summit, an extra pound in your pack feels like an anvil.

In the same way, words have value. The right words can right your balance. The right words can light your way. But words also have weight. In our life and work, we have to carry what is essential, and leave much of the rest behind.

In these letters I've tried to strip these thoughts to their bare essentials. You'll decide which ones are worth packing for your journey.

— 5 —

One of the most famous scholars of the ancient world — and, I think, one of the most insightful — was Edith Hamilton. This passage is from her to you. "When the world is storm-driven and the bad that happens and the worse that threatens are so urgent as to shut out everything else from view, then we need to know all the strong fortresses of the spirit which men have built through the ages. The eternal perspectives are being blotted out, and our judgment of immediate issues will go wrong unless we bring them back."

I want to call your attention to one of Hamilton's phrases: "fortresses of the spirit." Cut off from the wisdom of the past, we can feel overwhelmed by the incessant clatter of the present. But look: those who went before us left us a gift.

— 6 —

A truly new and original book would be one which made people love old truths.

— MARQUIS DE VAUVENARGUES (1715–1747)

One of the good things about BUD/S, about training in and around the ocean, about having to swim fifty meters underwater or having someone rip your mask from your face and turn off your tanks when you are swimming deep, is that it gives you a healthy appreciation for oxygen.

Surrounded by oxygen, we rarely notice it, though we desperately need it. At a moment of exhaustion, we take a long, deep breath and we feel better. Try it now. True?

The same can be said for wisdom. We are surrounded by an abundance of wisdom that, if not as close as air, is almost as accessible.

Seneca was a Roman philosopher who wrote down his thoughts on living in letters to his friend Lucilius. The problem, Seneca was told, was that a lot of his advice was, well, obvious.

Seneca had a great response: "People say: 'What good does it do to point out the obvious?' A great deal of good; for we sometimes know facts without paying attention to them. Advice . . . merely engages the attention and rouses us, and concentrates the memory, and keeps it from losing its grip. We miss much that is set before our eyes."

If a piece of wisdom has survived for generations — if it has helped make sense of lives separated by vast distances of time and space — that's a sign that it *works*. The new has no special claim on the true. As you read through these letters, you'll find that I haven't "uncovered" a secret formula or "revealed" a hidden way. Instead, I'm just trying to direct your attention to the wisdom about resilience that is already all around us.

— 7 —

So now, step back with me for a minute as I try to explain what we're doing here together.

These letters, the back-and-forth, the discussions, this is philosophy.

Today we think of philosophy as something that happens in a classroom and nowhere else. We think of philosophy as a discipline of sitting and thinking, reading and arguing. But there was a time when philosophy was more than just talk.

During the Golden Age of Greece, philosophers were less interested in sitting and thinking. They were more interested in thinking and living. As a practical matter, the Greeks usually did not "read" philosophy in the way that you are reading this letter — silently and to yourself. Reading philosophy meant reading aloud to others; practicing philosophy meant living in a community.

The emphasis was not on the words alone, but on the effect of the words. Did a philosopher help people to examine their lives? Did that examination lead to happiness, to flourishing, to meaning? If it did, it worked. If it didn't, then it didn't matter how clever the words were.

Of the ancients who practiced this kind of life, one of my favorites is Epictetus, who started life as a slave and ended it as the wisest philosopher of his day. Here's what he told his students about what they were trying to do together: "A carpenter does not come up to you and say, 'Listen to me discourse about the art of carpentry,' but he makes a contract for a house and builds it . . . Do the same thing yourself. Eat like a man, drink like a man . . . get married, have children, take part in civic life, learn how to put up with insults, and tolerate other people."

The test of a philosophy is simple: does it lead people to live better lives? If not, the philosophy fails. If so, it succeeds. Philosophy used to mean developing ideas about a life worth living, and then living that life. It still can.

The intention in reading and thinking and living this way is not so much to build an argument as it is to open a door. There is no fancy talk here, nothing that requires any specialized knowledge to understand. Philosophy can be done in what my high school English teacher Barbara Osburg used to call "simple nickel words."

Philosophy should speak to the worries of ordinary people. And good philosophy—hard, clear thinking—will address ordinary things in an insightful way. It will show us new possibilities for living.

— 8 —

The question is not whether you have a philosophy. Everyone has a philosophy. Some people live the philosophy, "I'm going to accumulate as much money as I can before I die." Some people live the philosophy, "I've gotten good at one thing, and I don't want to try anything new." Some people live the philosophy, "I'm going to keep my head down and not upset anyone."

Of course, when you spell it out like that, a philosophy can look a little ridiculous. But that's the point—we learn a lot about the philosophies we're living if we spell them out. Ridiculous philosophies, dishonest philosophies, destructive philosophies have their tightest hold on us when they're invisible.

Then there are philosophies that work, that produce what they're supposed to produce: real happiness. Thoreau said that the best philosophies "solve some of the problems of life, not only theoretically, but practically." We can tell a philosophy is working, he said, if it produces "a life of simplicity, independence, magnanimity, and trust."

The question is, are you aware of the philosophy you have—the assumptions, beliefs, and ideas that drive your actions? Are you aware of the way those assumptions, beliefs, and ideas add up to shape your life? Can they stand exposure to the light of day?

— 9 —

The worst form of stress is an absence of stress, because
the feeling that there is no life before death gives rise to a
despairing feeling of emptiness in the face of the void.

— BORIS CYRULNIK

There are a few things that human beings must do to live well: breathe, sleep, drink, eat, and love. To this list I'd add: struggle. We need challenges to master and problems to solve.

If we are trapped in a life where everything is provided for us, our minds fail to grow, our relationships atrophy, and our spirits deteriorate.

We can last only a few weeks without food, only a few days without sleep or water, only a few minutes without oxygen. Without oxygen, sleep, water, and food, our minds and bodies begin to break down. If we go without any of these for too long, we die.

I believe it's also true that without some sense of meaningful struggle in our lives, something inside us begins to break down, a part of us begins to die. Yet it's amazing how adaptable human beings can be. When we are kept from doing hard and meaningful work (perhaps by living in a prison of idle comfort, by drinking to excess, or by spending endless hours in front of video games or the Internet), people still find ways to eke out an existence. In the long run, though, deprivation of purpose is as destructive as deprivation of sleep. Without purpose, we can survive—but we cannot flourish.

When I was twenty, I lived and worked in a Bosnian refugee camp.

All the refugees had seen brutality and destruction. They had lost everything they ever owned. Many had lost friends and family. And now they were trapped in a camp, living in shacks, feeding on bread and rumors. Everyone suffered. Because I was young, there was a lot that I probably didn't see accurately, and there was certainly a lot that I didn't know. But I was struck by one thing. It seemed that the people who were doing best in the camp were often the parents and grandparents of very young children. They knew that they had to wake up every day and be strong for someone else.

The people who had the hardest time were the young adults and older teenagers. They felt that their lives had been cut short. They woke up every day with no prospects for a job or for school. Marriage seemed to make little sense. I remember them at a party in the camp's common room: downing their beers and then smashing the bottles on the concrete floor. The war had made them aimless, and aimlessness hurts.

The teenagers who were doing the best were often those who found something else to do. They volunteered in the kindergarten or coached the youngest kids as they played soccer.

The people who did the best, in other words, found a way to live for something at a time when a lot of people around them didn't know why they were alive at all.

Would you spend a weekend in the backyard with a cooler full of beer if you knew that your neighbors needed you? You told me yourself that when you started coaching you began to see more clearly and to live more cleanly. You need to be needed. Everyone does. You need a worthy struggle in your life.

And look, Walker, this isn't a problem just for refugees or for you. In the most prosperous moment in human history, tens of millions of people fail to flourish for lack of noble work to do, for lack of meaningful, hard, struggling engagement with the world.

We all need something to struggle against and to struggle for. The aim in life is not to avoid struggles, but to have the right ones; not to avoid worry, but to care about the right things; not to live without fear, but to confront worthy fears with force and passion.

One of the reasons you are suffering right now is precisely because the *purpose* of your struggle is unclear. What are you working toward? What are you fighting for? Who are you going to be?

These are big questions, and you can't answer them quickly or glibly.

But if you want to live a flourishing life, you will have to answer them. That's where philosophy can help.

What you will become is a result of what you are willing to endure. Are you willing to work hard? To think hard? I know that you are. You always have been.

What Is Resilience?

There are some things which cannot be learned quickly,
and time, which is all we have, must be paid heavily for
their acquiring.

— ERNEST HEMINGWAY

Walker,

I want to share a story written by a fellow veteran named Sophocles.

The Trojan War was the great war of the ancient Greek world, and at its beginning, thousands of warships set sail to assault the city of Troy. On the way, the Greeks stopped to rest on the island of Chryse. Sophocles wrote a play about what happened there, and about the struggles of a man named Philoctetes.

Philoctetes was a great archer, blessed with a magical bow that never missed its mark. But at Chryse, he stepped by accident onto ground that was sacred to the gods and a venomous snake bit his foot. His wound was no ordinary wound. It festered and rotted and gave off a smell so foul that other men could not stand to be near Philoctetes. His wound would not heal.

Odysseus ordered his men to row Philoctetes to a nearby deserted island and abandon him there. The army set sail for war. Over the next ten years, Philoctetes remained stranded on the island with a wound that never healed. The pain was unrelenting and at times so sharp that he lost consciousness.

Alone and forgotten, Philoctetes brooded over his wound and cursed his former friends.

In those same ten years, Odysseus and his warriors fought at Troy, but even after all of their struggle, the war remained at a stalemate. They consulted a prophet who predicted that the Greeks would remain powerless to win without Philoctetes and his weapon.

Odysseus and a select unit returned to the deserted island with a simple mission: get the bow and Philoctetes back. They found Philoctetes still wounded and bitter, and they begged him to sail with them to Troy.

Enraged by his abandonment, Philoctetes refuses to help. He wants only to go home to Greece, to be healed and left alone. At the moment Odysseus is about to give up, Heracles — once a hero and now a god — appears from the sky. He commands Philoctetes to fulfill his destiny:

> Be certain that to you too it is owed to suffer this —
> to make your life glorious after and through these labors.

Heracles tells Philoctetes that only if he lets go of his grudge and joins the Greeks at Troy can he be healed.

Philoctetes chooses. He and Odysseus set sail — and eventually, as the prophecy promised, the Trojan War was won.

Sophocles, who handed down this story, was more than a playwright. Like Aeschylus, his older countryman, Sophocles had known war. So had the people in his audiences. And when the Athenian audience came to hear the retelling of the story in their open-air theater at sunrise — the time when tragedies were traditionally performed — the spectators surely heard echoes of their own sacrifices, and of the wounds that they and those they loved had suffered.

The Athenians honored Sophocles for his ability to depict it all with such honesty. After one of his most popular plays, they elected him to the office of *strategos,* a very important post in Athens, which brought with it the responsibility of leading troops in battle.

Perhaps this was simply a vote for a celebrity. But perhaps it also reflected something deeper: the understanding that someone who could write with such wisdom about the hardships of war and the responsibilities of community could also lead with wisdom.

What is the wisdom in *Philoctetes,* a play Sophocles wrote toward the end of a long life? We cannot hope to be victorious if we abandon those who are wounded. As the poet Robert Bly wrote about this play, "The wounded man knows something." When Odysseus abandons Philoctetes, he abandons the very person he needs to win the war.

In *Philoctetes* we find a man who, despite his pain, still has something powerful to offer, something that will redeem his countrymen.

Sophocles's play is not a fairy tale; it's a complicated, messy work of art. But I take two things from it.

First, as a community, we cannot abandon our wounded. They still have something to offer — perhaps the very thing we need.

Second, our wounds and mistreatment — whether the ten-year abandonment of Philoctetes or the much smaller wounds of our lives — do not wipe out our obligation to serve. Being hurt by life does not diminish our duty to others. Even wounded and mistreated, we owe to others the labor that can make our lives glorious.

And keep in mind the one thing Philoctetes did during his ten years of pain: he stayed alive. Suicide isn't what warriors do, because the first purpose of the warrior is to protect others; suicide makes that impossible. In suicide, we take our pain, multiply it by ten, and hand it to everyone who loves us. What was hurting us becomes hell for them. There is something selfish about this.

This is hard to write, Walker. I've known some veterans who have committed suicide, and you've known a few too. I say this not because I want to criticize the dead, but because I want to help *you*. Suicide is not what warriors do.

— 2 —

There is only one road to true human greatness:
the road through suffering.

— ALBERT EINSTEIN

So, Walker, you remember in BUD/S when we all had to pass the Dive Physics test? Remember how a group of us used to stay back in the classroom and study, eating MREs while the rest of the class ran to lunch? At night we'd study in the barracks. A lot of guys were more afraid of the equations than they were of the ocean.

One of my proudest moments in BUD/S was when every person in our class passed the Dive Physics test. The instructors went back and checked the records. They couldn't find a class in BUD/S history that had ever done that.

So forgive the bragging. But I'm proud of that. We took something that looked complicated and made it simple so that all of our friends could be successful.

I want to dig up some physics again.

When people hear the word "resilience," they often think of "bouncing back." How many times have you heard that phrase?

And whether we know it or not, when we think "bouncing back," we're thinking physics. When Isaac Newton published his great work on mathematics and physics, the *Principia Mathematica,* in 1687, he did more than explain some of the fundamental laws of the universe. He also set off something of a physics fad: suddenly everyone wanted their thinking to be as logical, as precise, and as clear as Newton's. If there were laws that ruled the orbits of the planets, surely there had to be laws that explained the human mind, human actions, and human societies.

The problem is that most of life just isn't as black and white as Newtonian physics. And trying to treat human beings like variables in an equation leads to some bad thinking.

You can still see the influence of this hunger for the precision of physics if you look up "resilience" in the Merriam-Webster dictionary. One of the first definitions you'll find is this: "capability of a strained body to recover its size and shape after deformation, especially if the strain is caused by compressive stresses—called also *elastic resilience.*"

Resilience as elasticity. That's a physics definition, but when most people think of resilience as it applies to humans, they still have some variation of this definition in their minds. They think that resilience means "recovery" or "bouncing back" after stress. They think that resilient people are the same before and after hardship.

If we limit our understanding of resilience to this idea of bouncing back, we miss much of what hardship, pain, and suffering offer us. We also misunderstand our basic human capacity to change and improve.

Life's reality is that we cannot bounce back. We cannot bounce back because we cannot go back in time to the people we used to be. The parent who loses a child never bounces back. The nineteen-year-old marine who sails for war is gone forever, even if he returns. "What's done cannot be undone," and some of what life does to us is harsh.

You aren't going to be the same man you were before your brother died. Your parents aren't going to be the same parents. You know that there is no bouncing back. There is only moving through.

Fortunately, to be resilient we don't need to go back in time.

What happens to us becomes part of us. Resilient people do not bounce back from hard experiences; they find healthy ways to integrate them into their lives.

In time, people find that great calamity met with great spirit can create great strength.

Here's one other way that thinking about physics leads to sloppy thinking about life:

We know that physical objects in our lives tend to come to rest when they're overcome by friction. Strike a cue ball as hard as you want, and it still eventually putters to a stop. It's natural to think of ourselves in the same way, to imagine human beings as objects that eventually, even naturally, come to rest. And when we're *not* at rest — when we're struggling, agitated, anxious — we think that something must be wrong.

But in human life there is no state of rest. Children grow as they sleep. Our bodies — themselves host to tens of thousands of microscopic cells and other living organisms that live and die every day — are in a constant state of activity. At "rest," we are still aging; at "rest," our minds are organizing our memories. When we exercise, it's the period of recovery — time that looks like rest — in which our muscles grow stronger.

And what is true for us as individuals is true for our community, our country, our world. The forest does not rest, the sea does not rest. The ground beneath us is always moving, shifting, even if we are not aware of it. Your life moves forever in time.

So why this long discussion about rest?

Just to make this simple point: when pain hits you, it hits a moving target. And since you're already moving, what will change is not so much your state as your trajectory.

Don't expect a time in your life when you'll be free from change, free from struggle, free from worry. To be resilient, you must understand that your objective is not to come to rest, because there is no rest. Your objective is to use what hits you to change your trajectory in a positive direction.

—3—

In Cambodia, I watched girls who'd lost limbs to land mines walk miles on prosthetic legs. I saw young girls who were survivors of polio, whose legs were bent and weak and shriveled, stand up in orthotics and walk proudly. The disease hadn't taken their dignity or their determination.

Most of those girls came from families who lived on less than one dollar per day and were growing up in a culture where the disabled are often viewed as a burden. The world had hammered those girls with hardship, but they didn't make any excuses.

I read a little Hemingway in high school—*The Old Man and the Sea*, the short story "Hills Like White Elephants"—the usual stuff. At the end of college, a year or two before I went to Cambodia, I dove deep into Hemingway. I think I read everything he wrote. Everything. I read his famous novels and his bad novels. I even read his very bad poems. I read his books on hunting and bullfighting and war. I read the violence and the allusions to sex, and I liked the simple, direct, disciplined language that he used in his early work. I liked the way he wrote about food.

Like a lot of young guys, I was attracted to the macho in Hemingway, to the adventure. I can still picture one trout-fishing scene where a guy plunges his arm into an icy river. But the more I read and the older I got, what made Hemingway endure for me was his compassionate sense for the struggle in every good life. And when I saw those girls in Cambodia, it reminded me of this: "The world breaks every one and afterward many are strong at the broken places."

That line of Hemingway's is famous for good reason. What sticks in most people's minds is the phrase "strong at the broken places."

It's also important to remember his qualifier: many. Not all.

Not all of us are strong at the broken places. To be strong at the broken places is to be resilient. Being broken, by itself, does not make us better.

Hardship can create a helpless person or a heroic one. Some people are made stronger by suffering. Others are defeated. The difference is resilience. So now let's consider what separates those who are weakened by hardship from those who are strengthened by it.

— 4 —

Resilience begins with you, Walker. It would be easy to pass over this point too quickly.

Too often, when we talk about the challenges we face, that our children face, that our coworkers and colleagues and friends and fellow citizens face, we begin with a description of the world. We name and describe all the things that have contributed to our difficulties. What we usually overlook (or ignore) is what we have done to contribute to our situation. To put it another way, at the center of everything that happens to you is you.

So let's make an obvious point: *you* are the place you need to start if you want to become stronger in the face of adversity.

— 5 —

Resilience is distinct from mere survival, and more than mere endurance. Resilience is often endurance with direction. Where are you headed? Why are you going there?

No one, of course, can give you your "why." This letter certainly can't do that for you. You have to create your "why."

Start by asking yourself: Where am I headed?

It's not enough to *want* to be resilient. What do you want it for? What are you enduring for? Philoctetes spent ten years marinating in his pain, believing he had no direction. How many years will you spend marinating in yours?

And — I know you know this — you aren't a character in one of Sophocles's plays. Heracles isn't going to come down from the heavens, hand you a magic bow, and point you toward the right fight. Where are you heading now? Where do you want to head?

— 6 —

The first step to building resilience is to take responsibility for who you are and for your life. If you're not willing to do that, stop wasting your time reading this letter.

The essence of responsibility is the acceptance of the consequences — good and bad — of your actions. You are not responsible for everything that happens to you. You *are* responsible for how you deal with what happens to you.

Even when we recognize the limits of our own power to shape the world, we can still strive to be masters of ourselves. And that is more than enough work to fill a whole life.

History is full of those who have tried to escape the burdens of responsibility. At the extremes, some have even traded their freedom for obedience to tyrants. One of my favorite streetwise philosophers, Eric Hoffer, studied the reasons why people voluntarily give away responsibility and join mass movements and mobs. One quote he collected came from a young German who explained that he joined the Nazi party to be "free from freedom."

The desire to avoid responsibility can be overwhelming. That desire is so great that it has fed some of the greatest epochs of tyranny and acts of brutality the world has ever known. It is a desire so pervasive, so delicious, that tyrants have been able to rely on it in every era of human history. Responsibility is a heavy burden.

But responsibility also offers power. If we take responsibility for ourselves, we become not victims, but pioneers. The victim falls prey to fear and delights in blaming others. The pioneer forges his own path: more difficult, but much more rewarding.

So you ask yourself: Am I willing to take responsibility for my life, in word and in deed? If not, your chances of living a rich and fulfilling life are almost zero. If so, you have the potential for a joyous journey ahead.

— 7 —

Being resilient starts with a choice. Philoctetes must choose either to let his pain consume him or to find strength in his pain and serve a purpose larger than himself.

On all of our different frontlines, we will be faced with choices like this. We can choose the path of excuses. On this easy path, we soon find ourselves surrounded by the vultures that feed on excuses: blame, self-pity, whining, wallowing. It's a direction that leads to weakness, cowardice, and a miserly spirit. Excuses are incompatible with excellence.

The other path is to move through pain and hardship, fear and suffering, tragedy and trauma, so that we grow wiser and stronger. I know there are times when you've chosen that path. In the face of pain, you've asked: Will this break me or make me stronger? Will I get back up? Will I try again?

— 8 —

Resilience is a virtue. What is a virtue?

When we read the Greek philosophers, the word "virtue" shows up a lot. The word that's usually being translated is *arête*. *Arête*, however, meant something slightly — but significantly — different from the word "virtue" as we use it today.

Arête really meant something closer to "excellence." For the Greeks, no part of life was considered "moral" life or "ethical" life. It was all simply life. Just as a person could be excellent at running or pottery or writing plays, he could also be excellent at making the kinds of decisions that today we call "moral": decisions about how a person, a family, or a community can create and live a good life.

Even our word "virtue," which comes from Latin, originally meant "the excellences of a man." *Vir* meant "man," and a virtue was a character trait that a man needed to live his life well. Today we recognize that men and women all need certain kinds of excellences to live well. The key point is this: a virtue is an excellence that we can develop like any other excellence.

When we think of a virtue as an excellence, it changes the way we look at the world and at ourselves.

We begin to see that virtue is not necessarily something that we have, but something that we practice. With practice, we may become better at running, better at pottery, and better at writing plays. Without practice our skills deteriorate.

Walker, you and I have done this before. We spent long hours together learning to count our kicks in the pitch-black water of San Diego Bay. We learned to navigate steep, briar-tangled mountains with a compass, a map, and the stars. We spent days learning how to pull a trigger properly.

Resilience isn't any different. Aristotle taught that we aren't born with virtue; we're born with the ability to practice virtue. Practice builds habits. Our habits are our character. When it comes to virtue, practice "makes a very great difference — or rather, all the difference."

You weren't born with resilience, any more than you were born with
the ability to use a compass or aim a rifle. Resilience is an excellence
we build. We can practice it in the choices we make and the actions we
take. After enough practice, resilience becomes part of who we are.

I want to pause here to make an important point. When we understand a virtue as an excellence that we practice, three other things
will happen.

First, you will gain a great sense of power. You will recognize that
you have more ability than you thought to shape your character and,
with it, your fate.

Second, you will become more forgiving of others. Let me explain
how:

Imagine a great runner. She is fast and agile. When she runs, her
heart pumps, her legs turn, her arms glide, and her feet strike the
ground so smoothly and cleanly that she seems to fly through the air.
Now imagine that on the day of an important race — after years of dili-
gent practice and successful competition — she blasts out of the blocks,
sprints to the front of the pack, establishes a commanding lead, and
then crashes like a sack of limbs on the track. The other runners pass
her. She stumbles to regain her footing. Maybe she's bleeding, broken.
She finishes last, or maybe not at all.

Is she a bad runner? Of course not. She had a bad race.

The Greeks recognized that great people could fail terribly and still
be great. Wise people could sometimes be dumb. Courageous people
could be cowardly. Honest people could lie, and compassionate people
could be cruel.

Today, in a culture that should know enough to be forgiving of
human weakness, we often fail to remember that people are not great
all the time. People practice greatness. They perform with greatness.
People practice courage. They perform with courage. And then, one
day, they don't. This does not make them cowards. It makes them
human.

Third, we begin to see the power, fun, majesty, and beauty in virtue.
Virtue is not about what you deny yourself, but what you make of yourself.

In our culture, virtue is respectable, but boring. For us, virtue has
come to be associated with "not." Virtue is about what you should
not do. The "virtuous man" is somebody you'd like to teach your

kids' Sunday school class. But he might not be somebody you'd want to hang out with.

Speaking broadly, the ancients saw things differently. The virtues were exactly what was required to live a full and exciting life. Someone who had the virtues had energy and exuberance. He or she could fight with courage, love with passion, seek adventure with spirit—could know what it takes to create beauty and to live fully. The "wicked" were "those who haven't developed the knack of fine living—those who botch the business." Put most simply, to be virtuous meant that you were brilliant at being human.

We become what we do if we do it often enough. We act with courage, and we become courageous. We act with compassion, and we become compassionate. If we make resilient choices, we become resilient.

Let's not breeze through that too quickly. "If we make resilient choices, we become resilient." It sounds simple, like stating, "If I put on shoes, I'm wearing shoes." But there are three important points of emphasis here.

First, *you* can develop resilience. Anyone can do it. No one can do it for you. You and you alone have to do the work.

Second, you *can* develop resilience. It's possible to build virtues. It's possible to change your character. It's possible, therefore, to change the direction of your life.

Third, you can *develop* resilience. Resilience cannot be purchased or given to you; you have to do the hard work of building excellence in your life.

— 9 —

Many virtues—like courage or compassion—can be displayed in a moment. If we see a fearful child stand up to a bully, we recognize it immediately as a clear example of courage. Resilience takes longer. To endure pain and then turn that pain into wisdom, or to endure hardship and grow through that hardship, takes time. The fruits of resilience grow slowly.

Because of this, we learn best about resilience not when we focus on dramatic moments, but when we take in the arc of whole lives. Resilience is cultivated not so that we can perform well in a single instance, but so that we can live a full and flourishing life.

— 10 —

Zach, do you remember the Stockdale Paradox?

They taught it to us in Survival, Evasion, Resistance, and Escape school. Before we went out in the woods to starve for a week, then get captured, locked in small cages, beaten during interrogations, and blasted at night by the sounds of crying children pumped through loudspeakers, they wanted us to learn a lesson from Admiral James Stockdale, a pilot whose plane was shot down over Vietnam in 1965. He endured seven and a half years of captivity and torture as a prisoner of war. He organized a system of discipline and coded communications for his fellow POWs. He refused, even under torture, to offer intelligence to his captors. For his resilience in captivity and his leadership of his fellow prisoners, Stockdale earned the Congressional Medal of Honor.

Stockdale observed that the POWs who broke the fastest were those who deluded themselves about the severity of their ordeal. They imagined that they would be freed next week, or next month, or by Christmas. But he lasted unbroken for seven and a half years because, in part, he refused to lie to himself.

Here's how he explained the Stockdale Paradox: "You must never confuse faith that you will prevail in the end—which you can never afford to lose—with the discipline to confront the most brutal facts of your current reality, whatever they might be."

In the face of hardship, you have to maintain a clear focus on your harsh reality. It does you no good to sugarcoat the facts. It does you no good to fantasize about what might be. You have to maintain clarity about your reality. The paradox, however, is that at the very same time you have to find a way to maintain hope.

Walker, you used to ignore your own brutal reality. I remember you telling me that you were working, taking care of the family, paying the mortgage, getting stuff done, and drinking on the weekend. After one beer you'd be bitching about all of the guys who'd come home from the war and were whining about PTSD. You'd pretend that you had it all together. You were lying to yourself.

Soon enough, reality kicks down your front door, and then you can't pretend anymore. Pain is real. And we do better dealing with it when we acknowledge it. When we acknowledge pain, we shine a light on it.

Pain doesn't like this. Pain prefers to slip quietly into your psyche and breed with fear. Pain would rather lurk in the shadows and ambush you. Pain doesn't like to be seen or understood.

Stockdale said that you must confront the brutal facts of your reality. When we stop running from pain and acknowledge it, we see it for what it is. Often, under our gaze, it freezes in place. Then we can face it.

I love these lines from Archilochus, a Greek mercenary and poet:

Heart, my heart, so battered with misfortune far beyond your strength,
up, and face the men who hate us. Bare your chest to the assault
of the enemy, and fight them off. Stand fast among the beamlike spears.
Give no ground.

Pain comes in many forms. Fear does too. But some people would rather face spears than face facts. Confronting your current reality requires discipline and courage.

(Of course, none of us are perfect. Archilochus also wrote a great poem about throwing down his shield and running away:

I threw it down by a bush and ran
When the fighting got hot.
Life seemed somehow more precious.
It was a beautiful shield.
I know where I can buy another
Exactly like it, just as round.

So don't expect yourself to be perfect every time you act.)

Keep in mind, though, that there is a big difference between acknowledging pain and wallowing in it. Wallowing in pain is a life trap, the quicksand of achievement.

How do you know the difference between acknowledging pain and wallowing in it? There's no precise test. But if talking about or "examining" or "understanding" your pain has become an excuse you use to avoid doing what you need to do, then you are probably wallowing.

Don't wallow in pain. Confront it. Do it for yourself. Do it for your family. Do it so that you can grow and create happiness. Now let's begin.

Beginning

Please, dear Lord, don't let me f*** up.

— ALAN SHEPARD, *first American in space, seconds before liftoff*

Hey, Walker,

The other day you were telling me about all the things you're worried about, all the things you're afraid *might* happen if you start the new job you've been thinking about.

I said then, and I'll say now: The choice you have to make isn't really about the job. The choice is about whether or not you're going to live in fear for the rest of your life.

You responded, "When you said I could feed my fear or be the courageous Zach Walker you've always known, I basically heard you calling me a pussy."

Well . . . you have to choose. Beginning brings fear.

It doesn't matter whether you're launching yourself into space, standing waist-deep in grab-your-bones-and-make-'em-shake freezing water on the first night of Hell Week, sitting down to write a novel, applying for a job, or thinking about starting your own business — you'll feel fear.

You feel it now. That's good. It tells you that you're on the cusp of something worthwhile. If you continue to live a good life, you'll feel this fear time and time again.

But the longer you hesitate, the hairier and scarier the fear becomes. The longer you hesitate, the more likely you are to turn around and crawl back under the covers.

Screw that, Walker. It's time to begin.

— 2 —

I've been afraid of beginning many, many times. I certainly haven't mastered that fear, but I'll offer you a few thoughts about beginning that I've found helpful. First, when you begin, begin with humility.
   Start with the humility to recognize how little you know.

I begin with humility, I act with humility, I end with humility. Humility leads to clarity. Humility leads to an open mind and a forgiving heart. With an open mind and a forgiving heart, I see every person as superior to me in some way; with every person as my teacher, I grow in wisdom. As I grow in wisdom, humility becomes ever more my guide. I begin with humility, I act with humility, I end with humility.
   That's my humility mantra. I usually read it twice a day at the beginning of the day. I feel a little exposed handing it to you like this. I wonder what you'll think of it. But I share it with you because I think that humility is the virtue from which true, well-rounded, meaningful excellence begins.
   If you start with humility, you see every person as your teacher. If you start with humility, you recognize that you have something to learn.
   Maybe you like it. Maybe you don't. Maybe it just seems weird to you. But this is what works for me. Something else might work better for you.

I remember talking with a boy in a refugee camp near Goma, just over the border from Rwanda. It was less than a year after more than 800,000 people had been slaughtered in the genocide. This boy was sixteen, and he was the clear leader of a group of fifteen boys who had lived through disease, hunger, thirst, and deprivation.
   I asked him to tell me about the other boys. It may have been a quirk of the translation, but he described each boy as powerful: "He is powerful with making fire and cooking. He is powerful with the soldiers from Zaire — they like him. He is powerful with singing." And it struck me that one of the habits of the truly powerful is that they have the humility to recognize the power in everyone.
   Arrogance is the armor worn by hollow men, Walker. Their bragging and puffery is usually just a display meant to mask their own weakness.

* * *

Have the humility to admit to yourself that, of all the things you need to know and don't, one of the things that you don't know well enough is yourself. You perceive that something is missing in your life. It worries you that you cannot name it or define it precisely.

Welcome to the club, mate.

That's not an excuse for not starting, that's the *point* of starting. If you were whole, perfect, without need, desire, or fault, you wouldn't have to begin anything.

Of course you begin with doubts. We can be in awe of how much we don't know. "This feeling of wonder shows that you are a philosopher," said Plato, "since wonder is the only beginning of philosophy."

Wonder at what you don't know is the source of the wisdom you might one day achieve.

— 3 —

In *Prometheus Bound,* Aeschylus tells the story of Prometheus, the Titan who stole fire from heaven as a gift for mankind and saved us from extinction.

In punishment for his theft, the god Zeus orders Prometheus chained to a mountain crag. Each day, an eagle lands on him and devours his liver; each night, his liver grows back so the eagle can consume it again. Alone, immobile, exposed to the elements, Prometheus stays full of defiance. (The guy won't stop fighting. Remind you of anyone?)

Prometheus is chained, but noble. He is tied down and tortured, but still heroic. Prometheus is imprisoned, but his story is ultimately about the salvation of humanity and the possibility of human progress.

Life places limits on all of us. Yet even under the severest limits, we can still struggle valiantly, and in that struggle reach new heights of nobility and wisdom.

This lesson is the foundation of the idea of tragedy, which Aeschylus helped to embed in our culture. By "tragedy" I mean that Aeschylus saw all of us — you, me, our friends, our neighbors, the men and women we served with, our leaders — as imperfect creatures with mental, emotional, moral, physical, and spiritual limitations.

But these limitations enrich our lives with precious possibility, just as they enriched Prometheus with his strange grandeur. In a world without imperfections, the virtues would not be required.

Joy is a practice we build in a world where we feel pain. Resilience is a practice we build in a tragic world, where every one of us is limited in time, knowledge, and ability.

Remember how much we used to laugh in BUD/S? It was extreme pain, and yet it was a ton of fun—the best time you never want to have again. There's a line between tragedy and comedy, and it's thin. There's also a thin line between tragedy and determination, between tragedy and optimism, between tragedy and laughter. If you think about it, I bet some of the funniest people you know have also been hurt badly.

It's not a coincidence that the funniest president we've ever had, Lincoln, also had the most tragic sense of life—as well as a lifelong bout with depression. So did Winston Churchill, who was also known for his wit. Recognition of the tragic character of life is part of what spurs art, energy, comedy, courage. Would you love people the same if they could never die?

Edith Hamilton observed that the two greatest eras of tragic drama, the Golden Age of Athens and Shakespearean England, were times of great optimism, energy, trade, and exploration.

> Far from being periods of darkness and defeat, each was a time when life was seen exalted, a time of thrilling and unfathomable possibilities. They held their heads high, those men who conquered at Marathon and Salamis, and those who fought Spain and saw the great Armada sink. The world was a place of wonder; mankind was beauteous; life was lived on the crest of the wave. More than all, the poignant joy of heroism had stirred men's hearts. Not stuff for tragedy, would you say? But on the crest of the wave one must feel either tragically or joyously; one cannot feel tamely.

The other day, you told me that before you went to Afghanistan, you weren't sure that you really believed or understood that evil existed. You'd never seen the kind of vicious cruelty you saw there. And you said that when you came home, you were more sensitive to what was going on around you. You paid attention to the news and saw pain in the world in a way that you hadn't seen it before, and that was hard —you were suffering, fearful, sometimes paranoid.

Soon after I first got to Iraq, an assault team brought back photos from a house they'd raided. It was a torture house, and one photo showed a room full of human heads lying in a pool of blood. I felt the same way: evil is real.

Remember Adam and Eve, who ate of the tree of the knowledge of good and evil? What happened to them? They were banished from paradise and cursed to sweat and scratch for a living. Was Adam's choice a tragic one? Was Eve's? You can read reams of theology about the meaning of that choice, but what I know is this: that choice was, for them, also a beginning. The beginning of knowledge. The beginning of what it means to be human.

Now is, for you, a beginning. There is no going back to your pre-Afghanistan world. That certainly wasn't paradise, but it had some beauty to it. This new world also has some beauty to it, even if — and maybe especially because — it's a world in which you're newly aware of evil and pain in a way you weren't before.

Adam and Eve left the Garden and went out into the world: tilled the earth, had children, made a life. The knowledge of real evil and the experience of pain are always harsh. Often they're also a beginning.

When we build resilience in our lives, we come to see that pain is not something to be eliminated so that we can have joy, any more than fear is something to be eliminated so that we can have courage. Courage overcomes, but does not replace, fear. Joy overcomes, but does not replace, pain.

When we realize this, we feel the moments when we meet our limitations not as times to retreat, but as opportunities for happiness, meaning, engagement, exploration, creativity, achievement, beauty, and love.

— 4 —

Part of why I've thought about this stuff is because I've struggled so much with it myself.

Rilke, in his *Letters to a Young Poet,* put it this way: "Do not believe that he who seeks to comfort you lives untroubled among the simple and quiet words that sometimes do you good. His life has much difficulty and sadness . . . Were it otherwise he would never have been able to find those words."

I don't have it all figured out. I still often balk at beginning what I have to begin. And one of the reasons I struggle is that I want to wait for the world to change before *I* begin. I can complain about . . . anything, and I can use the way of the world as a way to excuse my own cowardice.

Even writing these letters to you. I've left these thoughts sitting for weeks. "Well, as soon as . . . *then* I'll write to Walker." Or, "After they finally . . . *then* I'll write to Walker." It's all whining and waiting. I let the work pile up for no good reason whatsoever, waiting for the world to change so that I can do what I need to do. It gets me nowhere.

When we accept what we cannot change — that some pain cannot be avoided, that some adversities cannot be overcome, that tragedy comes to every one of us — we are liberated to direct our energy toward work that we can actually do.

No doubt you've read this famous prayer: "God, grant me the serenity to accept the things I cannot change, the courage to change the things I can, and the wisdom to know the difference." One of the first times this prayer was seen in print was in 1944, in a book handed out to Army chaplains and soldiers fighting in the Second World War.

But the basic thought — the necessity of accepting pain in our lives — goes much further back. There's a version of the prayer in Arabic, written in medieval Spain by Solomon ibn Gabirol, a Jewish scholar and poet. He taught that wisdom and peace lay in "being reconciled to the uncontrollable." Ibn Gabirol knew tragedy: sickly and orphaned at a young age, he lived to see the assassination of his closest patron and mentor.

The idea of courageously and wisely accepting the pain we cannot change is not some piece of theological fluff. Such pain strengthened soldiers who fought to a vicious victory when the fate of the world was at stake, just as it comforted a young poet a thousand years ago who suffered and still went on to compose works of lasting beauty.

The right acceptance of what must be accepted will allow you to begin what must be begun.

We begin by accepting that we have problems, that we're miles away from perfect. But some people take this too far: they turn acceptance of the world into an excuse for passivity in the face of their own failings, and even in the face of evil. Yes, you have to accept some unpleasant, upsetting, tragic facts about life. But you also have to accept your responsibility to act in the world.

I like how Joseph Campbell explained this: "You can't say there shouldn't be poisonous serpents—that's the way life is. But in the field of action, if you see a poisonous serpent about to bite somebody, you kill it. That's not saying no to the serpent. That's saying no to that situation."

So let's accept what must be accepted, without letting our acceptance justify inaction.

Don't wait for the world to change. Kill the serpent.

— 5 —

Remember Land Nav, when we were taught how to use a compass?

We learned that we could point a compass in a given direction, pick a landmark along that bearing, walk to it, pick another landmark, walk to it, and by doing so we could follow a bearing through a forest, through a desert, over mountains, and—at the end of the day—we'd end up in one very particular place.

But if, at the beginning of our journey, we decided to change course by just a few degrees, and again we walked that new path through a forest, through a desert, over mountains, then—at the end of the day —we'd end up in a completely different place.

Great changes come when we make small adjustments with great conviction.

You want to transform who you are right now and the role that you play in the world—in your community, in your family, with your fellow veterans. I know you, Walker, and you want to get all of this done yesterday. You think that you can already see and hear and smell and taste who you want to be—you feel a new life ready to burst forth. That's good. That you is out there, on the horizon. To get there, all you have to do right now is make a slight change of course. Point yourself in a new direction and start walking.

In my work with other veterans, I've seen how only a few degrees of change—a slight reorientation of the spirit followed by consistent practice on a new path—has helped people rebuild their lives. We pray in the evening right before bed. We exercise. We sleep just half an hour longer. We eat dinner twice a week with our friends and family. We forgive. We take two minutes every morning to give thanks for those we love and the happiness we enjoy. These are quiet changes in the context of all the things we do in a day, and yet, applied consistently over time, they transform our lives.

Here's another way to think about it: Human beings are not caterpillars. We don't crawl into a cocoon and come out a different creature weeks later. When people begin, they are often too hungry for immediate results. When real transformation does occur in someone's life, it usually happens through evolution, not revolution.

Every time we make a choice to confront our fear, our character evolves and we become more courageous. Every time we make a choice to move through pain to pursue a purpose larger than ourselves, our character evolves and we become wiser. Every time we make a choice to move through suffering, our character evolves and we become stronger.

Over time, through a process of daily choices, we find that we've built courage, strength, and wisdom. We've changed who we are and how we can be of service to the people around us. What choices will you make today?

— 6 —

At the start of many important endeavors, you'll often think: How can I do this? I don't even know enough to begin. It's a common excuse, and it's often a mask for cowardice. When we say that we don't know what to do, it's often not information we're lacking, but courage.

When we begin, we sometimes lack the skills, knowledge, and experience to carry out even the most basic tasks. Of course we do. If we had the experience we needed, we'd already be done.

Not knowing everything cannot be an excuse for not doing anything.

— 7 —

You've heard it said that the journey of a thousand miles begins with a single step. That's true. It's also how the journey to nowhere begins. Action without direction rarely leads to progress.

You don't need to know everything to begin, but you do need to know something. Good intentions that are ill informed will not create good results. So what do you need to know? Just this: enough to tell better from worse.

You don't need to know what perfect looks like, just what better looks like. Better is your bearing. Better is enough to point you in the right direction.

It's like getting in a rowboat and setting out for a far shore. In the beginning, you see it dimly, but that's all you need. With effort and a steady bearing, the far shore comes into focus. It grows clearer with every pull on the oars.

— 8 —

You are human. You are imperfect. You don't begin with perfectly pure motives. If you're like most of us, your motives are probably almost embarrassing next to the excellence you want to reach. You look in the mirror and you know this to be true. And guess what?

It's not a secret.

Get started anyway. Begin where you are. It's the only place where you can begin.

To begin where you are, you have to be where you are.

This sounds a little abstract. Maybe it is. I'm only trying to point out that to begin at the beginning you have to *be* at the beginning. Too often we enter a new endeavor and imagine that we have more skills, more knowledge, more ability than we actually do. Focus on the fundamentals. We will fail if we expect to be good before we've even begun.

So start at the beginning. Approach each day as if you have something new to learn. Your task is not to begin in a noble place, but to end up in one.

— 9 —

Human motivation is rarely one thing. And where it is one thing, that one thing is rarely simple.

Writers on spiritual life, from Saint Ignatius of Loyola to T. S. Eliot, have spoken of "the purification of the motive" on the journey to wisdom. We don't start with the motives of a wise person. (If we had them, there'd be no need for the journey.)

Instead, we begin with the selfish motives of a fallible person. Perhaps there's someone we want to impress. Perhaps we're inordinately impressed with ourselves. Perhaps we're interested in the wrong kind of success, or a false version of happiness.

It doesn't matter. As long as we have enough wonder and humility to start the journey and to correct ourselves when we go wrong, our motives don't have to be pure. Finding better, more selfless, more meaningful reasons for what we do is exactly why we set out. And one day we can look back and laugh at the foolishness we once carried. That's the surest sign we're growing in wisdom.

One of the most famous spiritual journeys was made by Saint Augustine, who lived in the fifth century. He wasn't always a saint. He fathered an illegitimate child with his mistress, and was known for the prayer "Grant me chastity . . . but not yet."

He was also a voracious reader of rhetoric and philosophy — not, at first, because he wanted to live philosophically, but because he was brilliant and ambitious and he wanted a plum job at the Roman emperor's court. But even after he'd won his dream job, he continued to read and study, and the more he reflected, the more he realized there was a hole in his life.

At the age of thirty-two, he experienced a religious conversion and was baptized. But it was not until two years later, when his teenage son suddenly died, that he chose to give away his possessions and fully commit himself to the spiritual life. Augustine went on to write some of the world's most profound books of theology — including the *Confessions,* the story of his spiritual journey and the first autobiography ever written in the West. When he reflected on all the selfish ambition he began with, and all the false starts and doubts on his path, he could only say to God, "I have loved you so late."

It hurts to realize how much time we have wasted. It hurts to realize how foolish we were when we began. And yet, the only thing that hurts more is not beginning at all.

You don't need to be a golden boy. You don't need to be a hero. You don't need to pretend — to yourself or to anyone — that you're showing up with perfect motives.

If you wait to begin until you've mastered your intentions, you'll never begin. Selfish, silly, vain desires can create real growth when you subject them to discipline.

Accept that you are imperfect and always will be. Your quest is not to perfect yourself, but to better your imperfect self.

— 10 —

Know this: anyone who does anything worthy, anything noble, anything meaningful, will have critics. You are a man who does things that are worthy, noble, and meaningful. You will have critics.

Some people try to live a life without criticism by shrinking themselves. They try to make themselves invisible. And you know what happens then? It's not just that they diminish themselves, fail to live their best lives, and squander their time. All of that happens, of course. But you know what else happens? People criticize them for being invisible.

You can't escape criticism. You can't please everyone because very many people are not pleased with themselves. People who hate something in themselves are often harshly critical of others. And people who hate something in themselves find it hard to see honor in someone else.

Fortunately, it works the other way as well. People who are confident of their goodness have an ability to see the quality and potential in others. The essayist Montaigne put it nicely: "The confidence in another man's virtue is no light evidence of a man's own."

Walker, it might give you some comfort to know that even Mother Teresa had many people who hated her.

You know that I worked briefly in one of Mother Teresa's homes for the destitute and dying in Varanasi, India. I also had the chance to see her briefly in Calcutta shortly before she died. You mentioned that experience the other day, and I'm going to rewrite here what I wrote before about the work she inspired:

> In a humble building not far from the River Ganges in Varanasi, India, Mother Teresa's Missionaries of Charity run a home for the destitute and dying. Their mission is simple: help the poorest of the poor die with dignity. Many of the patients are seriously physically ill, while some are severely mentally ill, and together, they live in a small concrete compound that is unadorned and true to the mission of the sisters who have pledged to live just as the poorest of the poor do.
>
> I had expected to see only adults in the home, but one boy lived there also. Mentally and physically disabled, he had been abandoned and for

years before coming to the home he had begged on the street. He squatted in the home just as he had squatted on the street as a beggar, and he had squatted for so long that he could no longer straighten his legs. He smiled often, but the only word he could say was "namaste." Each time he said it, he would offer the traditional Hindu greeting and bring his hands together in front of his chest and lower his head. The namaste greeting has a spiritual origin that is usually understood to mean, "I salute the divinity within you." . . .

I had expected to find an atmosphere of sorrow and penance and heavy burden under the shadow of death in this home. This was a place where people had come to die, and the dying were tended to by sisters of the Missionaries of Charity, who express their faith by living in absolute poverty and extraordinary hardship.

These sisters, I knew, washed everything by hand just as the poor did. They owned three saris and a pair of sandals and nothing more. But I saw that the sisters sometimes skipped and ran through the home. They shared jokes with the patients. They laughed out loud. They did work that most of us would consider onerous — cleaning vomit from the face of a dying man — and they did it with a sense of great joy and light.

People *criticize* this. And not just under their breath, Zach. They publish articles. They write books. They go on television. And it started well before Mother Teresa became famous.

When Mother Teresa was a young and unknown nun starting her work, she faced serious criticism from the leaders of the community where she was pulling dying people from sewers and giving them a place to die with dignity — because people in the community felt that Mother Teresa was implicitly criticizing them for not caring for their own poor.

You might have to read that twice to untangle their craziness. Why does this make me so perversely happy? Because it's so ridiculous. Mother Teresa spent a lifetime doing some of the hardest and most needed work on earth, and people who hadn't spent a month doing anything like it criticized her while entombed in their own comfort. Now, you're not Mother Teresa and neither am I. I'm just using this example because it goes to show that anyone who does anything worthy will attract critics. Begin anyway.

And let me make a note here about heroes. Read about them. Really study their lives. Make sure that your kids do too. One of the problems with the teaching of history today is that we often talk about heroes as if they were never hated. Children come to think that to be heroic is to be liked a lot. They then make the natural mistake of conflating popularity with purposeful living. They should hear how heroes were criticized, see how heroes were attacked, and feel how heroes suffered.

> You have enemies? Why, it is the story of every man who has done a great deed or created a new idea. It is the cloud which thunders around everything that shines. Fame must have enemies, as light must have gnats.

> — VICTOR HUGO

Three more things about critics and criticism, Walker. First, many critics are cowards. Not only do they snipe at lives that they are unwilling to live themselves, but they'll mouth off for years and never once have the courage to sit down with you, face to face, and tell you what they think. If you let them direct what you do, you are turning your life over to cowards.

Second, as with all fears, we have a tendency to imagine the worst. I like how Thomas Jefferson put it: "How much pain have cost us the evils which have never happened!" Are you going to let what someone *might* say prevent you from doing what you *must do?*

Finally, of course there is such a thing as constructive criticism. Everyone likes to say that they are offering constructive criticism. But you know what's really constructive? Work. There are simple standards for measuring the worth of people's critiques. Do they actually care about you? Do they just talk at you, or are they willing to sweat with you? Have they put any effort into what they are saying to you?

Someone who cares about you, sweats with you, and corrects you when you need to be corrected is one of the most precious things in life: a true friend.

— 11 —

This is from George Garrett, a novelist and amateur boxer:

> Most of the fighters I knew were wounded people who felt a deep, powerful urge to wound others at real risk to themselves. In the beginning.

What happened was that in almost every case, there was so much self-discipline required and craft involved, so much else besides one's original motivations to concentrate on, that these motivations became at least cloudy and vague and were often forgotten, lost completely. Many good and experienced fighters (as has often been noted) become gentle and kind people.

Accepting our imperfections — accepting that we can start on the right journey for the less-than-right reasons — does not take away our responsibility to stop being selfish.

Selfish, silly, and vain desires can produce extraordinary achievements. We don't have to spend too much time looking at the ranks of the highest achievers to find some ugly personalities.

What a selfish desire cannot do is produce meaning.

It's possible for people of high achievement to remain selfish. It's also possible for people of high achievement to remain miserable. The happiness of excellence, like every happiness, finds its highest expression when we apply ourselves to a purpose beyond ourselves.

— 12 —

We can hope to leave behind our selfishness and our vanity. When we consider, even for a moment, our own very, very small place in the sea of the universe, the *idea* of being vain, of being selfish, seems irrational and ridiculous. But irrationality— like pain and fear — is not something we set out to eliminate. It is something we can make use of, that can help us build a meaningful life.

Great endeavors are usually fueled, at least in part, by an irrational passion. Let's not glorify irrationality, but let's recognize that if you look rationally at the odds of succeeding at *anything* worthwhile, you'll often end up with a rational decision to surrender. To go on anyway, you have to be a little crazy.

Harness that crazy. That's what some of the giants of history were so great at — not at being more rational than the rest of us, but at putting their crazy to work.

Isaac Newton spent just as much time obsessively decoding biblical prophecies and predicting the end of the world as he did revolutionizing our understanding of physics. Florence Nightingale revolutionized the practice of health care even as she was racked with intense despair for much of her life. She wrote in a letter, "Why, oh my God, can I not be satisfied with the life that satisfied so many people ... ? Why am I starving, desperate and diseased on it?" John Nash, the founder of game theory, was a paranoid schizophrenic; he said that "rationality of thought imposes a limit on a person's concept of his relation to the cosmos."

I'm not telling you to go out and contract a case of clinical depression or paranoid schizophrenia. I'm just reminding you that excellence is often irrational. Greatness is often strange. Beauty is often odd.

So even if your irrationality doesn't run to those extremes, remember: we can seek to conquer what is selfish in us without eliminating what is unique about us. To make the world excellent, great, and beautiful, we may have to be a little irrational, a bit strange, and sometimes odd. That's OK. Hold on to that.

— 13 —

You will fail. Especially in the beginning. You will fail. And that's not just OK, it's essential. Without resilience, the first failure is also the last — because it's final.

Those who are excellent at their work have learned to comfortably coexist with failure. The excellent fail more often than the mediocre.

They begin more. They attempt more. They attack more. Mastery lives quietly atop a mountain of mistakes.

The exceptional artist throws away hundreds of photographs. The exceptional writer wears out the eraser. The exceptional investor puts money into losing ventures. If every risk you take pays off, then you probably aren't actually taking risks. We don't want to excuse recklessness and foolishness as "just taking risks," but we should understand that those who have built true excellence in their lives are always fighting at the edges of their ability.

What distinguishes the exceptional from the unexceptional? A willingness to fail, and an exceptional ability to learn from every failure.

I know some SEALs who are no longer willing to step into a ring or a dojo. Not because they weren't strong and skilled. Not because they didn't win dozens of fights in their time — but because they did. They succeeded at something and became paralyzed by their success. They've become so attached to their reputation as tough, successful guys that they can't handle the thought of losing. They don't want to fail in front of others. The risk to the ego is too great. So they stop trying. They won't start a new career or even a new hobby. They won't go back to school.

The success of their past should be the foundation of their present. Instead, they've built their lives so that their past hangs over their future like a guillotine and they aren't willing to stick their neck out.

When I came home from Iraq, I thought a lot about taking up tae kwon do. But I kept putting it off. I was a boxing champion, a Navy SEAL. What was the point in learning a whole new discipline, beginning again, getting my ass kicked for months in a row until I figured out what I was doing?

I finally got over myself and found a dojang and discovered that I was right. I did get my ass kicked. I had the grace and flexibility of a drunk elephant. Now it's a couple of years later and I'm still not great. But I'm learning and having a great time at it.

Defeat is real. It is also temporary. We have to understand both. Faced for what it is, absorbed and met without self-deception, defeat can offer wisdom and motivation.

Begin even though you know that you will suffer failure and defeat along the way.

— 14 —

Move and the way will open.

— ZEN PROVERB

Remember that deciding is not doing, and wanting is not choosing. Transformation will take place not because of what you decide you want, but because of what you choose to do.

Do me a favor, Zach, and read this twice:

Until one is committed, there is hesitancy, the chance to draw back, always ineffectiveness. Concerning all acts of initiative (and creation), there is one elementary truth the ignorance of which kills countless ideas and splendid plans: that the moment one definitely commits oneself, the providence moves too. A whole stream of events issues from the decision, raising in one's favor all manner of unforeseen incidents, meetings and material assistance, which no man could have dreamt would have come his way. I learned a deep respect for one of Goethe's couplets:

Whatever you can do or dream you can, begin it.
Boldness has genius, power and magic in it!

— W. H. MURRAY, MOUNTAINEER AND WRITER

Happiness

✳

Walker,

You and I have been through rough times, and we spent the last couple of letters talking about why rough times demand resilience. Now I want to talk about something bigger and even more important.

You need resilience not just for the hard times. You need resilience if you're going to be happy.

So let's talk about a funny thing. You ask most people, "Do you want to be happy?" They say, "Yes."

Then you ask, "What does it mean to be happy?" And you get blank stares. You get some umming and aahing.

Now, not everything that is good, useful, or beautiful can be defined. Can you define jazz, or ballet, or painting? I certainly can't. So we shouldn't be surprised that we can't come up with a set of words to describe the art of living.

But "happy" is a word we throw around *a lot*. "The pursuit of happiness" is etched into the American mind right there next to "life" and "liberty." And if we're going to aim for something, work for something, then it might do us good to spend some time thinking about what we're aiming at.

And before we start, I want to be clear, Walker. I want you to be happy. Are you?

— 2 —

Are you happy?

It's a question you probably ask yourself. I know it's a question you ask your wife. It's a question she probably asks you.

But is it the right question? What does it really mean to be happy? (And while this is true of everything that I write to you, it's particularly true of what I'm going to write about happiness: I don't have *the* answer. And no one but you will have *your* answer.)

The guys you liked hearing from before—Aeschylus and Sophocles and Aristotle—had an interesting way of talking about happiness. Broadly speaking, in the Greek world, to live well meant to live a *flourishing* life.

What does it mean to flourish?

You were a logger. You know trees. And it's obvious to you when a tree is flourishing. Provided the right soil, water, and sun, a flourishing tree grows tall and strong. Its branches spread, its trunk grows thicker, its leaves come in green in the spring, and it produces seeds and sap and deep roots.

You also know when a tree is suffering. You know when it's dead or when it's close to dying. You don't need to ask the tree how it feels. You look at the tree and you know these things. The tree is flourishing or it's not.

Flourishing is a fact, not a feeling. We flourish when we grow and thrive. We flourish when we exercise our powers. We flourish when we become what we are capable of becoming.

Of course, people are more complex than trees, and it can be more difficult to tell when a person is flourishing. But it's not impossible—in fact, the basic idea is the same. As Edith Hamilton put it, the Greeks often thought of flourishing as "the exercise of vital powers along lines of excellence in a life affording them scope."

Let's look at this idea in some detail. You *exercise* your vital powers. Flourishing is rooted in action. That action might be meditation. It might be cooking a meal or teaching a class. It might be putting your daughter to sleep. But flourishing isn't abstract. It's a product of what we do.

You exercise vital powers. Vital to you. Vital to the world. You draw from your strengths to do worthy work in the world.

You work *along lines of excellence.* You don't just do things. You do them well.

Aristotle, who did more than any other thinker to develop our ideas of human flourishing, said that "happiness is a kind of working of the soul in the way of perfect excellence." It might be quality cooking, quality saxophone playing, or quality lovemaking — a flourishing life is a life lived along lines of excellence.

The Greeks recognized that true flourishing is not always within our control. The tree needs good soil and good sun. People need a life that affords them scope. Starving people find it hard to flourish.

Flourishing, then, isn't a passing feeling or an emotional state. Flourishing is a condition that is created by the choices we make in the world we live in.

Few people think of happiness in this way anymore. You see that it took me a couple of hundred words to break down what we mean by "a flourishing life." Aristotle and the Greeks expressed this idea in a single word: *eudaimonia.*

Isn't it interesting that we don't have any commonly used word or phrase for this idea in English? We find it hard even to *say* what it means to flourish, let alone to *actually* flourish.

— 3 —

And maybe here, Zach, is a good place to make a quick point about the limitations and possibilities of language.

When you write a word — say, "swim" — it represents an experience but isn't, of course, the experience itself. If we use words to describe the experience well — say, "in a cold black lake" or "on a warm blue beach" — we gain a more precise idea of the particular experience. The obvious limitation of language, however, is that no matter how well we write, our words can only be clumsy approximations of life.

Here we're talking about happiness, and we have a few different words we can use — meaning, purpose, joy, pleasure — but no set of words can fully capture something as simple, even, as rolling a piece of chocolate around on your tongue. One consequence of this is that these letters in general, and this description of happiness in particular, will never be as full or precise as your own life. There will always be something missing.

At the same time, one of the great possibilities of language is that it can draw our attention to parts of life that we might not have noticed on our own. Ancient writers, both Western and Eastern, often wrote using analogies. They did this because of what an analogy offers: an angle.

Analogies help us to consider things in a way that we might not have considered them before. This can be extraordinarily helpful, and when language is used in this way it seems not clumsy, but clever. No matter how useful the analogy, however, we always have to remember that an analogy offers an angle, not an answer. We have to live our answers.

— 4 —

To say that someone is flourishing or not flourishing is different from saying that someone is good or bad. An ill old man, in pain and dying at home, might be dignified, just, and virtuous. Such a man might be an example of what it means to die well; he could be a perfect example of courage in the face of adversity — but it does not make sense to say that he is flourishing when he is dying.

The difference is worth thinking about. We might want our children to emulate the old man's courage, but we would not want our children to be in his condition. And here we begin to see one of the critical differences between flourishing and being good. Flourishing is not a virtue, but a condition; not a character trait, but a result.

We need virtue to flourish, but virtue isn't enough. To create a flourishing life, we need both virtue and the conditions in which virtue can flourish.

— 5 —

If you ever need a reminder that life isn't fair, Walker, just visit some schools around the country. The other day, I visited a junior high school in North St. Louis, a poorer part of my hometown. The whole time I was there, I didn't hear a single kind word from a teacher to a student, or a single word of instruction. I heard a lot of yelling. I saw students who skulked through the halls and teachers who could reach them only through fear and threats.

Those kids simply don't have the chances to flourish that I did. What could they have done with the education I got? What would I have become with the education they're getting?

Good actions are not always rewarded. Good people suffer, and resilient people do not always flourish.

Resilience is a virtue required for flourishing, but being resilient will not guarantee that we will flourish. Unfairness, injustice, and bad fortune will snuff out promising lives. Unasked-for pain will still come our way. I say this not to discourage you, but to be honest with you. We can build resilience and shape the world we live in. We can't rebuild the world.

Let's follow this strand of thought about the power of fortune for a minute. When you read the *Iliad,* the *Odyssey,* or even the Old Testament, you may notice one of the most striking differences between ancient and contemporary life: the amount of time and effort that people put into placating the gods or God. Think of the Greek army sacrificing oxen in the shadow of the Trojan walls, Odysseus tossed in stormy seas at the mercy of Poseidon, Abraham building altars to God in the desert with his own hands. With prayer and sacrifices, rituals and rules, people tried very hard to please the divine, because they believed that their lives depended on it.

This made a lot of sense. In the ancient world, survival and happiness hinged on what nature and agriculture provided. There is a healthy dose of realism that comes from life lived on the land, the kind of life you grew up with. The hunter masters his skills, yet still loves a stroke of luck. The farmer learns that despite his best efforts, pests descend. Despite his most fervent hopes, the rains don't come — and when they do, they can come in a flood. Worse still, an evil man can reap a bounty while a good man (think of Job) can suffer torments.

People who live close to the land tend to harbor a sense of realism about the role of luck in their lives. Reynolds Price, a novelist and one of my college teachers, put it well: "Scratch a farmer and find the tragic sense of life. You can't convince a farmer that life is just one big Coors beer bash . . . They live according to the laws of sun, ice, and water."

But those who are cut off from the land, except as a place to relax and recreate, are often afflicted with urban idealism. More and more people today live in a world of streets and houses and buildings and stadiums and schools. Stores and shops provide their food. All of these have been built by man, and it can lead us to an unnatural conclusion, even if we are unaware of it: that man has the potential to create a paradise.

Human beings have produced wonders. We've cured diseases and reduced hunger, charted outer space, expanded the prospects for long and joyous lives. Were we to return to ancient Greece with all of our technology, we would indeed seem godlike.

But we are not gods, and fortune is not ours to direct. Idealists forget this, and they are more easily ambushed by life. Realists remember this, and realism often accompanies resilience.

Fortune will play her hand. And when she stands between us and flourishing, all we can do is live our best life.

One of the reasons why so much of the wisdom about resilience is in fact *ancient* wisdom is that it comes from a time when human beings put less stock in their power to control the world. And that's why it's still valuable to us at those times — and there are many — when events seem beyond our power to control.

— 6 —

Think about all the different ways that you're happy.

You have the happiness of eating good ice cream, the happiness of a dinner with old friends, the happiness of a walk in the woods, the happiness of a hard-won victory, the happiness of a prayer that brings you peace.

If we imagine a Mayan farmer, an ancient Burmese bricklayer, an Egyptian scribe, a Roman chef, a Spanish monk of the Middle Ages, and a modern American mechanic, we begin to see the wildly diverse beauty that exists in human life. There are many different ways to live and, even in the span of a single life, many different kinds of happiness.

Given how varied and beautifully diverse human life is, we could say that there are as many kinds of happiness as there are colors: an infinite palette of joy that colors our world.

— 7 —

In fact, thinking about color can lead us to a good analogy for happiness. The human eye can perceive millions of colors. Yet we know that we can create this wide range of colors largely from just three primary colors: red, yellow, and blue.

In the same way that an infinite variety of colors can be created from three primary ones, we can think about the full range of happiness by looking at three primary kinds of happiness: the happiness of pleasure, the happiness of grace, and the happiness of excellence.

I think it's fair to say that people who are flourishing usually have all three kinds of happiness in their lives. Let's consider them one at a time.

— 8 —

The happiness of pleasure is easy to understand and easy to experience. We find it in a plate of good food, in a crackling fire, in a sound night's sleep under a sturdy roof. Just as the primary colors have many shades, the intensity of our happiness can be heightened or dampened depending, for example, on the quality of the food we eat or the softness of our bed.

The happiness of pleasure is also shaped by our condition and our context. You never had to go to Survival, Evasion, Resistance, and Escape school. I don't know how you managed that, but I remember my week in SERE well. You get dropped in the woods as if you're behind enemy lines — for us it was in the scrub desert mountains in winter — and you have to evade capture. Then, when you do get captured, they put you in a POW camp. (I know what you're thinking: How'd you get captured, G? Well, everyone *has* to get captured at some point.)

That whole week in SERE school, all I had to eat was half a carrot, half a cup of rice water, and an apple. But man, that apple was good. That was the sweetest, most satisfying, most succulent apple I've ever had. I loved that apple. I think that apple might have even loved me, it was so good. And I ate all of it. All of it except the stem and maybe a few of the seeds. Even the core was precious. The happiness I took from that apple during a week of starvation was completely different from the happiness of the apple I might have tonight after dinner.

Some people — especially philosophers who get wrapped up in the life of the mind — have a tendency to deny or degrade the value of this kind of happiness. They refer to such pleasures as "animal" or "base" or "low," and they consider other kinds of happiness to be of a higher value.

One philosopher to argue for this view was John Stuart Mill. He believed in "higher" and "lower" pleasures. Here's the most famous thing he said about pleasure: "It is better to be a human being dissatisfied

than a pig satisfied; better to be Socrates dissatisfied than a fool satisfied. And if the fool, or the pig, are of a different opinion, it is because
they only know their own side of the question."

Now, Mill was undeniably a genius. He was *raised* to be a genius,
subjected to a rigorous program of education designed by his father.
It was so intense, in fact, that he had a nervous breakdown when he
was twenty years old. Yet here, I think, you begin to see part of Mill's
blindness. So much of his training, his suffering, and his pleasure was
rooted in the mind that he failed to understand the life of the body or
to appreciate the value of pleasure.

Those who deny that pleasure is real happiness have probably never
gone a few days without food or weeks without warmth. Much of the
world goes without the material things we take for granted: a bed to
sleep in, a roof to sleep under, suitable clothes to wear. And while we
might call a roof a necessity and candy a luxury, both provide real
pleasure.

Let me share one story to explain why I think this way. I was in India.
It was night, and I'd been riding the overnight train to Bombay in the
cheap seats.

I'd often buy bread when I traveled, and that trip I had a loaf of
bread with me that I hadn't eaten. I stepped off the train amid the hot,
exhausted rush of hundreds of other human beings and saw a kid—
maybe he was ten—lying under a blanket in the station. The children
who lived on the streets of Indian cities were some of the hungriest I'd
seen. The boy was half asleep. I walk over to him and gently tap his
shoulder with the brown bag. He barely opens his eyes, and it seems
as if he's thinking: Who's this white guy waking me up? Crazy dream?
And then he realizes I'm handing him the bag, and he takes it in his
hands and can feel that it's bread. He looks in the bag, and his mouth
opens wide, and he's looking at me with wild, happy surprise.

Mill can call that whatever he wants, but it's happiness. Real happiness. And it's just as good and real as the happiness of hard thinking.

— 9 —

Walker, the second kind of happiness is harder for me to wrap language
around. I'm calling it the happiness of grace, but your pastor might

throw a fit because of the different meanings people ascribe to the word "grace."

Without getting into the theological details, grace is often considered to be a free gift from God that comes to us even though we haven't earned it. And there is a happiness that comes to human beings when we are grateful for the gifts we have received. You might also call this the happiness of gratitude.

Think of the sense of joy and peace that comes over us when we pause, even for a moment, and genuinely say "thank you." We may experience this kind of happiness in prayer, reflection, or meditation. Some people experience it on long walks. Others experience it when they see their children smile or when they see their spouse soundly asleep.

This sort of happiness is often associated with a religious experience, but it usually happens outside the context of organized religious life. In order to say "thank you," we have to thank someone or something. This means that we have, at least at that moment, some kind of relationship that is larger than ourselves. When we say "thank you" we acknowledge a rightness in the world. The whole world might not be right, but we are thankful for at least one thing that seems fitting.

In every civilization we find evidence that human beings have long sought and long enjoyed the happiness of grace: the sense that there is an order to the cosmos, an awareness of the gift of life, and an appreciation for our own place in it.

Seneca wrote beautifully about this feeling, the awe at looking up and realizing that the universe, as huge and complicated as it is, somehow works. Maybe you've felt it deep in the woods or floating in your kayak on the sea:

> This swift revolution of the heavens, being ruled by eternal law, goes on unhindered, producing so many things on land and sea, so many brilliant lights in the sky all shining in fixed array . . . Even the phenomena which seem irregular and undetermined — I mean showers and clouds, the stroke of crashing thunderbolts and the fires that belch from the riven peaks of mountains, tremors of the quaking ground . . . these, no matter how suddenly they occur, do not happen without a reason.

— 10 —

Walker, you told me that some of your happiest kid memories were of diving for abalone. Most abalone divers in California put on a fancy wetsuit first. But not you—you'd dive off a rock in your Levi's, kick until you were fifteen or twenty feet under, pry the abalone off the seabed, and thrash your way back to the surface on a single breath. Then you'd do it again. And each time, you'd push yourself to dive deeper, hold your breath longer, bring back more. This is the kind of thing that regularly gets people killed—and you were doing it in jeans.

I have one question for you: What the hell were you doing?

If you'd needed food, you could've gone to the store. But, of course, you weren't doing it for food. You were doing it because it made you happy. Because you understood what Aristotle understood: pushing ourselves to grow, to get better, to dive deeper is at the heart of happiness. This is why kids climb trees, and why it's often a mistake when people yell at them to get down.

This is the happiness that goes hand in hand with excellence, with pursuing worthy goals, with growing in mastery.

And what's key here, Walker, is that you were happy while you were diving. It is about the *exercise* of powers. The most common mistake people make in thinking about the happiness of excellence is to focus on moments of achievement. They imagine the mountain climber on the summit. That's part of the happiness of excellence, and a very real part.

What counts more, though, is not the happiness of being there, but the happiness of getting there. A mountain climber heads for the summit, and joy meets her along the way. You head for the bottom of the ocean, and joy meets you on the way down.

To be more precise, you create joy along the way. Some psychologists, like Mihaly Czikszentmihalyi, talk about the concept of flow, the kind of happiness that comes when we lose ourselves through complete absorption in a rewarding task: "These periods of struggling to overcome challenges are what people find to be the most enjoyable times of their lives. A person who has achieved control over psychic energy and has invested it in consciously chosen goals cannot help but grow into a more complex being. By stretching skills, by reaching toward higher challenges, such a person becomes an increasingly extraordinary individual."

These moments of immersion, of engagement, of clear focus — moments that can last for hours, occasionally days — are some of the best times of our lives.

I want to be clear about this point. Pursuing excellence, stretching and straining our minds, bodies, and spirits, isn't like eating your vegetables. I'm not talking about this pursuit because it's good for you. I'm talking about it because it's *joyful* for you.

Let me quote one other bit about the idea of flow, from the psychologist who first popularized the term: "Contrary to what we usually believe, moments like these, the best moments in our lives, are not the passive, receptive, relaxing times ... The best moments usually occur when a person's body or mind is stretched to its limits in a voluntary effort to accomplish something difficult and worthwhile."

You already know this. In your moments of growth, you feel fully present, fully alive. You know those times when you look up and think, It's been eight hours? When you're pushing yourself, absorbed, lost in time, that's happiness. It's the happiness that resilience helps us to achieve.

Joy, like sweat, is usually a byproduct of your activity, not your aim.

Remember what comes first. A focus on happiness will not lead to excellence. A focus on excellence will, over time, lead to happiness.

The pursuit of excellence leads to growth, mastery, and achievement. None of these are sufficient for happiness, yet all of them are necessary.

The happiness of excellence comes from deep engagement with the world. And when we're engaged in service to others, we find that this happiness takes on a whole new dimension: meaning.

It's one pleasure to dive for abalone. It's another pleasure to dive for abalone to feed a hungry family. My grandmother-in-law knits. She's great at it, and I know that trying to master new patterns and products gives her pleasure. I also know that knitting for a friend in hospice or for her great-grandchildren provides her a deeper satisfaction that comes with doing work that's meaningful.

And that combination — outer service and inner growth — is one of the most beautiful things we can create in a good life.

— 11 —

We can push that analogy between happiness and the colors a bit further. If you lose one of the primary colors, you lose a big part of the color spectrum. If you lose yellow, you also lose every shade of green.

In the same way, our lives lose something without all three kinds of happiness. Those who do not have worthy struggles in their lives never enjoy the pleasure of celebrating a hard-won victory. They don't know the satisfaction that comes from growth, or the happiness of friendships formed when people help each other in hard times.

We can all think of people — whether they're people we've been lucky to know or people we know from history — who made great sacrifices in their search for a purpose, because they knew that their lives wouldn't be complete without one.

One of those people was Hannah Senesh. When she left her native Hungary to emigrate to Palestine, she wrote in her diary, "I've become a different person, and it's a very good feeling. One needs something to believe in, something for which one can have whole-hearted enthusiasm. One needs to feel that one's life has meaning, that one is needed in this world."

She lived by those words. A few years later, at the age of twenty-three, she volunteered to parachute into a war zone, sneak behind Nazi lines, and rescue Hungarian Jews on the verge of being sent to Auschwitz. She became a symbol of heroism and purpose to those who came after her and learned her story.

I was one of them. I learned about Hannah Senesh as a kid in Sunday school, and as you can see, her story stuck with me. The lesson I take from her is that the pull of purpose, the desire to feel "needed in this world" — however we fulfill that desire — is a very powerful force in a human life. You don't have to die in pursuit of excellence, Walker. We all want you around for a while. But you do have to recognize that the drive to live well and purposefully isn't some grim, ugly, teeth-gritting duty. On the contrary: "it's a very good feeling." It really is happiness.

— 12 —

Lots and lots of red will never make blue. In the same way, because physical pleasure is fundamentally different from the pursuit of excellence, the happiness of pleasure can never replace the happiness that comes from the pursuit of excellence.

But people still try. When people lose the pursuit of something worthy, they often try to replace that pursuit with some kind of pleasure.

We can pursue pleasures all we like. But having a lot of the wrong thing doesn't make it the right thing. Pleasures can never make up for an absence of purposeful work and meaningful relationships. Pleasures will never make you whole.

Some veterans come home from war and turn to alcohol or drugs: you've been there, and thousands have been there before you. Why is it that the toughest people we know — people who went without a soft bed, a home-cooked meal, and comfortable clothes for months at a time — suddenly can't go a day without a bottle?

A lot of people think veterans turn to drink and drugs to forget what they experienced in war. And some do. But that's only a partial and distorted truth. More often, veterans turn to drink and drugs to replace what they experienced in war.

A veteran who comes home from war is returning from one of the most intense experiences a human being can have. Even if he was not under fire every day, he woke up every morning as part of a team. He started every day with a purpose, and a mission that mattered to those around him.

Even in the middle of the desert, when it's a hundred degrees at ten a.m. and your nostrils are full of sand, there's happiness. Real happiness. It comes from working together, hurting together, fighting together, surviving together, mourning together. It is the essence of the happiness of excellence.

The conditions might be miserable, the larger mission might be misguided, but your purpose is usually clear every day, even if it is only to bring your friends home with honor.

I have always had a preference for Spartan living, and in the military the simplicity of your environment matches the clarity of your purpose. When I was in Iraq, we knew that our work was saving the lives of American marines. We woke up every day to live a life that mattered.

When you come home from war, all of that — the adrenaline, the love, the purpose, the pursuit, the nobility, the calling — vanishes. The happiness of excellence, of purposeful endeavor, is gone.

At the same time, you've been laboring in an environment with few pleasures. So you reach for a beer. You indulge in a meal. You make love. The first night home, this is all good. Life is good. Life is very, very good.

But if you've been home for a year, and you are still drinking hard every night, then you have a problem. And the problem, truth be told, isn't what happened in the war. The problem now is what you've decided to make of your life since you've been home. Alcohol and drugs can soothe us, but only temporarily. TV and video games can distract us, but they can't trick us into thinking we've found meaning.

You've lived this, Zach. People all around you are living the same thing every day on their own frontlines. Athletes who leave the game because of injury or the natural decay of their skills are living it. People who lose their jobs are living it. Workers who retire and can't think of how to fill their days are living it. Elderly people who outlive their friends are living it.

What the hell, they all wonder, *am I here for now?*

But there is no purpose to be found at the bottom of a whiskey bottle. The happiness of pleasure can't provide purpose; it can't substitute for the happiness of excellence.

The challenge for the veteran — and for anyone suddenly deprived of purpose — is not simply to overcome trauma, but to rebuild meaning. The only way out is through. Through suffering to strength. Through hardship to healing. And the longer we wait, the less life we have to live.

— 13 —

There is happiness in struggle.

I ran my first marathon when I was sixteen, and I came to love the fun and struggle of long-distance running. Fifteen years and many races later, I set a goal to run a three-hour marathon. I bought the right shoes, ate all the right foods, did all the right training with some very fast friends. I even picked a flat, fast course with the perfect conditions: Arizona in January. I went to sleep every night for months thinking of the date circled on my calendar.

I crossed the finish line in three hours . . . and twelve seconds. That sucked.

I decided to try one more time. And I decided that if I was going to break through the three-hour wall, I needed to do something harder, maybe a little crazy. I couldn't just "take" the time. I'd have to earn it.

I'd been reading about Emil Zátopek, one of the greatest runners of all time—and one of the most intense. The training run I copied from his regimen was the 80 x 400. He would run 80 times around a 400-meter track, with a 60-second rest between each lap. And he'd run each lap at a sprint.

I have no idea what the physiological value of that training was. I'm not sure if my body changed. But my mind did. I discovered I could run faster and harder than I thought I could—faster and harder than I had in Arizona. And when the next marathon came, I thought about Emil Zátopek, pushed a little harder, and broke through that wall.

I like Zátopek because he's a great example of resilience and happiness working in tandem.

Emil Zátopek did not set out to be a runner. He was forced into his first race in 1940, at the age of eighteen, by a coach at the Czech shoe factory where he worked. Somewhere before the finish line of that first race, he discovered that he wanted to win more than anything. "But I only came in second," Zátopek later remembered. "That was the way it started." His life had a direction.

Soon he was training insanely hard, developing a regimen and a running style all his own. Where other runners paced themselves in training, he sprinted. He ran in the snow and in his army boots, so that running 10,000 meters in clear conditions in track shoes felt like "a relief" by comparison. Within four years, Zátopek was setting Czech records, then world records. Asked the secret of his success, he responded: "Simple. I run, and run and run."

In the 1952 Olympics, after winning gold in the 5,000- and 10,000-meter races, Zátopek decided on a whim to run his first marathon. His strategy: find the fastest runner and keep pace with him. With a third of the race done, Zátopek turned to his closest competitor at the head of the pack and asked if he was running at the right pace. The leader replied, "Too slow," hoping to trick the Czech into exhausting himself. Instead, Zátopek sped up—and crossed the finish line with a world record.

Emil Zátopek was never a graceful runner. His head lolled from side to side as he ran, and his breaths came in gasps so loud his competitors could hear him coming. He wore all the pain of running on his face.

You can imagine him in sight of the finish, pain clawing through his thighs, the rhythm of his heart pounding in his ears, his lungs on fire.

That's very real pain. And a very real pleasure. It's a purpose and a happiness only possible with resilience.

When we rob people of their pain — when we don't allow them the possibility of failure — we also rob them of their happiness.

We are meant to have worthy work to do. If we aren't allowed to struggle for something worthwhile, we'll never grow in resilience, and we'll never experience complete happiness.

— 14 —

It's natural to ask: If we need all three kinds of happiness, why do we see and hear so much about the happiness of pleasure and so little about the happiness of grace and the happiness of excellence?

Today we are sold to at a frequency and intensity unmatched in history. On television and radio, the sides of buses, fliers on our cars, entire sides of buildings, billboards, mailings, targeted ads in our in-boxes — there are fewer moments than ever before when our senses are not bombarded by advertising.

Think of the happiness of pleasure from the perspective of someone responsible for those ads. Happiness is attainable: anyone can buy it. And those ads offer a vision of happiness that's relatable — "you're so close" — and vivid — "it'll feel so good."

But pleasure has its limits. There comes a point of excess, a point of exhaustion. And the constant *pursuit* of pleasure can actually distract us from enjoying what we already have. Epicurus, maybe the greatest philosopher of pleasure, understood this. "Not what we have, but what we enjoy, constitutes our abundance."

The constant promise of pleasure can blind us to the fact that there are other kinds of happiness that we need for a full life. We begin to believe that one more purchase, one more meal, one more trip, one more *thing* will finally make us complete.

Why sell something no one can buy? The happiness that comes from the pursuit of excellence cannot be advertised — because it is not for sale. It is unsellable because we create it, or not, for ourselves.

* * *

Constantly pursuing pleasure puts too many lives out of whack. "Look at all the shades of red I have!" people say. "I have auburn and burgundy and cardinal and crimson and maroon and raspberry and rose and rust and . . ." And you may be blind to everything else.

Excellence and grace are often missing from the stunted version of happiness people want to sell us.

— 15 —

Finally, Walker, it's important to remember that all the talk about colors is only an analogy, and every analogy has its limitations. Where on the color wheel are your friends, your kids, your wife, your parents?

They are, of course, in everything. But you and I know it would be false to say only that our kids make us more grateful, that our friends make us more excellent, or that some of the people in our lives make it more pleasurable. It's true that they do these things, but there's a happiness in our relationships that is deeper, wider, and more profound than anything we've touched on here. We can talk more about relationships and resilience later. For now, I just want to make the point that these letters will have their limitations: maybe the most important is our inability to adequately express or theorize how crucial love is to happiness.

Models

> You know by instinct that it is impossible to "teach"
> democracy, or citizenship or a happy married life . . . They
> come, not from a course, but from a teacher; not from a
> curriculum, but from a human soul.

— JACQUES BARZUN

Walker,

My boxing trainer was a guy named Ariel Blair. His mother named him Ariel, which, he often told us with a smile, meant "the Lion of God."

When he was growing up in Washington, D.C., during the Depression, most of the kids he played with couldn't pronounce his name, so "Ariel" became "Earl." In his teens he worked odd jobs — cleaning an excursion boat, shining shoes, washing dishes, busing tables. He joined the (segregated) military at the end of World War II, and when he came home from the war he had several careers: in construction, cleaning and testing air cylinders, as a mobile messenger delivering telegrams. When I met Earl he was working in a warehouse during the day and teaching boxing at night.

You and Earl look pretty different. He's a half century older than you. He's black. You're white. He's urban. You're rural.

But you and Earl have more in common than a lot of people I know. You've both had calluses on your hands since you were fourteen years old, and you both instinctively distrust people who haven't had to work as hard as you. You've both lived hard lives, punctuated by tragedy. And you are both very aware that your time on earth is limited. You both joke a lot and laugh hard, but I don't know many people who think as seriously about what it means to live well. You both wake up in the middle of the night wondering if you're doing it right.

You both grew up in schools that didn't know what to do with boys who had more energy than patience. You managed to graduate from high school—which Earl never did—yet both of you feel that you're missing something. Sometimes you think of yourselves as uneducated. You've both been unfairly judged for it, and you've felt that prejudice rub against you for a long time.

You share some fears. You're both gifted with words, but afraid to write. You've both built up stores of wisdom, but too often you're afraid to share what you've learned. Earl has to be coaxed to walk into a school and speak to young people. You, a man who patrolled the streets of Afghanistan, are afraid to travel to a city *in the United States* and talk with veterans who want to hear your story.

And in this way, both of you—tremendously courageous men most of the time—sometimes act out of fear when everyone needs you to stand with strength.

There are elementary school children in Earl's neighborhood who need to hear some of his stories. They should hear about the time when Earl was on Okinawa, "the Rock." He complained about segregation in the Army and was thrown in the stockade for insubordination. One of his friends slipped out of the barracks at night and low-crawled to the fence line outside Earl's cell. Earl crawled out and they whispered through the wire. His friend told Earl that he'd overheard the commanding officer say they were going to find a way to provoke Earl when he was on a work detail, make Earl attack one of the guards, and then they'd shoot him. They said, "That man will not leave the Rock alive." They also need to hear Earl tell his story about the Jewish doctor on the base who didn't want to see anyone punished on account of prejudice. The doctor risked his own career, got Earl off the Rock, and saved Earl's life. He also—to hear Earl tell it—changed Earl's own prejudiced view of people who were Jewish.

A lot of men who live hard lives withdraw into themselves. For them, a nod can constitute conversation. You and Earl both admire and appreciate such men because you've spent a lot of time around them. But you also recognize that these men, while they can set a great example, too often die without sharing what they've learned.

You and Earl both became trainers. As soon as you made it back from Afghanistan, you signed up to be a SEAL trainer. There are still many frogmen who know how to think under fire and how to fight as a team because of what you taught them.

Earl trained men to box, and perhaps more important, he trained them in how to live well. Earl said he wasn't a coach: "A coach makes you more skilled, shows you how to be better at a certain activity — maybe it's running, maybe it's throwing, maybe it's boxing. But what's the point? The point is, after a coach coaches you, you can go and do whatever you want with your new skill. You learn to run, you can go rob a store. You learn to fight, you can go fight in the street. But that's not what I'm about. I am not a coach with players, but a teacher with students. I teach my boxers not just a set of skills, but a way of living."

So I want to write about one of the first lessons about living I picked up from Earl. It's pretty simple. But if it were obvious, I wouldn't have needed Earl to teach me.

— 2 —

I started boxing with Earl when I was nineteen. I was a sophomore in college.

During the day, on campus, I studied Aristotle. Aristotle told his students that "what is valuable and pleasant to a morally good man *actually is* valuable and pleasant." In other words, you know what the good thing is by seeing what the good person does. If you want to know how to live well, don't make things more complicated than they need to be. Just look at a model of someone who's already living well. Start there.

After reading Aristotle in class, I'd drive into Durham and make my way to a small boxing gym tucked in a corner of a rough neighborhood. There Earl and I would train with Derrick.

Derrick, my training partner, worked in construction. He was six-two and had the powerful build of a tall, fast fighter. He fought professionally. He was a young guy at the time — twenty-six — but since I was seven years younger, it seemed to me that Derrick had a whole planet of experience underneath him.

When I asked Earl, "How do I throw a jab?" he said, "Watch Derrick. *Do* as he does."

When Earl let me start training on the heavy bag, he'd have me watch Derrick. He'd say, "There's your picture, Eric. Watch how Derrick works the bag."

Derrick was my model, and I learned faster by watching and imitating him than I ever could have done by reading a book or listening to a coach alone.

Earl and Aristotle. They both said the same thing: Find a model. Do as they do.

— 3 —

Walker, let's remember that "stupid hurts."

Human beings learn by imitating other human beings.

Probably the most complex intellectual feat any of us will ever achieve is learning to talk. And we do it simply by listening to others, trying to do what they do.

We survive because we imitate. We pass on cultures and languages and common sense because we imitate. And what we imitate are not only skills — how you ride a bike or climb a rope — but ways of being. How do you talk to your neighbor? How do you carry yourself on patrol? How do you press on when your body is begging you to quit? You watch someone else do it, and you imitate.

What's strange about the way most of us live is that we know how important it is to have models. Everyone wants their children to look for good "role models." Yet once we become adults, we stop looking. That's just stupid. And it leads to a lot of unnecessary pain.

Karl Marlantes, a Vietnam veteran, wrote an excellent book called *What It Is Like to Go to War.* It starts with this:

> Any fool can learn from his mistakes. The wise man learns
> from the mistakes of others.
>
> — OTTO VON BISMARCK

When we did something dumb in BUD/S, remember how the instructors would say, "Well, if you don't want to be smart, then you better be hard"? Then they'd make us do 237 burpees in the sand, or run in and out of the ocean a dozen times.

The lesson was: Stupid hurts. Be smart.

That's still true today, Walker. You've written to me a lot about your brother Ed. You told me that after he died, "my world turned upside down":

I didn't know what else to do when I fell on hard times, but drink. So drink I did, and did it often, and to extremes. I drank like a whale, not a fish. I denied myself the ability to feel, and when drinking stopped working I drank some more. When drinking more stopped working, I tried drinking even more. I would black out in my backyard and wake up facedown next to my barbeque pit, then walk to the store to buy more beer.

Now, Walker, what is that? Read your own writing above. How would you describe it? I write this loving you, but this above is only one thing and you know it. It's stupid.

I have two brothers. Both of them, thank God, are alive and healthy. I don't know what it's like to lose a brother. But I do know this: You are not the first person to lose someone you love. You are not the first person to lose a brother.

In all the times that you've written to me about Ed, you've told me about what happened to *you*, what *you* did, what *you* felt, what *you* wished you had done, what *you* failed to do.

Never once have you told me about someone you admire who learned how to endure a brother's death. In all this time, I've never heard you refer to someone else's story or struggle.

You've been trapped in your own mind and your own life and your own story. Of course you didn't know what to do. You've never had to do this before.

But other people *have* had to deal with this. So learn from them.

— 4 —

You've already done the hardest thing, Walker. You've started. You wrote:

I didn't know that I was reaching out for your guidance and wisdom when I asked you for that letter of reference, but I was . . . I now have the strength to act on the wisdom you know I have . . . I will achieve resilience through my hardship. I will persevere. The time for Zach Walker to be the resilient man I know I can be and am is right now. Not tomorrow, not in ten minutes, right this second.

So what's next? What do we do first?

Let's find a model. Now, how do we do that well?

If I sat down in your living room and placed a giant bag of jigsaw puzzle pieces on a table in front of you and asked you to put all of the pieces together, what's the first thing you'd ask for?

(First you'd probably ask for a reason. "Why are you askin' me to do a puzzle, G?" But if for the moment you accept that you're going to do the puzzle, what would you ask for?)

I'm guessing you'd ask for a picture. You'd want to know how all of the pieces come together. You'd want to know what you're trying to make.

Here's the thing: life only hands you pieces. You have to figure out how to put them together.

Your life doesn't come with a picture of what it's supposed to look like on the box. You have to — you get to — choose that picture for yourself. And you choose it by looking for a model of a life well lived.

"There's your picture, Eric. Watch how Derrick works the bag."

What's powerful about this simple idea is that, over time, you'll begin to find models for almost any part of your life that you want to make excellent. And because of this, in any well-lived life, you'll likely not have one model, but many.

— 5 —

Let me tell you a bit about how I've used models in my life. In the summer of 1994 I went overseas to work with Bosnian refugees. Bosnia had been racked by vicious campaigns of ethnic cleansing. I lived and worked in refugee camps, and it was in those camps that I tried to do my first documentary photography work.

I wasn't a great photographer. I certainly wasn't anything close to being professional, but after seeing how the refugees lived, I knew — in general terms — what I wanted to do. I wanted to show people that even in times of great hardship, men, women, and children can live with courage and dignity.

I also knew that I wasn't the first person to try to do this. So I read *Let Us Now Praise Famous Men*, an unorthodox, deeply felt work of reporting and photographs that brought the lives of Depression-era tenant farmers, in all their struggle and pride, to the American public.

I read James Agee's firsthand account of the farmers' lives; I studied Walker Evans's black-and-white photographs.

I looked for other models too: Dorothea Lange's iconic images of the American Dust Bowl; Sebastião Salgado's remarkable panoramas from Brazil. I read *Down and Out in Paris and London*—a book George Orwell wrote about his time living among those who had been forgotten.

Not everything I studied or read proved to be a good model for me. I photographed in black and white, and so I studied Ansel Adams. I looked at his work, bought his books, went to his exhibits, and ... nothing. His work just didn't seem to be the right model for mine. He photographed landscapes, I photographed people. He photographed from far away, I took pictures up close. It's not that I didn't recognize the genius in his work. I did. It's just that it wasn't the kind of genius that I sought to emulate. I mention it because you should keep in mind that not everyone is, can be, or should be a model for you—even if they are great.

Later, when I went to Rwanda, Bolivia, Cambodia, India, Mexico, Albania, and Gaza, I tried to photograph like Salgado and Evans. I tried to capture honest personal photographs of people living noble lives through incredible trials. And I tried to do this in a way that would give others some insight into, connection with, and respect for the lives of others.

What I produced was uniquely my own. Evans and Salgado couldn't take the photographs for me. And, over time, I developed my own style. I look at Salgado's work in *Terra* and it's obvious how far away I am from his excellence, but my own work was better because I had his model to aim at.

There's no excellence in a vacuum. Look at the most original people you can think of—the pathbreaking scientist, the profound artist, the record-setting athlete—and you'll find people who started by copying.

"Start copying what you love. Copy copy copy copy. At the end of the copy you will find yourself." That's from Yohji Yamamoto, an influential fashion designer. I'm guessing that this is the first time in recorded history that one SEAL has given guidance to another by quoting a fashion designer, but, hey man, what's true is true.

What's true is that the way to excellence starts by copying the excellence around you. "Those who do not want to imitate anything, produce nothing." Salvador Dalí said that, and if anyone should know about originality, he should.

Before he wrote the symphonies that would revolutionize music, Beethoven copied Mozart's style. Before he pioneered cubism, Pablo Picasso mastered the realistic style of the painters who came before him. Before he wrote the dialogues that made Socrates immortal, Plato spent nearly every day just listening to Socrates talk.

So copy, day after day. And one day you'll take stock and find that what started out as copying—whether it's your writing, or your way of being a dad, or your way of facing up to loss—has become something uniquely your own.

— 6 —

Now, let's say that you look around for a while. You read, you talk with friends and family. You search. How do you know if you've found a model?

It's pretty straightforward: when you find yourself reflecting on someone's positive example to guide your thinking and your actions and you begin to imitate him, then you have a model.

When you ask most adults "Who are your role models?" they hem and haw and then, after a few moments' pause, say, "My parents."

If you push them on this, they will, revealingly, start to talk about someone who was a role model for them when they were a child or a young adult. They'll tell you about how the person influenced their life many years ago. But they rarely tell you about how they are modeling themselves after someone today.

We don't grow in courage or wisdom or resilience by thinking alone. We grow in these virtues by observing how they are embodied in courageous, wise, resilient people of flesh and blood, and by emulating them.

A model can be living or dead. A model can be someone you have never met, or a person you live with. A model can be any age, any race, any gender, someone who has achieved monumental greatness, or someone who has lived a quietly honorable life. What all good models share is an excellence that draws us to emulate them.

— 7 —

The writer Hunter S. Thompson once set out to learn the secrets of F. Scott Fitzgerald's *The Great Gatsby,* the book he admired more than any other. So he typed out the entire book for himself—because, he said, he wanted to understand what it felt like to write a masterpiece, word by word.

That might strike us as more than a little crazy. The goal is to learn from our models, not to make ourselves into identical copies of them. Yet I think there's some wisdom in Thompson's practice. He was trying to get into the mind of his model, to know how it felt to type a perfect sentence.

Over the past few weeks, Walker, you've been asking me to give you some guidance about how you can become a leader in your town, how you can organize people to clean up parks, to build monuments, to raise money for good causes. You want to know what to do first, second, and then third. And I haven't really answered you.

Here's why: It's not because I don't want you to become a leader in your town, or because I think you can't do it. It's because you're asking the wrong question. The question isn't, "What do I do?" The question is, "Who do I learn from, and how do I learn from them?" Learn from a model, and you'll know what to do.

Remember the jigsaw puzzle? Who's your picture? Who leads in your community in a way that you admire? How are you going to learn from them?

Thompson wasn't trying to write *The Great Gatsby.* That book had already been written. But he was trying, in a devoted way, to imitate his model's process. You won't achieve exactly what your model has achieved. But by learning the habits, disciplines, and practices that made their accomplishments possible, you'll find your way to accomplishments of your own.

Rather than ask, "How can I achieve what they achieved?" try asking, "How can I create myself as they created themselves?"

— 8 —

After I was hit by the suicide truck bomb in Iraq, I felt—for a few days at least—that I'd lost part of my hearing. When I went to the VA for a hearing test, they told me I was fine. But the experience made me think about what I'd do if I went deaf.

One thing I'd definitely do would be to read a biography of Beethoven. When he was thirty-one, and it became clear that he was losing his hearing for good, he thought long and hard about killing himself. He even sat down to write a suicide note. But instead, the note became a testament to his decision to keep living. He saved it among his papers, and it was only discovered after he died of natural causes twenty-five years later. He wrote: "Oh fellow men, when at some point you read this . . . someone who has had misfortune may console himself to find a similar case."

He's telling us: I've been there. You're not alone.

Think about all the ways models help us learn resilience.

Models offer hope. After an entrepreneur goes bankrupt, a soldier loses a limb, or a mother loses a child, it may feel to each of them as if joy has been permanently crushed from their life. But if they meet another business leader, another soldier, another mother who has passed through similar hardship and still built a meaningful life, they may come to see how much is still possible. When we see what others have done, we begin to ask what we might do. We begin to see a way through.

Models offer practical wisdom. The closer the model's experience is to yours, the more practical advice you may find. You can benefit from the example of your model's mistakes and learn from the example of your model's strengths. No one can speak to a wounded veteran like another wounded veteran. No one can speak to a family that has cared for a desperately ill child like another family that has done the same.

Even if we are unable to find someone who has struggled as we have struggled, we still have no reason to feel alone. We have no excuse for failing to learn. As long as we can read, we have access to models from all of recorded history: biographies that are reservoirs of insight, stories of human tragedy and human possibilities.

Literature and history are among our greatest resources in this regard. By immersing ourselves in stories, we learn to exercise the moral imagination. By putting ourselves in someone else's shoes — by trying to see what she saw and hear what she heard and feel what she might have felt — we expand our sense of what is possible in our own lives. When we learn how to enter into the stories and experiences of others, we're learning some of what they learned.

It takes humility to realize that your story is not unique. It takes empathy to realize that the stories of others matter as much as your own. Reading literature and history — starting to learn the stories of others as early as we can — fosters those virtues.

Let me offer another thought for you. Think about what it means to have a liberal arts education. The word "liberal" has, at its root, *liber* — the same root, of course, as the word "liberty." The idea of learning literature and history is that they *free you* to see how you might live. They *free you* to live a better life, informed by all of the accumulated knowledge and wisdom available to you. They *free you* from living inside the narrow confines of your own story.

— 9 —

People can have one virtue without having them all. Those who are brave might also be impatient. Those who are patient might also be unjust. And even when people exercise one virtue in one context, they often fail to exercise the same virtue in another. The disciplined athlete is the undisciplined spender. The courageous soldier becomes the frightened father.

We don't choose our models in a spirit of passive, all-consuming admiration, as a child does. We must choose actively, as an adult does. We're seasoned enough to know that no one exercises a perfect and complete set of the virtues. We can select the qualities we want to emulate, leaving aside the rest without regrets.

We can admire the profound wisdom of Plato without accepting or ignoring his deep elitism, which held that many of us have no hope of achieving wisdom at all. We can admire the freethinking genius of Thomas Jefferson without accepting or ignoring his ownership of other human beings. We can admire the audacity of Richard Wagner, a nearly self-taught musician who became one of history's greatest composers, without accepting or ignoring his hatred of Jews.

We can admire without ignoring, because we are adults, and that is what adults are capable of.

— 10 —

As a kid, I loved Aquaman. I thought he was the best. I'm sure that you had your own superhero too. As children, we like to believe in the shining, flawless hero.

That belief is entirely appropriate to childhood. But in time we have to "put away childish things." Our lives change, and our models should change with them. I'm not still going around jumping off the couch wearing Underoos and idolizing Aquaman. (Though truth be told, I'm looking forward to having kids old enough to jump off couches with me.)

The models you choose for your life should match the challenges you're facing. Right now, you might have a model for how to deal with your brother's death, a model for how to serve in the community, and a model for how to be a father.

Over time, you'll grow. Your sense of self will change. You'll have new challenges, and you will choose new models of excellence to help you meet them. The model who was perfect at one time in our lives can turn imperfect as our lives and our needs change. The model who taught us courage may be ill suited when the times demand patience.

At each stage, we pursue different dreams, learn different ways of living a good life, and pass through different trials. So we cannot hold inflexibly to our models. We cannot make them into idols. And when times change, we have to let go of our models with gratitude.

The most important thing to let go of — the thing so many of us struggle to let go of — is the idea that our heroes are flawless. We have to put that idea away, if only because such a view of heroes begins to limit our view of our own lives.

If we believe that our heroes are flawless, we begin to believe that we, being flawed, are incapable of heroism. In this way, a belief in the perfection of others can inhibit our own growth.

Adult heroism is different. The adult knows that all heroic lives are, in a sense, a heroic struggle to overcome our own limitations.

Believing in the perfection of heroes can hamper us in another way. When we finally find out that our heroes are not perfect, but human, we can be tempted to dismiss all that is heroic about them. Sometimes people do this to comfort themselves. If no one is heroic, they think, then why should I try?

Flawed heroes are still heroic. Every Achilles has an Achilles' heel.

Your hero is flawed. So are you. Congratulations, you have that in common. Now, make yourself similar in another way: go be heroic.

Identity

> Be less concerned with what you have than with what you
> are, so that you may make yourselves as excellent and as
> rational as possible.
>
> — SOCRATES

Walker,

We talked about this the other day, but I want to put it down in a letter so that you can look at it again.

You were telling me about how the docs at the VA kept asking you how you were feeling. You'd tell them that you were feeling good one day and bad the next, feeling good in the morning and then bad at night. Then the next day it was bad in the morning, better in the afternoon, and worse at night. You were feeling bad, then better, but mostly still bad. You felt trapped by what you were feeling.

And then I interrupted: "Walker, how you feel is not important right now." I told you to take out a piece of paper. We wrote down three words, in this order:

FEELINGS
ACTION
IDENTITY

That is the trap that your docs and your choices have put you in. In our culture, we teach people to put feelings first. It's the first thing people ask you, especially when they think that something might be wrong. "How are you feeling?" It's often a sucker's question, because the next thing they do is to help you to think about what you should do. "Well, if you're feeling this way, then . . ."

In the end, we tend to assume, without really thinking about it, that everything starts with our feelings, that our feelings are in control. Feelings lead to action. Action shapes our identity. So if you're feeling angry, jealous, frightened, gluttonous . . . well, you'll be more likely to act that way, and that's who you become.

I told you that I was less interested in how you feel and more interested in who you want to be.

We talked about this for a while, and here's what you wrote to me later:

> Good talking with you today, old friend. That said, I feel like radioactive waste right now. I thought I made it through the worst of my lows, but can't help but think there's a mighty shit storm building up somewhere with my name spelled out in its clouds. A lot of what you said today got me to thinking. Who am I? What do I identify myself as? What type of man? It brought me back to who I was when I was in the Teams. Thanks for clearing that up for me. It seems as though I need a reminder every once in a while. Anything is possible, my friend.

Then, a few days later, you wrote to me that you'd made a decision: "I don't have to live in fear. I am in control of my mind."

I asked you to write down those same three words in the opposite direction. It's the direction that holds the most promise for your life:

IDENTITY

ACTION

FEELINGS

You begin by asking, "Who am I going to be?" You decided to be courageous again.

So what's next? Act that way. Act with courage. And here comes the part that's so simple it's easy to miss: the way you act will shape the way you feel. You act with courage and immediately your fears start to shrink and you begin to grow.

If you want to feel differently, act differently.

This ain't complicated, my friend. But it's amazing how many people get it wrong for so long.

Let me tell you a little about someone who *didn't* get it wrong. In one of my letters I mentioned Cato, the ancient Roman who died fighting against Julius Caesar's dictatorship. Cato was an inspirational figure for the people who founded our country — George Washington even staged a play at Valley Forge about his fight for liberty.

Cato was a man who decided at an early age what kind of person he wanted to be — someone who was stoic, tough, self-sacrificing — and then he set out very deliberately to become that person. He was born into a wealthy family, and he could have chosen the easy life of luxury lived by most of Rome's young men as the Republic fell apart. Instead, wrote an ancient biographer:

> He built up his body by vigorous exercises, accustoming himself to endure both heat and snow with uncovered head, and to journey on foot at all seasons, without a vehicle. Those of his friends who went abroad with him used horses, and Cato would often join each of them in turn and converse with him, although he walked and they rode . . .
>
> He would often go out into the streets after breakfast without shoes or tunic. He was not hunting for notoriety by this strange practice, but accustoming himself to be ashamed only of what was really shameful, and to ignore men's low opinion of other things.

In this translation of the biography, we read that Cato was "accustoming himself." The translator might have said that Cato was "training himself." He chose a noble identity and then used his actions to make himself into the person he had resolved to be.

— 2 —

When you put identity first — when you start from your conscious choice to be a certain kind of person — the way you think about achievement changes too. You see that character precedes achievement.

I don't mean that good things only happen to good people, or that there's no such thing as luck. I only mean that while what we accomplish is sometimes beyond our control, we can always shape who we are. We can't promise achievement. But we can become the kind of people who are worthy of achievement.

Here's Washington's favorite quotation from the play he put on at Valley Forge: " 'Tis not in mortals to command success, but we'll do more . . . we'll deserve it." It's a fitting line for a guy who, in the winter of 1778, had no idea if he was going to win the war.

This seems like obvious advice, until you realize how easy it is to get caught up in measuring ourselves against others' accomplishments. When we look at other people, we see what they've *done*: the business they've built, the family they've raised, the meal they've cooked, the race they've won. It's a lot harder to see *how* they've done what they've done.

But that's what you have to look for, Walker, in your models and mentors, and in yourself. Make yourself into the kind of person who is capable of building the business, holding down the job, and teaching the kid, and the results will come in time.

— 3 —

Putting feelings in the right place doesn't mean that feelings aren't important. I care about how people feel, and I know that you do too. The technical term for someone who doesn't care about how other people feel is "jackass." At the extreme, a person who doesn't care about others' feelings is a sociopath.

Almost everyone who has ever written thoughtfully about ethics has recognized that our feelings for others — beginning with empathy — are at the heart of living well. A disciple once asked Confucius, "Is there a single word that can be a guide to conduct throughout one's life?" Confucius answered, "It is perhaps the word '*empathy.*' " We can't treat others as they deserve unless we can feel what it's like to be in their shoes.

But — and this is where ancient wisdom tends to diverge from modern thought — all of this goes hand in hand with the belief that your emotions can be harnessed and your feelings can be trained.

Plato had a nice way of thinking about this. When we think of the soul, he writes in his dialogue *Phaedrus*, let's imagine it as "a pair of winged horses and a charioteer." The charioteer, who controls the horses and steers the chariot, is your reason. The two horses are our emotions: one, Plato says, stands for our nobler emotions, such as our desire for honor, and the other stands for our baser passions and appetites.

But notice: both horses are required to pull the chariot forward. Emotions can drive us in a way that reason alone cannot. And we need the drive of the emotions to live a flourishing life.

One of the beauties of Plato's analogy is that he makes it clear that you are *not* your emotions. There is a difference between *feeling* jealous, angry, gluttonous, greedy, or slothful and actually *being* jealous, angry, gluttonous, greedy, or slothful.

If you *feel* jealous, you're human. If you *are* jealous, then you're losing control of your life; your horses are running wild.

The analogy works in another way as well: you can train your horses.

And you, my friend, have some serious horsepower to work with. Your emotions run deep. It's part of what makes you such a good friend and good father. It's part of what makes you so outrageously courageous and, on the flip side, so prone to fear and even paranoia. It's part of your rock-solid sense of justice, but it's also part of what makes you a little too quick to fight.

If you want to think about harnessing your anger, you can learn something from Gandhi. Gandhi, my friend, was an angry man. I know you're thinking: Really? The guy who spun his own clothing and told everyone to practice nonviolence—he was *angry?*

Yes. Read a good biography of Gandhi and you'll begin to understand why. When he was a young man living in South Africa, he was thrown out of a first-class train car reserved for whites. He was beaten by a stagecoach driver for refusing to give up his seat to a European. Years later, in India, he lived through the massacre of hundreds of peaceful protesters.

Here's what Gandhi said about his anger: "I have learned through bitter experience the one supreme lesson to conserve my anger, and as heat conserved is transmuted into energy, even so our anger controlled can be transmuted into a power which can move the world."

So let's talk for a minute about harnessing your horsepower.

— 4 —

The horses run wild when we decide that feelings come first. We come to believe that feeling a certain way demands acting a certain way. We start to think of ourselves as passive: victims of whatever mood takes us.

Plato is telling us that it's not that simple. We control our emotions as much as our emotions control us. The way we feel is often a product of the way we act. Our actions often *create* our feelings.

If you sleep for eight hours, you *feel* differently than if you sleep for two. Everyone knows and accepts this. It's also the case that if you, Walker, help out the young Army Ranger you met who's struggling to patch his life back together, you will *feel* better afterward. You'll feel stronger, more centered, more purposeful.

Sleeping, eating, exercising — these actions shape how you feel. Acting with compassion, courage, grace — these actions also shape how you feel.

Here's where this gets tough. Imagine that a friend tells us, "I feel depressed every morning."

Society has taught us that we're supposed to say, "I'm sorry you feel that way." And that's a fine thing to say. But then we're supposed to ask

> WHY: *"Why do you feel depressed?"*
> WHAT: *"What makes you depressed?"*
> WHEN: *"How long have you been depressed?"* Sometimes we'll even ask
> WHO: *"Have you talked with anyone about your depression?"*
> WHERE: *"Is it only in your house? In bed? Do you feel better at work?"*

The question we almost never ask, however, is the only one that really matters:

How: "How do you do that? How do you make yourself depressed every morning?"

That sounds like a harsh thing to say to someone who is down. It certainly is a hard question to ask. The only thing harsher is to not ask the question.

When we fail to ask that last question of people we care about — or when we fail to ask it of ourselves — we fail to give the struggling person the thing he or she needs most: control.

David Burns is a psychiatrist who's pioneered a new way of treating depression. Rather than taking the patient's negative emotions for granted, he challenges them. Rather than using drugs, he uses reason. He finds that many of the painful things we believe about ourselves are wrong, or at least exaggerated. Over time, through deliberate action and thought, we can change how we feel.

A reporter went to a psychiatry conference and watched one of Burns's training videos:

> The patient looks around frantically. She is sobbing, panicking, overwhelmed by anxiety. She says she can't breathe; her lungs are about to collapse; her heart is about to stop. She feels like she is going to die.
>
> Listening to this . . . Burns calmly asks, "Do you think you could exercise strenuously right now?" Terri doesn't know; she just feels so bad. "Why don't we find out?" Burns suggests . . . and then asks her to try some jumping jacks . . .
>
> "Could you do this if you were dying?" he asks Terri. "Can you see yourself in an emergency room doing jumping jacks?" Hesitantly, she begins to laugh. Soon she's belly laughing. The joy she feels surges off the screen. Turning from the video to the therapists, Burns says *that's* the kind of dramatic change he wants them to achieve. Terri had been experiencing five paralyzing panic attacks a week. She's had only one since Burns taped the session they've just viewed — and that was 20 years ago.

That change didn't come from taking a pill or from taking painful emotions for granted. It came from a simple action, jumping jacks, and a simple question: If you're really about to die, how can you be doing jumping jacks?

When you feel miserable — even when you feel you're going to die — that's not the end of the story. It's time to start asking the hard questions. How much of your pain is out there in the world? How much is in your mind? What is within your power to change? If the feelings you have are killing you, how can you change them?

— 5 —

I recently took my preschool teachers to lunch. Most of them are quite elderly now, and I wanted to be sure that I had thanked all of them while I had the chance.

One of my teachers, Betty Greenberg, told me a story. She said that I'd been punching another kid in class and she stopped me. She took me out of the room and told me that I was not to hit other children, that I should not harm other people. After she explained this, she asked me if I understood. I told her yes, I understood. Then she told me that I could go back into class.

I walked straight up to the kid and punched him again. Now, this is just one incident from when I was three, but self-control is something I struggled with when I was young. In high school, I was an unremarkable soccer player, but I did set the school record for yellow cards, mostly for play that was too aggressive.

When I was growing up, my mom used to say she was worried that I'd end up in jail. I think that's probably the case for a lot of moms of future SEALs, but I want to make it clear that this isn't abstract for me. What I'm writing to you comes out of my own struggle to get this right.

My school friend Mike had grandparents who lived on a farm, and when I was thirteen I stayed with them for a few weeks during the summer. I had never ridden a horse before, but Bob and Jane, Mike's grandparents, let me take a filly named Kate out to ride. I rode everywhere on that horse. And Kate and I raced down streets, over hills, across fields.

I didn't know how to ride, Walker. I still don't. Mostly I just got Kate up to full speed and grabbed the saddle horn with one hand and a fist full of her mane with the other. Over time, though, Kate and I learned to ride together.

When we were walking, I'd make a short, sharp clicking sound out the right side of my mouth. She'd start to trot. I'd click again and she'd start to canter. I'd click again and she'd be flying at a gallop, raising dust, and I'd be hanging on for life, wearing a smile wider than a horseshoe.

When it was time to slow, I'd say "Whooooaa" and brush her neck, and she'd settle down into a walk.

Now, someone who knows something about horses would probably cringe reading this. But to me, that's a symbol of wild power, disciplined over time.

Walker, all analogies have flaws and limitations, and we've probably pushed the emotions/horses one about as far as makes sense. But before we leave it, I want to make one more point. Imagine you've trained two brilliant horses. Championship horses. Beautiful horses. Swift horses.

They respond not to the whip or even the reins, but simply to the sound of your voice, to the tilt of your body.

Now imagine that you put those horses in a barn and leave them there—for a year. The horses are fed and watered and their stalls are cleaned. But for a year you don't exercise them. For a year you don't train them. You take 'em out of the barn after a year. How good are they going to be?

Some things in life need to be done only once and they're done forever. This isn't one of them. This is a practice that—like eating well, like keeping yourself clean—demands daily attention.

And that also means there's no getting to perfect. There's no point at which you've cleaned yourself so well that you never have to shower again. You never win an award for mastering your emotions and call it a day.

And if this is something you tackle every day—some days better, some days worse—then in the awareness of your own struggle you'll find room to be forgiving of yourself and of the people around you.

— 6 —

Actors in ancient Greece put on masks before walking onstage. The mask did two things. For the audience, the exaggerated facial features allowed them to see the mood of the character even from the cheap seats at the back of the theater. For the actor, the mask helped him transform. It helped him become the character. The actor put on an outer mask to create an inner character. As long as the mask was on and he recited his lines, he could feel for a time as if he actually was Achilles or Odysseus or Philoctetes. That's not magic—it's just theater.

Now think about cops and firefighters. They wear uniforms. Why? Most people would say it's so that others—the public—can see who they are and react appropriately. And that's true. But it's only half the reason. When they put on the uniform they often become a different person. Remember how you felt the first time you put on camouflage before a night patrol? What does Clark Kent do to become Superman? He changes his clothes.

In BUD/S, Master Chief Will Guild taught us that if you're having trouble finding "it" inside, then "put on your game face." He reminded us that when Achilles puts on his helmet, he *becomes* a warrior.

Contemporary actors know that when they want to create a feeling, they act out the body's emotional language. If they want to act angry, they purposefully furrow their brow and take shallow breaths. If they need to act impatient, they might start tapping their foot. The furrow of a brow when angry, the tapping of a foot when impatient, the deep sigh when worried—these actions don't just *express* emotional states, they *create* emotional states. That's not unique to actors: your actions shape your state.

Here's an experiment. Smile. Really smile. Try to genuinely smile for fifteen seconds. If you're like most people, you'll feel better. Smiling for a few seconds doesn't transform you, but it does change you.

This works in lots of ways. Take fear. If, when you're afraid, you slow and deepen your breathing, you'll gain control over your mind.

Remember the fifty-meter underwater swim? How do you swim fifty meters on a single breath? The trick is to slow your breathing, calm your mind, and lower your heart rate. As your heart rate drops, so does your rate of oxygen consumption. Guys who began the swim with hearts pounding in fear often passed out before they made it to the other end of the pool. Guys who began calm and unafraid swam the entire fifty meters underwater.

That was the lesson of the test: Jump in calm and you'll make it. Jump in fearful and you'll fail.

You've trained your emotions before. You'll be able to do it again.

—7—

Smiling and breathing. These are simple things.

Exercising and serving. These are simple things.

Being grateful and gracious. These are simple things.

Acting with humility. Acting with courage. These are simple things.

Some people try to make this business of living too complicated, Walker.

It's hard, but it doesn't need to be complicated. Decide who you want to be. Act that way. In time, you'll become the person you resolve to be.

When you act this way, you're going to feel like a fake at first. When you want to kill someone, but instead act with kindness, you'll feel like a fake. When you want to hide in your bedroom, but instead go to work, you'll feel like a fake. The first few times—the first dozen times, or the first hundred — it will feel like a lie, a trick. It will feel like putting on a mask.

But this is exactly how we consciously create our own character. "Be what you would like to seem." Wear the mask of the virtue you want until it's no longer a mask.

One day, it will no longer be you putting on the mask of resilience. It will be you, resilient.

— 8 —

Here's the thing, Walker: you already know this. I know you know this because you've written to me about the power of identity. I love your letters about growing up in a logging town. I want to point out that what you said about identity is just as true today as it was for seven-year-old Walker. Here's some of what you wrote about swimming in the river dam not far from your house:

I remember conquering fears of diving and flipping off the diving board and getting up the courage to grab my first crawdad barehanded. These accomplishments themselves weren't significant. Most kids I grew up with from surrounding areas all caught the same critters and learned to dive and flip off of docks and diving boards, but the coaxing we used was highly unique to Cazadero and logging communities like it . . .

If somebody chickened out on a dare, we'd simply tell them, "You're not a logger." It didn't matter what it was. These were some of my first memories.

Everyone knew how to swim before they remembered anything in their lives, so daring someone to swim was out. Of course not every seven-year-old wanted to go off the "top knot" of the rope swing, dive off the diving board, or catch a turtle that had the capacity to snap off the end of your pinky finger, so for all of these normal activities, you simply weren't a logger if you didn't do it. Not being a logger was about the worst thing you could call someone . . .

Those were the days. They really were. All you had to do was focus on being a logger and you could conquer any fear. The day would soon come when I would enter the brush and see firsthand just what type of "normal" activities a big timber logger encountered on a daily basis . . . "You're not a logger" was the catch phrase of my youth. The fact is, if you're the kid who freezes when you hear that, you're not going to be prepared for the woods.

How did those kids get you to jump off the rope swing or catch a turtle? They didn't reason with you ("Don't worry, no one gets hurt jumping off the rope"). They didn't threaten you ("Jump off the rope or I'll kick your ass"). They talked about *identity*: "You're not a logger." For someone who looked up to loggers as models of what it meant to be brave and tough, "You're not a logger" was the worst thing you could hear. You'd do anything to prove that you were a logger. And ten years later, when you grew up and went into the woods, you were ready.

Our sense of ourselves shapes what we do. When you claim that identity—whether it's a logger, a scholar, a SEAL, or a father—you're also claiming the commitments and expectations and values that go with it, and you're making a promise to live up to them. And yes, when you claim that identity, you're faking a bit. You definitely weren't going to go into the forest and cut down a redwood when you were seven. You *weren't* a logger. But you became one.

This is something kids understand but a lot of adults forget. When kids play, when they shoot hoops or push a stroller or jump off a rope swing, they're trying on new identities. What would I do if I were a basketball player? What would I do if I were a dad? What would I do if I were a logger?

Becoming someone new will sometimes feel like play. That's a good thing. A lot of adults think that the opposite of play is work. And they think that if something is serious or important that it should be treated as work. But think about when you were a kid. Or think about the last time you really played—at diving, at running, in the backyard with your son. In play we're engaged. In play we create joy.

The opposite of play isn't work. The opposite of play is disengagement. Creating who you are is a serious and important endeavor. But engage with it and it'll feel fun, playful.

The other day, Walker, you reminded me that there are lots of identities we don't claim for ourselves. You told me you didn't choose to be an alcoholic, but it's part of who you are.

And, of course, you're right. We don't create ourselves from scratch. Some roles we're born into — son, brother, cousin — and we have to play them our whole lives. But have you ever watched two different actors play the same role? We still have great freedom to shape the parts we're given.

You don't have a choice about being an alcoholic. But you do get to choose what kind of alcoholic you're going to be: the kind who lets his addiction define his life, or the kind whose life is too rich and purposeful to be defined by addiction.

Sometimes, Walker, you will fail to live up to your own standards. You will fail to be your best self. Welcome to the club. Resilient people are able to quickly and powerfully remind themselves — or be reminded by others — of who they are.

Things are going better for you right now, and I'm very glad for that. But there will come a moment when you are in a metaphorical firefight. You'll smell the gunpowder in your nostrils, you'll feel the fear, you'll start to sweat. You might not want it to ever happen again, but it likely will. When it does, how will you remind yourself of who you want to be?

What will you say to yourself? Will you say, Remember, you are Zach Walker, Navy SEAL? Remember, you are a father, setting an example for your children? Remember, be a leader; act with courage? Remember, be a warrior; serve with pride?

You know why a lot of people don't do this, Walker? Because they are embarrassed to think of themselves as being more than they are today. And here's the crazy part: they don't have to share this with *anyone,* and yet the very idea that they might think of themselves as capable of greatness causes them to imagine a thousand critics, and they constrain their own sense of who they can be. Shot down by a ghost sniper of their own creation.

Forget that, Walker. People need you to be strong. Your family, your community, your country. So envision yourself as strong. Remind yourself that you are strong. Become strong.

— 9 —

Tools help to make us successful. We aren't stuck with what nature gave us. We build on what we've been given.

We invented spears to bring down mammoths, compasses to cross oceans, printing presses to communicate across continents. Our lives are longer, more comfortable, and more prosperous because of the tools we've invented.

But it's also a human tendency — and a pronounced tendency in

America — to become enamored of our tools and lose sight of their place. Think about a couple of the basic functions of any community: educating children and policing the streets. Today we spend huge effort and millions of dollars to bring more technology into the classroom, when the great majority of students in the great majority of circumstances can learn almost all of what they need to know with a supportive family, a pencil, some paper, good books, and a great teacher. The schools that produced Shakespeare and Jefferson and Darwin had some writing materials, some printed books — and that was it.

Imagine you're a fourteen- or fifteen-year-old school kid at Radley Hall in England in 1837. Here are some of the questions on your winter exam:

- Why is not virtue either παθος or δυναμις?
- Give Aristotle's reasons (4) why true self-love cannot exist in vicious men.
- Find the length of an arc whose chord is 18, and the chord of half the arc 10⅓.
- Give the characters of Alfred the Great, Cardinal Wolsey, Henry the Eighth, and Queen Elizabeth.
- How are Peterborough, Constantinople, Edinburgh, and Paris severally situate[d] with regard to London?

Can you imagine passing that test, Walker? I can't.

I don't want to argue that nineteenth-century England was some kind of educational golden age. Even to qualify for a school like that, you had to be a member of the privileged class. My point is that you don't need any special technology to master Aristotle or geometry, or to think seriously about virtue.

You find the same thing in policing. After I had worked with the Baltimore Police Department for a few years, I was invited to speak at the Major Cities Chiefs of Police Conference. Almost every speaker or panel addressed some new piece of technology: advanced surveillance systems, new nonlethal weaponry, robotic cameras, gunshot detection systems. These tools can be helpful, but only if those who serve as police officers have the basic skills of communication, teamwork, physical fitness, integrity, courage, compassion, cleverness, and fairness.

Think about what made the SEAL teams work. Even with access to the most sophisticated technology in the world, we had a simple mantra: "Humans before hardware."

Millions of people, in all walks of life and in every endeavor, create distractions and excuses for themselves by focusing on tools rather than on character. They'd rather, as Socrates warned, focus on what they *have* than on what they *are*.

But you know better than that. No tool can take the place of character.

This also applies to writing. You told me that exchanging these letters has reminded you of how happy writing makes you. You also told me how hard it is to write in a small house full of kids. Well, for fun if nothing else, try to remember all the incredible books that were written, or at least started, in miserable conditions. You don't need a comfortable writing desk or a well-stocked library or pots of coffee — or even, sometimes, paper — to come up with a masterpiece.

In the year 524, the philosopher Boethius was imprisoned for treason against the king of Italy. As he waited to be executed, he wrote *The Consolation of Philosophy*, a record of his struggle to find meaning in his fall from power and security. Even though the *Consolation* is largely and sadly forgotten in our time, it was among the most copied, most read books in the Western world for nearly a thousand years.

In 1602, Miguel de Cervantes sat in a Spanish debtors' prison. He was broke and he couldn't use his left arm, which had been wounded in battle. As he passed the time in his dungeon cell, he imagined the story of an old man who comes to believe he is a knight. That was the start of *Don Quixote*, the first (and for some, still the greatest) modern novel.

In 1849, Fyodor Dostoyevsky was arrested on suspicion of plotting to overthrow the Russian tsar. He was blindfolded and put in front of a firing squad — but was saved at the last minute when a letter arrived announcing his new sentence, nine years of exile in Siberia. That's a hell of a lot of time to think. The writer who came out of exile was a lot different from the cocky young man who was arrested. When he got back to the world, Dostoyevsky wrote *Crime and Punishment, The Brothers Karamazov*, and the other novels that put him on the list of the greatest authors of all time.

My point, Walker, is that none of these people had many tools to make their work easier. Their work didn't happen at a comfortable writers' retreat or in a nice little café. It happened in dank cells and in prison camps. They made do with scrap paper or, when paper ran out, relied on memory.

But they produced masterworks, because what was most important about them could not be separated from them as long as they lived: their character, their experience, their hard-earned wisdom.

Humans before hardware, Walker.

Habits

We sow a thought and reap an act;
We sow an act and reap a habit;
We sow a habit and reap a character;
We sow a character and reap a destiny.

— ANONYMOUS

Walker,

Do you remember when we went to Camp Pendleton and they taught us how to shoot a rifle? We were pretty pumped. After months of runs, swims, and rounds on the obstacle course, finally we were going to get a chance to actually shoot.

One of the first things we did was to lie prone in the mud. We rested our rifles on sandbags, looked down our sights, fired at targets twenty-five meters away, and made adjustments until we'd each sighted in. When we got up we were covered in mud like a bunch of happy pigs. We walked around with our rifles and didn't have to say a word to each other. This was cool. We'd earned this together. Now this was gonna start being fun.

Then one of the instructors called us over and he lay down on the ground. He modeled for us how to properly fire from the prone position. Then they took us back to that long cement alley that ran behind the targets. They told us to lie on our stomach and bring the rifle up to firing position with our elbows arrowed into the ground. We lay there. And we lay there. And we lay there, looking down the sights of our rifles as our weight and the weight of the rifle ran through our elbows into the concrete.

At first we didn't mind. It was uncomfortable, but we'd been uncomfortable many times before. It was an irritant to the elbows no worse than an itch. But we held that position, and as the minutes passed, the sensation grew into pain. We didn't dare move. Then it started to burn a little. A few minutes more and it felt as if the bone of my elbow was going to cut through my skin. We were all thinking, If we move, are they going to beat us?

Then, finally, somebody in our class whispered what we'd all been thinking: "Why does *everything* at BUD/S have to suck?"

Later that day, they taught us the concept of "natural point of aim." Your natural point of aim is the point toward which your bullets will fly when everything else is steady.

Lying on the ground and holding your rifle firmly, you focus on your front sight. You close your eyes. You breathe in, let the breath out slowly, and then—at rest—you open your eyes. Now everything—you, the rifle, your breathing—is at rest. You look down the sights of your rifle to see where your bullet will fly: you're looking at your natural point of aim.

Small modifications can alter the trajectory of your bullet—up to a point. But if you really want to change your results, you have to reset your natural point of aim.

Your life has a natural point of aim. It flies in the direction of your habits. To change the direction of your life, you have to reset your habits.

— 2 —

Never cease chiseling your own statue.

— PLOTINUS (205–270)

You have enormous potential to create yourself.

Human beings have enormous potential for self-sacrifice, for courage, for feats of extraordinary endurance, for works of breathtaking beauty. Yet human beings also abuse and torture—sometimes with creativity and delight. They enslave and exploit their fellow human beings. They enact elaborate schemes to inflict pain in the lives of others.

The extremes of which we are capable could fill you with joy or with angst, with hope or with fear. They should, at least, fill you with seriousness about your own possibilities to create yourself.

Every time you act, your actions create feelings — pleasure or pain, pride or shame — that reinforce habits. With each repetition, what was once novel becomes familiar.

If you are cruel every day, you become a cruel person. If you are kind every day, you become a kind person. It is easier to be compassionate the tenth time than the first time. Unfortunately, it is also easier to be cruel the tenth time than the first time.

When a habit has become so ingrained that actions begin to flow from you without conscious thought or effort, then you have changed your character.

If we are intentional about what we repeatedly do, we can practice who we want to become. And through practice, we can become who we want to be.

— 3 —

Walker,

Do you believe that magicians can saw people in half and put them back together? Do you believe that magicians can levitate in the air or make whole buildings disappear?

Of course not. You recognize these tricks as illusions.

Now, if you're like me, you still enjoy the shows. It's fascinating to see how magicians make us see things that can't possibly be true. It's fun, even if I'm aware that I'm looking at illusions.

Today I want to talk about one of the illusions that distort how we see our lives. It's called "the critical decision."

When people tell the story of their lives, or stories about their families, their companies, their communities, or their country, they like the stories that come to a suspenseful climax.

It's just how good stories go: "And then he made his fateful decision . . ." And whether you are talking about a bedraggled Army crossing a frozen river to win a revolution, three hundred warriors standing shoulder to shoulder against invasion, or Zach Walker leaving the Teams and coming home to Cazadero, we like to tell stories that focus on these isolated moments.

When I was in college, we used case studies to examine "critical decisions" in ethics. Sometimes we'd be given fictional scenarios and then asked, "What would you do?" This is all good and healthy. Stories told like this can impart wisdom, and decisions studied like this can provide insight. And, more than good and healthy, sometimes such stories are also accurate. There are times when the world holds its breath, waiting to see what men and women of courage will do. There are times when "one man with courage makes a majority." There are choices made by individuals and small teams that shape the fate of the world and alter the course of human progress.

Three hundred Spartans did make a stand at Thermopylae. Caesar did cross the Rubicon. Washington did cross the Delaware.

All of these moments are fascinating. But here's the rub: most people, most of the time, are not confronted with "critical decisions."

The vast majority of us, the vast majority of the time, simply have to live our lives well. We have to make many important decisions, of course, but the fate of our lives rarely hangs in the balance.

We decide to get married or divorced, to have children or not, to go to school or drop out, to move across the country, to join the military, to take a job, to pursue a relationship, to open a business. It can be tempting, in retrospect, to single out one moment and declare, "That was when everything changed."

But it's not true. Most lives aren't that neat. When you read a good biography, or you come to know a good friend, what you begin to see is that the direction of that person's life is shaped not by a single turning point, but by thousands of days, each filled with small, unspectacular decisions and small, unremarkable acts that make us who we are.

You'll understand your own life better, and the lives of others better, if you stop looking for critical decisions and turning points. Your life builds not by dramatic acts, but by accumulation.

Why, then, do people like to believe in the big decision or the critical moment? Why do people think the only way to change is through some sort of earthshattering conversion experience?

Because magic's fun. It's fun to watch a person get sawed in half and put back together. And it's fun to think that after a lifetime of laziness someone can suddenly produce great work. It's easy and comforting to believe that a single moment's kindness can wipe out a lifetime habit of cruelty. It's fantastic to believe that the man who's always been a coward will awaken and find courage.

People like to imagine that they will "rise to the occasion." They taught us in the Teams that people rarely do. What happens, in fact, is that when things get really hard and people are really afraid, they sink to the level of their training.

You train your habits. And if a critical moment does come, all you can be is ready for it.

People do change their lives. Sometimes radically. Ask *some* recovering alcoholics. Ask *some* former prisoners. Ask *some* women who have left abusive husbands. Thousands of people do this. But there's only one way it happens. It happens through hard work.

You've never been afraid of hard work, Walker. And that's the only kind of magic you need to believe in. You don't need a turning point, an epiphany, a miracle moment to change your life. How many people have put off the necessary, unglamorous work of building habits because they spend their lives waiting for an epiphany that never comes?

Don't wait. Don't wait a single day.

Live.

— 4 —

Some people think of habits as patterns of action that enslave us. They see someone who acts out of habit as an automaton who lives without choice. But consider the ways in which habits can liberate you.

A life without habits — in which we had to consider from scratch each day which shoe to tie first and how we want to brush our teeth — would leave us exhausted. By relying on habits, we free our minds to focus on what matters most.

In the middle of Leonardo da Vinci's famous notebooks, there's a section called "The Practice of Painting." It's full of pages and pages of advice to beginners from a master. Look at it for a few minutes, and it's obvious that you're reading the work of a man beautifully obsessed with his craft.

Leonardo starts from the beginning: how to trace and copy the work of a great artist before you. Then he writes about mastering the details of human anatomy:

It is indispensable to a painter who would be thoroughly familiar with the limbs in all the positions and actions of which they are capable, in the nude, to know the anatomy of the sinews, bones, muscles and tendons so that, in their various movements and exertions, he may know which nerve or muscle is the cause of each movement and show those only as prominent and thickened, and not the others all over, as many do who, to seem great draftsmen, draw their nude figures looking like wood, devoid of grace; so that you would think you were looking at a sack of walnuts rather than the human form, or a bundle of radishes rather than the muscles of figures.

Before you can paint, he says, you have to know the nerves and tendons and muscles behind *every* movement. The lesson goes on and on: how to set up your studio; whether to paint alone or with friends; how wide to open your studio's window; the best kind of light to paint in; "how to draw a figure on a wall 12 braccia high which shall look 24 braccia high"; where to find a good mirror; why some shadows are more pleasant to look at than others; how to paint skin; why faces look darker when seen from farther away; how to depict anger and despair; how to paint a flood or a man making a speech; how, even in your spare time, you should come up with games to test the sharpness of your eye and the steadiness of your hand; how, when you close your eyes to go to sleep, you should see in your mind's eye the figures you painted that day in all their detail.

Here's the thing, Walker: Do you think Leonardo had to think much about *any* of that when he sat down to paint his masterworks? I doubt it. He had been studying and practicing and building habits his entire life. When he sat down and took up his brush, all of that, *all* of it, was a part of him. He had attained a level of unconscious competence.

What do you see when you watch a painter like this humming away at his work? Do you see a slave, a robot? Or do you see someone finally free to do what he was put on earth to do?

— 5 —

Generally speaking, children have a greater capacity for resilience than adults. This is not just because they are younger. And it is not just because they have different bodies or more supple brains. It's because, in my opinion, adults have forgotten how to fail.

Many adults are fearful of failure, while children have to be familiar with failure. What is growing up except failing over and over again — at walking, at tying your shoes, at reading, at riding a bike, at doing math, at writing a sentence?

If you're growing, you're likely failing. If you're not failing, you're likely not growing.

(And one caveat here: I'm not really sure that many American children today *are* more resilient than adults. When we swaddle our kids in bubble wrap, keep red ink off their school papers to spare their feelings, rush to pick them up every time they fall, don't let them climb trees, and give them trophies for everything they do — we have stopped letting them fail.)

Are you still willing to fail, Walker?

As time passes, some people become especially fearful of failure. They seek to protect what they've accumulated. They lose the hunger and daring of their early days. Comfortable in a cocoon, they experiment less. They try fewer new things. They embrace fewer adventures.

As we become older, it is comforting to know that we have earned a measure of proficiency and mastery through years of practice. It is fine and fitting to be proud of what we've done. But adults can come to stake their identity on the success they have attained, while losing the very spirit and character that made success possible in the first place.

The prospect of a new adventure promises a confrontation with our inadequacies and failings. Adventure can throw our comfortable sense of self into doubt. No wonder, then, that many people have only one or two or zero adventures in their lives. Too often we see people, by the end of their lives, balancing atop an ever narrower set of experiences and teetering like an elephant on a stick.

We can make a different choice. We can choose, at any age, to have adventures and growth and happiness. We can begin again. We can have all of this, as long as we are still willing to fail.

> And happiness . . . what is it? I say it is neither virtue
> nor pleasure nor this thing or that, but simply growth.
> We are happy when we are growing.
>
> — JOHN BUTLER YEATS

We should be, in part, beginners for our entire lives. Beginning anew refreshes the habit of learning.

To begin again does not mean that we start something new every day. That is not to begin, but to bounce. Nor does it mean that we abandon what we learned at each new beginning. But if every few years we dedicate a part of ourselves to a new endeavor, we find that we are again disciples, and that the habit of beginning is renewed. We are reminded of how we grow, we are reminded that we *can* grow, and we are reminded of how we profit from growth.

Or, we can decay.

Virtues that are not practiced die. Resilience that is not practiced weakens. The only way to keep resilience alive — through success, through temporary comfort, and through the challenges of age — is to engage ourselves in purposeful learning at every step of life. Every master must still have a master. Every good teacher must still be a student.

– 6 –

To learn resilience, children must be exposed to hardship. If they don't meet hardship early, they'll certainly find it later. And if they haven't built a habit of resilience and earned some self-respect by then, the adult pain they meet probably won't strengthen them. It will likely overwhelm them.

You know how a vaccine works. We build a healthy immune system not by staying clear of germs and pathogens, but by exposing ourselves to them. A vaccine — usually a small, weakened form of a virus — allows our immune system to build the resistance that inoculates us for when we meet the virus full force. Without the benefit of a vaccine in childhood, a virus can kill us when we're adults.

Protecting children from all suffering is, in fact, one of the only ways to ensure that they will be overwhelmed and badly hurt one day. They will have none of the resources, the experiences, the spiritual reserves of courage and fortitude necessary to make it through future difficulties. You wouldn't want that for your kids, and I don't want it for mine.

There's one sure way to build self-respect: through achievement. A child who learns to tie her own shoes grows in confidence. So does a child who learns to spell his name. So does a student who learns to stand in front of class and read his poem.

Self-respect isn't something a teacher or a coach or a government can hand you. Self-respect grows through self-created success: not because we've been told we're good, but when we *know* we're good.

Not everyone gets a trophy, because not every performance merits celebration. If we want our children to have a shot at resilience, they must learn what failure means. If they don't learn that lesson from loving parents and coaches and teachers, life will teach it to them in a far harsher way.

Children need to be loved. And part of loving is to comfort, hug, and hold them when they are hurting. Both you and I know that, especially as parents, it is our job to provide love at all times and in all circumstances. But as guys who want to protect other people, we have to realize that we can overdo this. As hard as it is to do, part of loving someone means letting her experience hurt in the right way.

In trying to protect too much, kind people can inflict great cruelty.

I cracked up reading your letter about playing "football" with your buddy Kevin as a kid in Cazadero. I'm putting "football" in quotes, because traditionally football fields don't include water hazards and a three-foot drop.

Kevin's nickname was "Wart," mine was the less flattering "Droopy," but when we stepped on the football field, together we were "the Gut Brothers." . . . The field we played on was a pasture that sheep grazed on, which doubled as clay pigeon cemetery. The uphill side got steep, but if you had the energy to run up the hill, there was no out of bounds. On the downhill side there was a three-foot drop onto the dirt driveway that led up to Kevin and Randy's house. The south side of the field had an end zone marked by a large fig tree which hung over a stream that split the pasture, and the northern end zone was a three-foot butt-cut redwood log.

This all meant that if you had the ball you could be tackled into a steaming heap of sheep dung or stabbed by broken clay pigeons upon hitting the ground. If you were close to an end zone you ran the risk of ending up in a stream or pile-drived into a redwood tree, and if you were even remotely close to the road, you turned upfield and prayed that the larger guys running downhill at you didn't launch off the drop and send you into the dirt road ass over teakettle.

Worst of all was fumbling the ball or dropping a pass. If the ball hit your hands and you didn't catch it, you'd catch a whoopin' in the huddle.

Fumbling was worse. That gave the other team the ball, and you'd really get roughed up for that. We took our share of beatings for both of those offenses and still came back for more.

Some of these things happened to most of us every time we played, but being the smallest, slowest, and weakest brought about a knowing that one, if not all, of those things was going to happen to you every time for sure. You couldn't sell out, though. If you didn't play football, you weren't a logger.

It didn't take long before the word was out: the Gut Brothers didn't fumble and they could catch anything thrown in their vicinity.

Walker, do you wish that you'd had a well-meaning adult who shut down your football games so that you didn't get hurt? Of course not. You got roughed up, and it did you good.

Parents and safety have a place, of course. I remember one time when my friends and I were firing bottle rockets at each other. We were each armed with a Wiffle ball bat. The bats had a small hole at the base. We'd slide a bottle rocket into the bat, light the fuse, and run through the yard holding the bat like a gun and aiming the rocket until it fired at our friends. My friend's mom came outside and saw us. I'd never heard her yell before, but she screamed, "Mark Timothy"—she even busted out the middle name—*"get over here right now!"*

She was right. We could have blown each other's eyes out.

Extreme recklessness is dangerous. But extreme caution is dangerous in its own way. And I've seen our culture shift further and further toward extreme caution.

Now let's not get carried away: challenging our children can also be overdone. Let's be clear that challenging children works best when children are loved—and when they are challenged *because* they are loved.

There is a lot of evidence to suggest that the children who are most likely and most willing to take risks are those who know that they can return to loving parents and a secure home. We often venture most boldly when we understand that our ventures are not all or nothing—when we are confident that we have a safe and welcoming home to return to.

Resilience—the willingness and ability to endure hardship and become better by it—is a habit that sinks its roots in the soil of security.

The child who is always protected from harm will never be resilient. At the same time, the child who is never loved will rarely be resilient.

The goal, then, is to build as early as possible a habit of intelligent risk-taking. We learn to find the happy medium between fearfulness and recklessness.

There's a common misconception that wildly successful people are reckless. When Hernán Cortés arrived in Mexico, he supposedly ordered his crew to burn their ships — telling them, in other words, that there was no retreat from their mission to conquer the New World. They would win or die. As it turns out, that's a legend. And, true or not, it's a pretty poor guide to the art of intelligent risk-taking.

It's true that full commitment often breeds full effort. Armies, dogs, and people sometimes fight most fiercely when they're cornered. And great deeds sometimes do begin when we leave our pasts entirely behind.

But the grand gesture and the decisive moment demand a different approach from the good of every day. The reality is that great risk takers often have a safe place to retreat to, a place of confidence and security that enables them to dare greatly. Children who fall from the tree retreat to the arms of their loving parents. Adults retreat to their homes, to their spouses, to their friends, or to their hobbies.

For most people engaged in most pursuits of excellence, we are not dealing with a single important day of decision. We are dealing instead with days and weeks and months and years of accumulated effort, consistent practice, and wise habit formation.

That kind of effort demands great reserves of energy, and even those who take huge amounts of energy from their work frequently build oases of safety, set aside from their risk-taking. That, too, is part of the habit of resilience.

When you leave for work every day, you don't burn your house down.

If there's one thing I hope you'll take from this, it's the promise that you don't have to serve your habits. Your habits can serve you. They can strengthen and reinforce the kind of person you want to become.

You have power over your habits. That also means you're responsible for your habits. So let's talk about what it means to be responsible.

Responsibility

Walker,

In my previous letter I wrote about the importance of habits, and I mentioned a few — a willingness to fail, a willingness to begin again — that are essential to resilience. Today I'm writing about the single most important habit to build if you want to be resilient: the habit of taking responsibility for your life.

There is no easy formula for predicting someone's resilience. Sometimes the people we most expect to grow through hardship snap under pressure instead. And sometimes the people we most expect to crack surprise us with their strength.

But I do believe that there is one question that can tell you more than any other about people's capacity for resilience. Ask them: "What are you responsible for?"

The more responsibility people take, the more resilient they are likely to be. The less responsibility people take — for their actions, for their lives, for their happiness — the more likely it is that life will crush them. At the root of resilience is the willingness to take responsibility for results.

Walker, you know perhaps more than most that life can do cruel things to people. Life is unfair. You are not responsible for everything that happens to you. You *are* responsible for how you react to everything that happens to you.

That's something I saw in the refugee camps. Thousands of men, women, and children were in the same miserable situation — uprooted from their homes, torn from their lives. Yet while some were beaten down by the misery around them, others stood proud. Some were withdrawn and some were engaged. Some sat in their trailers all day and smoked; others found children to teach, sports to organize, clothes to mend. Even at their most powerless, some found that they had a power that events could not steal from them.

— 2 —

The first word out of the mouth of the complainer is almost always "they." "They" were unfair. "They" didn't. "They" wouldn't. "They" can't.

"They" distracts from "I." "They" suggests that someone else is in control.

On the other hand, as soon as we say "I am responsible for . . . ," we take control of *something*.

Earlier, I told you about the Navy pilot James Stockdale. Stockdale was an ardent student of Stoicism, and when he ejected from his stricken plane over Vietnam in 1965, he had a moment to reflect as he parachuted into enemy hands and what would become punishing years of captivity. "I'm leaving the world of technology," he recalled telling himself, "and entering the world of Epictetus."

Stockdale was right: he was entering a world in which he would suffer more in seven years than most people would suffer in seven lifetimes. And as he drifted toward that suffering, he thought of Epictetus, and of all the ancient wisdom about resilience the Stoic could offer.

Epictetus was born a slave and crippled at a young age, possibly as a result of a severe beating from a cruel master. The story goes that when the master went to work on his leg, Epictetus said, in the most matter-of-fact way, "You're going to break it." And when the leg finally snapped, instead of screaming in pain, he simply said, "Didn't I tell you that you'd break it?"

This sounds like a Washington-chopping-down-the-cherry-tree tall tale to me. But the reason why people told that story about Epictetus was that it was symbolic of his philosophy: even in the face of a master who delighted in cruelty, Epictetus maintained mastery of himself.

Epictetus lived what he taught. After he was freed, he went on to become one of Rome's greatest philosophers. We live in an uncertain and hostile world, he told his students, but we alone are responsible for our happiness, because each of us is free to choose and judge. Whatever the world sends us, we have power over our intentions and our attitudes.

Epictetus said that "it is not things which trouble us, but the judgments we bring to bear upon things." That doesn't mean we sugarcoat things. That doesn't mean that we put on a big, fake smile and pretend that it's *great* that our legs are broken.

It just means that a lot of our suffering — or, as Epictetus believed, all of it — comes from our minds, from the way we turn things over and over, the way we worry, the way we fear things that haven't happened yet. Try to look at things as they actually are in this moment, stripped of fear and worry, and you're likely to find that you can better bear your pain.

Like Epictetus, Stockdale sustained a severely broken leg. He suffered regular beatings, imprisonment in leg irons, and solitary confinement in a cell three feet wide. But in a world in which virtually everything had been taken out of his power, he followed Epictetus's guidance and found ways to exercise responsibility. He kept his fellow prisoners organized and disciplined. He refused to offer intelligence to his captors, even under torture.

Throughout his ordeal, Stockdale maintained that he held more power over his suffering than his captors did: his ordeal would only become an evil if he let it. "I never lost faith in the end of the story," he said, "that I would prevail in the end and turn the experience into the defining event of my life, which, in retrospect, I would not trade." Stockdale refused to relinquish responsibility for his own thoughts and intentions.

Few of us will suffer the way James Stockdale did. Yet all of us are likely to find, as Stockdale did, that acceptance of responsibility is a powerful cure for pain. Even when seemingly powerless, the resilient person finds a way to grab hold of something — no matter how small at first — to be responsible for.

— 3 —

Taking responsibility requires courage, because the person who takes responsibility is very likely to feel fear. A good teacher will not only want his students to succeed; he will fear that he might fail them. A good doctor will not only want her surgery to succeed; she will fear that she might fail.

If you take responsibility for anything in your life, know that you'll feel fear. That fear will manifest itself in many ways: fear of embarrassment, fear of failure, fear of hurt.

Such fears are entirely natural and healthy, and you should recognize them as proof that you've chosen work worth doing. Every worthy challenge will inspire some fear.

A lot of the doctors of a lot of the veterans I know are pushing pills to help reduce anxiety. I don't doubt that they help sometimes, but too often the pills come with no demands that someone change his or her life, and so you end up with a prescription shortcut to nothing but more and more medication. You also end up with the false ideal that the good life is anxiety-free.

Yet if you come across a person or a team without fear, without anxiety, there is a good chance that you've run into ignorance or apathy. You've run into someone who doesn't know enough or care enough to be afraid. Neither is good.

Fear is a core emotion. A life without fear is an unhealthy life.

If you take your kids to the creek to swim, you'll have a lot of fun, but you'll also be on alert. That's good. That's proper. Fear is fine. You need it. If someone came to you at the creek and offered you a pill so that you won't worry as much about your kids, you'd tell 'em to shove the pill.

Proper fear is part of the package of responsible, adult living. Today, too many doctors, psychologists, psychiatrists, and well-intentioned do-gooders want to reduce anxiety or eliminate fear from decision making. They've got it backward. Focus not on wiping out your anxiety, but on directing your anxiety to worthy ends. Focus not on reducing your fear, but on building your courage — because, as you take more and more responsibility for your life, you'll need more and more courage.

Remember the two horses of the emotions we talked about, Walker? Fear is a motivator. It can propel you.

You know this. Anyone who's been through BUD/S knows it. Remember how the threat of being in the Goon Squad could make you run fast? They'd make us run for miles — over the sand berm, down the beach, back again. After a few miles, an instructor would plant himself on the course of the run, raise his arm over his head, and let it hang there like some kind of guillotine. If you made it past before he dropped his arm, you were fine, but if his arm dropped before you reached him, you were in the Goon Squad.

We did *not* want to be in the Goon Squad. While the rest of the class jogged in a circle, the Goon Squad would do fireman's carry drills up and down the beach, squats, pushups in the sand. They'd crab-crawl up and over the sand berm and back again.

I remember one run when I was feeling weak and dehydrated, and I was farther behind where I would have otherwise been. I wanted to be a leader, I wanted to be a top-of-the-pack trainee. I wanted to be a guy who pushed himself. None of those thoughts helped. I was smashed. But then one of the instructors mentioned the Goon Squad and I really started to run hard. I passed one guy, two, three. I remember thinking, Fear works.

Fear can make human beings do amazing things. Fear can help you to see your world clearly in a way that you never have before.

Fear becomes destructive when it drives us to do things that are unwise or unhelpful. Fear becomes destructive when it begins to cloud our vision. But like most emotions, fear is destructive only when it runs wild. Embrace the fear that comes from accepting responsibility, and use it to propel yourself to become the person you choose to be.

— 4 —

While fear can often be your friend, excuses are almost always your enemy. Faced with a choice between hard action and easy excuses, people often choose the excuse. You know this. I know this. We see people do it all the time. But why? Why are excuses so powerful?

Eric Hoffer said this: "There are many who find a good alibi far more attractive than an achievement. For an achievement does not settle anything permanently. We still have to prove our worth anew each day: we have to prove that we are as good today as we were yesterday. But when we have a valid alibi for not achieving anything we are fixed, so to speak, for life."

Excellence is beautiful and, like all beautiful things, temporary. One moment we are victorious. The next moment we *were* victorious. An excuse, however, endures. An excuse promises permanence.

Excellence is difficult. An excuse is seductive. It promises to end hardship, failure, and embarrassment. Excellence requires pain. An excuse promises that you'll be pain-free.

You look at it like that, and you begin to see why excuses are so seductive.

— 5 —

How do excuses take hold? An excuse starts as a protective measure. It shields us from pain, saves our pride, keeps our ego from being punctured, allows us to obscure the brutal truth. That feels like a relief at first. We avoided the pain.

Then we lay another excuse on top of the first. Then another. Excuses make us feel safe. So, we think, why not add another? Soon enough, you're wearing excuses like a knight wearing armor.

Well, what's the harm in that? You're a strong guy, Walker, but how fast do you think you'd be able to run wearing a suit of armor? How well could you climb a mountain? How well could you swim across a lake? How well could you hug your kids?

Excuses protect you, but they exact a heavy cost. You can't live a full life while you wear them.

You can take away someone's house. You can take their food, their money. You can take their clothes, their freedom, even their children. But you can't take away someone else's excuse.

We give up our excuses ourselves, or not at all.

And here's what's really difficult about excuses. You're the only one who can let them go, but other people offer them to you all the time. Excuses don't just tempt those who make them, they tempt those who hear them. Sometimes the world can't wait to give you an excuse.

Why? Because an excuse often frees *everyone* from responsibility.

If you grab an excuse, it can almost look generous. It can look as if you're giving not just yourself but everyone around you a break, and that makes it even more tempting.

— 6 —

A few weeks ago, I was talking with a group of eighty-some veterans in St. Louis who'd flown in from around the country. They were enlisted and officer, soldier and sailor, marine and airman. Many had been in combat. Most had been diagnosed with a disability.

I told them that one of the greatest dangers facing a veteran coming home is an onslaught of misdirected sympathy.

That's partly because, along with gratitude, the veteran is offered a raft of excuses. The world says: "Because of your injury (or your stress, or the friends you lost), you don't have to . . .

"Be there for your family."

"Show up for work on time."

"Treat your friends well."

"Serve anymore."

Excuses are usually offered with the best intentions. People want to be kind to those who are suffering. People want to reach out and do what they can — even when what they choose to do is worse than nothing.

They offer you an excuse because they don't want to add to your suffering. Or maybe they want to connect and don't know how. Maybe they want to express thanks, and think that letting you off the hook is a way to do that. (That happens more and more in a country in which soldiers and civilians are increasingly strangers to one another.) It comes from a place of kindness.

But it's kind poison. Don't drink it.

People who think you weak will offer you an excuse. People who respect you will offer you a challenge.

— 7 —

It's easy to say that "no one else understands." It's easy to imagine that, because you're a unique person, your pain is unique too. And it's easy to become isolated in your pain.

That, too, is fuel for excuses: you imagine that your pain is so special that no one can grasp it, your excuse so unique that no one can challenge it.

It's true that no one else has received your injuries. Yet every person shares with every other person an ocean of common experience. Love, fear, longing for life, dread of death, desire for affection, achievement, meaning, and friendship — all of these and more are universal. In your flesh-and-blood community — and in the larger community of history and literature — all of these things surround you.

Losing a friend in battle bears a likeness to losing a friend to cancer. And though the former is rarer than the latter, they share much in common. So there is a simple truth to tell those who cling to the excuse that "no one understands": your pain is real, but it is not unique.

— 8 —

Having been injured often provides an odd kind of comfort: it allows people the chance to hang out where they have been hurt. The hurt becomes a permanent excuse: "I can't [fill in the blank] because I've been hurt."

I did this a lot after I got divorced. Loving a person fully means taking risks. It means opening yourself to her love. It means being vulnerable in your weakness, sharing your imperfections. I was hurt and ashamed and scared. I didn't want to get run over by a train again. I found that, being divorced, I had a ready excuse to avoid anything painful. I'd say, "I don't want to go through that again," and people around me — loving people — would let me off the hook, even though finding someone to love and live with is the surest way to real happiness in life.

A broken bone takes longer to heal than a sprained ankle. The loss of a marriage takes longer to heal than the end of a promising fling. And just as you can't run on a broken leg, you shouldn't jump right back into trying to build a life of love after divorce. But there comes a time when enough is enough.

All of these injuries have a hard truth in common. In the long term, the obstacle that stands between us and healing is often not the injury we have received, but ourselves: our decision to keep the injury alive and open long after it should have become a hard-won scar. *It is not things which trouble us, but the judgments we bring to bear upon things.*

Sadly, our approach to struggling veterans often encourages them to "hang out in hurt." Men and women who once demonstrated remarkable resilience, who passed through trials unthinkable to most, are suddenly allowed to play the victim.

The struggling veteran's trauma is often genuine. The fear of crowds and loud noises, dreams of your battle buddies in distress, reaching under the bed for the gun in the middle of the night — these are all real and hard. They are also beatable.

In truth, it's not the trauma that's most harmful. The harm comes when we make trauma an excuse to avoid the activities, the relationships, and the purpose that are its only lasting cure.

— 9 —

Diabolos is the ancient Greek word for devil. The literal translation is "one who throws an obstacle in the path."

It's often easier to imagine that a guy with horns and a pitchfork has harmed us than to realize how we have harmed ourselves. Yet we are usually our own worst enemy. We throw obstacles in our own path.

If we had an external enemy who consistently forced us to make bad choices, to engage in self-destructive behavior, to be less than we are capable of, we'd declare war. Why should we act any differently when the enemy is inside?

You have to master the one who throws obstacles in your way. Master yourself.

Over the long term, you are responsible for your happiness. I don't say this to blame you for how you feel. I say it because in taking responsibility you will find freedom and power.

Vocation

Walker,

You will never find your purpose. You will never find your purpose for the simple reason that your purpose is not lost.

If you want to live a purposeful life, you will have to create your purpose.

How do you create your purpose? You take action. You try things. You fail. You pursue excellence in your endeavors and you endure pain. The pursuit of excellence forces you beyond what you already know, and in this way you come to better understand the world.

You do this not once, not twice, not three times, but three thousand times. You make it a habit.

Through action, you learn what you are capable of doing and you sense what you are capable of becoming.

You are — right now — in the process of developing your vocation. You are doing this *not* because you are working in the concrete industry, counseling your fellow veterans, or reading to your children. You are developing your vocation because — as you wrote to me the other day — you are *learning* in all of these endeavors. You're learning a new job. You're learning what it's like to help others again, rather than be on the receiving end of help. You've always loved your children, but now you're making a more sustained effort to be a good father every day and night. This is how vocations are created.

You act and achieve a small victory. This feels good. It reinforces your commitment. You act again, and maybe you fail this time. A defeat leads to learning, which leads to better action, which is followed by another small victory, which again reinforces your commitment. This cycle, repeated again and again, inches you closer and closer, minute by minute, day by day, to developing your vocation.

Slowly you create your passionate purpose through consistent, excellent work.

When we "do work," we too often think of it as a one-way affair. People think: I woke up and built a fence, or taught a class, or saw a patient; I made dinner for my family. We recognize that a fence now exists or that our family has been fed: we pay attention to the change around us, but not to the change within us.

Maybe you've heard this saying: What you work on, works on you. People are shaped by what they do. People who do work that hurts understand this: ask a roofer about his forearms; ask a waitress about her feet. But the work we do has an effect on our minds and our souls as well. A good writer will become more finely attuned to the way people use words. A good rabbi will learn to recognize pain before people say a word.

As ever, Walker, there is a wild diversity to life, and it makes no sense to say that roofers, teachers, nurses, engineers, or sheriffs *are* one way. That's not right. The point is that what you do will shape you as much as it shapes the world you live in.

What shape do you want that to be? How is the work you are doing today shaping who you will be tomorrow?

— 2 —

The word "vocation" comes from the Latin *vocare*, "to call." To have a vocation, then, is to have work that you feel you have been called to.

The notion of a calling has religious roots: it originally meant a call from God. Today, many people still testify that they feel called by a higher power to the work they do. What role God actually plays in this is far beyond my power to say. What I can tell you is that whenever I've met people who feel as if they've found their calling, they've told me stories of failure, confusion, purposelessness, even despair — stories of the hard work they did before and after they heard a call.

Think about the story of Newton and the apple. Newton told a few friends that he was walking in his garden when he saw an apple fall from a tree. He wondered why the apple fell straight down, and didn't fall up or sideways or at some other strange angle — and this started Newton on the chain of thought that would lead him to discover the laws of gravity.

Now, Walker, millions of people have watched millions of pieces of fruit fall from trees. If I had been standing next to Newton, my most profound thought would probably have been: Hey, apple. Yum. Newton was able to see what he saw only because years and years of study and experimentation and wonder had made him ready.

I think that being called to a vocation is a little like that. Maybe you'll have a revelation, an aha moment. But you have to make yourself ready to listen. The calling you hear is often the echo of your own efforts.

I'll tell you a little about how I've experienced this in my own life.

I've been doing work with returning veterans for about seven years. Two weeks before I flew home from Iraq, if you had told me I'd be doing this seven years after I got home, I wouldn't have believed you.

If I had an aha moment, it came when I went to the Bethesda Naval Hospital to visit with some recently returned wounded marines.

As I pushed open the heavy brown door of a hospital room, a young soldier lying in bed caught me with his eyes and followed me as I walked in. Gauze bandages were wrapped around his neck. He'd taken a bullet through the throat.

"How you doin'?" I asked, and he wrote on a yellow legal pad, "Fine, was actually having fun over there before this."

His young wife sat next to him with red-ringed eyes, her hand on his shoulder. Most of the Army's wounded were at Walter Reed, but this soldier — for some reason having to do with his care — had been brought to Bethesda. I joked that he was in enemy territory at a Navy hospital, and he wrote, "Navy actually OK, some of them," and he smiled. We communicated a bit more, and as I walked out of his room, I was thinking, What's this guy going to do next?

I walked into another room where a marine had lost part of his right lung and the use of his right hand. With his good hand, he took mine and shook firmly. His mother sat hunched at his side, and it seemed that she'd been there for a very long time, trapped in worry and confusion and heartache. I guessed that the marine was nineteen, maybe twenty years old. He reminded me of many of the men I had served with. I could picture him cleaning his weapon on a sweltering morning in Southeast Asia, turning a knob to check his radio frequency before a mission in Kenya, or strapping on body armor before a night patrol in Iraq.

We talked for a while about where he'd served, how he'd been hit, and where he was from. I asked him, "What do you want to do when you recover?"

"I want to go back to my unit, sir."

I nodded. "I know that your guys'll be glad to know that."

But the brutal fact was that this marine was not going to be back on the battlefield with his unit any time soon. So how could he maintain hope?

I wasn't conscious of it at the time, but my experiences with refugees had taught me something about suffering and hope. In Bosnia I had seen how people need a purpose to serve even — perhaps especially — when things are incredibly bleak. In Rwanda I had seen how, even in the face of unimaginable hardship, people could preserve their dignity and their compassion. In Cambodia I had seen how young girls who had lost limbs to land mines needed models of successful women to look up to.

Of course, I didn't live those experiences as neatly as they read on paper. Not every experience came packaged with a tidy lesson wrapped up at the end. I spent a lot of time confused. But it all added up to this: when I saw veterans lying in hospital beds, I saw them differently. I didn't see people who wanted charity, but people who needed a challenge. I saw people whose most serious injury over the long term was not going to be the loss of a limb or of eyesight, but the loss of their team and mission. To the extent that I had any insight, it came because practice and experience prepared me to see my fellow veterans differently than a lot of other people saw them.

A few days after my visit to Bethesda, I donated my combat pay to start The Mission Continues. I'm sharing this story not because I think it's unique or special, but because it's common: this is how people everywhere have found their vocations. A real accounting for vocation starts not just with the aha moment, but with all of the work that makes such moments possible.

* * *

You want to know what your purpose is. I can't tell you. I can tell you that, whatever it is, you'll have to work for it. Your purpose will not be found; it will be forged.

What people experience as revelation is often a result of their resolve.

3

The greatest definition of a vocation I've ever heard was offered by Reverend Peter Gomes. He said that your vocation is "the place where your great joy meets the world's great need."

Let's stop for a minute and think about that definition. In a true vocation, you find happiness in your work — not just in the rewards of your work, but in the work itself. And because your work serves a need, others take happiness from your work too.

My mom was a teacher for over forty years, and much of that time was in early childhood special education. She shaped the lives of hundreds of children. (When I was growing up, my dad and brothers and I would often refuse to go to the store with her, not because we didn't want to be with her, but because it was impossible to buy a dozen eggs without three families stopping us to update her on how the children she'd once taught were getting on.)

If anyone has ever had a vocation — a place where joy and need come together — it's my mom. Her work was often difficult, frustrating, sometimes infuriating on a day-to-day basis. But over the years she was sustained by joy. Your vocation can be, and should be, a source of joy for you. It's part of what sustains you.

There is nothing selfish in devoting great energy to creating and then practicing your vocation. Without a vocation, we can serve others in short bursts of enthusiasm, but before long we may wear out. It's usually only from within a vocation that we can serve with lasting energy and consistency.

Remember what it was like to be a new father? The sleepless nights, the worry, the burden of feeling totally responsible for a fragile human life, all balanced by overwhelming energy and love? Any vocation — like the vocation of parenthood — will demand its toll of struggle and sleepless nights. And it will be worth it.

— 4 —

Almost any activity, if you pursue it with purpose and attention for its own sake, can become a vocation.

When I was in college, one of my favorite philosophy professors was Alasdair MacIntyre. One of the things MacIntyre taught was the difference between "external goods" and "internal goods." External goods are the rewards we receive for pursuing an activity—money, prestige, promotions, and so on. Internal goods are the deep satisfactions of pursuing an activity for itself.

MacIntyre writes that you can train a child to play chess by offering her a piece of candy—an external good—every time she wins. But not until she discovers for herself the pleasures of developing strategies, reading her opponent's mind, and thinking three moves ahead will she become a real chess player.

There's a Jewish tradition that embodies this very wisdom. In the Jewish shtetls of Eastern Europe, mothers would prepare a treat for their children on the first day of school: cookies in the shape of letters of the alphabet. In some families, the new student would get a drop of honey for each letter he sounded out.

The lesson was easy enough for a six- or seven-year-old to grasp: learning is sweet. In time, children would learn that the real sweetness was in the knowledge they could unlock as they mastered their letters. They'd move from seeking external rewards to pursuing internal happiness.

Some jobs are just jobs—we work 'em for money in the way that a kid works for honey. But other jobs, over time, become part of us in a deeper way. We begin to study the job—we want to learn how to get better at it. We begin to enjoy the job and time seems to fly by at work. We begin to build friendships at the job—we find people we like and sometimes admire. And we begin to take pride in the job. We come to associate the work we do with who we are, and when we've found our vocation we're proud of both.

— 5 —

Today, almost any working person in any developed country can purchase almost any book for the equivalent of two or three hours of labor.

Those two hours' worth of wages are precious, but books are much, much cheaper than they used to be. In medieval Byzantium, for example, an average laborer would have had to work for two or three *years* to buy a single book.

Even in colonial America, a printed book was one of the greatest luxuries you could own. If a family owned only one book, it was usually the Bible. And if a home had two books, you could be almost certain that they were the Bible and *The Pilgrim's Progress*.

These days, not many people have heard of *The Pilgrim's Progress*. But this allegory by John Bunyan, an army veteran and a self-taught preacher, is among the most influential books ever written in English. For 335 years — from the day it was published — it has never been out of print.

Why did so many people spend so much of their hard-earned money to buy this book? One reason stands out: *The Pilgrim's Progress* described, better than any other book, the call of vocation.

Bunyan's book tells the story of an everyman, known only as Christian, who discovers one day an overwhelming sense of vocation to embark on a spiritual journey. He cannot shake it, try as he might to put it out of his mind: "The night was as troublesome to him as the day; wherefore, instead of sleeping, he spent it in sighs and tears. So, when the morning was come, [his wife and children] would know how he did. He told them, Worse and worse ... He would also walk solitarily in the fields, sometimes reading, and sometimes praying: and thus for some days he spent his time."

One of the reasons why this story has endured is that it is painfully honest about what it means to struggle with a calling we can't ignore. Christian pursues his calling at great cost. He leaves his world of security for a long and trying journey.

Everyone who has ever felt that they've been called to a vocation has endured similar suffering: leaving the comfortably familiar behind for something you know you have to do. When I started working with veterans, I lived for months on an air mattress in a near-empty apartment, wondering if my organization would survive. When a veteran lied to us and tried to steal funds, I wondered if the effort was worth it. When we were turned down by donors, I wondered why no one else saw value in what we were doing.

Working at your vocation doesn't mean that your life is going to be easy. In fact, in many ways it may be harder. And working at your vocation does not mean that you will always be happy. But such work is an absolute necessity for living the flourishing life I've been writing to you about — the kind of life in which you can exercise your vital powers to the fullest.

> With nothing meaningful in life, nothing is interesting.
>
> — DANIEL KLEIN

Fireworks are interesting. Once or twice a year, we might spend an hour or two watching in wonder as fireworks light up the night sky. But imagine two straight *days* of fireworks. You'd pass out from boredom.

A spectacle can capture our attention, but it takes meaning to sustain our attention. If we forget this, we are liable to hop from spectacle to spectacle, entertainment to entertainment, diversion to diversion.

People who lament, "I'm bored," are usually complaining about an absence of diversion, a lack of spectacle. But often, I think, they're really lamenting a lack of meaning. Without meaning, everything becomes spectacle, and spectacle becomes exhausting. In the long run, the only cure for boredom is meaning.

We all know what it's like to do work that doesn't engage us. Everything — the thought that you need to wash the dishes, a movement in the corner of your eye — becomes a distraction.

In response, distracted people often try to eliminate distractions. They create processes, rules, or tricks to help them do their work. This is helpful sometimes. But much of the time, the drive to kill distractions can be a huge distraction itself. There will always be distractions in life. We can be unnerved even by the sound of silence. Focus comes not from working without distractions, but with a devotion so intense that distractions fall from our awareness.

When we see people whose talents lie fallow, whose energy is engaged in pursuits they see as trivial — or worse, in pursuits others see as destructive — the problem usually isn't that they have too many distractions. The problem is that they have too few devotions.

— 6 —

I am a creature of God and you are a creature of God.
My work may be in the city, yours is perhaps in the field.

As you rise early to your work, so I rise early to my work.
As you do not claim that your work is superior to mine, so I
do not claim that mine is superior to yours. And should one
say, I do more important work and the other less important
work, we have already learned: more or less, it does not
matter, so long as the heart is turned toward heaven.

— TALMUD

Someone's vocation might be to make herself into an outstanding grandmother, a great coconut farmer, or a professional skier. There are poets, doctors, truckers, bankers, actors, cops, cooks, and teachers whose days fly by in a blur because they are in love with what they do. There are also neurosurgeons, astrophysicists, carpenters, hairdressers, and law partners who sullenly punch in every morning and watch the clock all day. Just as any work can be made into a miserable bore, any vocation can be a source of joy if it's pursued with passion and a love of excellence.

One of the things that's hard for you now, Walker, is that you are leaving a well-understood and almost universally admired profession — in your case that of Navy SEAL — and you wonder, Will I ever do anything as worthy again? That's true for a lot of veterans.

It's possible to get stuck there. The question is, where will your joy meet the world's need? As a coach? A father? A business owner?

As you think about this, you should also be aware of a few prejudices that cloud how we think about vocations.

First, we have in our culture a long-standing prejudice that places the professor above the plumber, the sage ahead of the salesman, and the abstract before the practical. It's one of the reasons why, today, many parents push their kids to become "knowledge workers" instead of artisans, even though the life of a skilled artisan often offers more prospects for freedom, satisfaction, and self-governance than that of many kids who end up stuck at a desk, drowning in debt, and afraid to offend their boss.

Another prejudice is that we often treat public service work as inherently more noble than the work of those who make service possible by building businesses and creating wealth. Almost every occupation can be a site of service if pursued with compassion. Conversely, people can treat any occupation selfishly, no matter how public-spirited the job title.

I think that we confuse ourselves when we make service the exclusive domain of certain professions. I admire many cops, teachers, nurses, and soldiers. I also admire many janitors, receptionists, launderers, and barbers. Nobility in work lies not so much in the work that we do, but in the excellence we bring to it. We hurt ourselves as a society when we imagine that service is something that select people choose to do, rather than the expectation of every citizen.

Is your service over because you left the military? I don't think so.

At the same time, it's important to realize that our vocations may be different from our jobs. My dad, for example, worked for the Department of Agriculture. I know that he took pride in doing his work well. But I also know that my grandfather died when my dad was six years old. Growing up without a father, my dad swore he'd be a father to his sons. He often left the house around four-thirty a.m. so that he could put in a day's work and still be home when we came home from school. He coached our teams. In many ways, being a father was my dad's vocation.

I think it's nearly impossible to know anyone's real vocation unless you really know *them,* and it's often a mistake to assume that what someone gets paid to do is the same as her life's work. People are complex and multilayered. Get to know them and you'll often find that their devotions differ from what *you* see them do. You may also find that they harbor reserves of courage and energy that you have never seen.

There are many beautifully diverse ways to live a good life, and you'll create one again.

—7—

Many people — in companies, on athletic fields, even in classrooms — speak about their work in the language of warfare. To them, the idea of the warrior suggests strength and conquest. They go to war with their competitors, tell their colleagues to fight like soldiers, and imagine that their leaders are generals. They can forget that what makes a warrior is not a weapon, a uniform, or a unit, but a cause worthy of sacrifice.

Rosa Parks, Mahatma Gandhi, Mother Teresa. They aren't often thought of as warriors, but they endured more hardship and inspired more courageous commitment than most generals. If people want to talk like warriors, they also have to embrace the true warrior's purpose: serving something greater than yourself.

Walker, when you joined the American military, you didn't take an oath to be a warrior. Everyone you served with took an oath to be a soldier or sailor or airman or marine who would support and defend the Constitution of the United States. When you join the military you pledge to serve something larger than yourself.

The warrior is not supreme. The warrior is a servant. If you're going to be a warrior, what are you going to serve?

Resilience is often strengthened by a sense of service. If you're going to be resilient, what are you going to be resilient *for?*

This is why having a vocation often strengthens resilience. Your devotion gives you something worth sacrificing for. Your desire to become excellent gives you a reason to develop your habits of mind, body, and spirit.

When I think of the Bosnian refugees who found purpose in the camps by caring for their families, when I think of the SEAL trainees who made it through Hell Week by stepping outside their own pain and fear to help the men beside them, when I think of the veterans who came home from war and found a new purpose in service, I'm reminded of what Nietzsche said: "He who has a *why* to live for can bear almost any *how.*"

If there is a purpose behind your pain, you can find a way through it. For all of us, developing a vocation helps to define and create that sense of purpose.

— 8 —

I think that you and I talked about Joseph Campbell once before. I really hope you'll pick up a book by him, Walker. He's helped two generations to understand the idea of the hero's journey. I'd recommend *The Power of Myth*, a book that's really the record of a long conversation.

Campbell was a scholar of mythology, and his big idea was that the myths of the world's cultures often tell a single, unified story. Though the surface details vary from culture to culture, the essential story remains the same: the journey of a hero who passes from ordinary life through a series of trials and finally returns to serve his people.

Here's how Campbell summarized this recurring myth: "A hero ventures forth from the world of common day into a region of supernatural wonder: fabulous forces are there encountered and a decisive victory is won: the hero comes back from this mysterious adventure with the power to bestow boons on his fellow man."

Communities spread across space and time seem compelled to tell versions of this story. We see its landmarks — such as the hero's call to adventure, or his symbolic death and rebirth — in everything from epic poetry to movies, from Odysseus to Luke Skywalker.

Given what we're talking about, having a vocation, one aspect of the hero's journey is especially important for you to grasp. "The ultimate aim of the quest," wrote Campbell, "must be neither release nor ecstasy for oneself, but the wisdom and the power to serve others." The hero engages in self-discovery and self-creation so that he can ultimately be more useful to others. The hero's journey gives him the power to serve, and he returns to use that power.

Of course, we live in the real world, not the world of myth. But diverse communities wouldn't tell and retell variations of this story if it didn't express something true about human possibilities. And at the crux of the hero's journey is this: the decision to return and serve. That's the real test of heroism.

And that's where your story is now, Walker. You left your world, you saw and experienced things that would have changed anyone, and you've come back. What have you brought with you? How will you use it to make your journey, and your return, heroic?

— 9 —

As I said before, Walker, you're not the first man to face what you're facing. Check out the painting called *The Veteran in a New Field*. It was painted in 1865 by Winslow Homer. The Civil War had ended. Robert E. Lee had surrendered. Lincoln was dead. Thousands of veterans had made their way back to their farms. This veteran, too, has headed straight for his field. He has tossed his military jacket and canteen behind him (in the lower right, though you may not be able to see them here).

There are some dark undertones. The farmer's scythe and the cut stalks remind us of the Grim Reaper — and of the hundreds of thousands of this man's fellow veterans who had given their lives in fields like this.

At the same time, look at that field. There's a big, beautiful crop in front of him. Wheat up to his ears! The sky (in the actual painting) couldn't be a more brilliant blue. A man who ventured to fight far from home has returned to bring in the harvest. Is it too simple to see hardship behind him and hard-won hope in front of him? Is it too simple for us to see the same things in our lives?

— 10 —

And finally, Walker, as we think about hardship and heroism and meaning and engagement, let's also remember fun.

Think about your kids. They're a ton of fun, aren't they? Children play sports. They learn new instruments. They read. They try new things. They learn. They build skills. They laugh.

And then, without our really noticing or deciding, this all slows down and grinds to a halt in too many lives. Not long after our bodies stop growing, our minds and skills stop growing too.

Part of what the old admire and sometimes envy in children is their energy, their curiosity, the fun they have, and their sense of wonder about the world. Where does all of that wonder come from?

A lot of adults think it comes from the fact that children know less of the world. Of course kids are energetic and fascinated and having fun, the thinking goes; they're experiencing everything for the first time.

But sadly, not all children have that wonder. I've worked with some of them—children who live on the streets of Bolivia, children who work full-time at hard labor. So consider this: maybe children don't have these qualities because they are young. Maybe they have them because of how their young lives are structured. Energy, curiosity, and wonder are not products of age. They're byproducts of what we do. Just as those qualities are not universally alive in children, they're not universally dead in adults.

Think about your own kids, Walker. They can be lost for hours in play and make-believe. Is that work saving the world? Certainly not. Not directly. So let's remember that much of the satisfaction we take in what we do comes from something other than its importance.

The good news is that joy, growth, and service tend to reinforce one another.

> The self becomes complex as a result of experiencing flow.
> Paradoxically, it is when we act freely, for the sake of action
> itself rather than for ulterior motives, that we learn to
> become more than what we were. When we choose a goal
> and invest ourselves in it to the limits of our concentration,
> whatever we do will be enjoyable. And once we have
> tasted this joy, we will redouble our efforts to taste it again.
> This is the way the self grows . . . Flow is important
> both because it makes the present instant more enjoyable,
> and because it builds the self-confidence that allows us
> to develop skills and make significant contributions to
> humankind.
>
> — MIHALY CSIKSZENTMIHALYI

You have significant contributions to make, my friend, and I hope that developing your vocation will bring you a lot of joy as well.

Philosophy

Most people imagine that philosophy consists in delivering discourses from the heights of a chair, and in giving classes based on texts. But what these people utterly miss is the uninterrupted philosophy which we see being practiced every day . . . Socrates did not set up grandstands for his audience and did not sit upon a professorial chair; he had no fixed timetable for talking or walking with his friends. Rather, he did philosophy sometimes by joking with them, or by drinking or going to war or to the market with them, and finally by going to prison and drinking poison. He was the first to show that at all times and in every place, in everything that happens to us, daily life gives us the opportunity to do philosophy.

— PLUTARCH (C. 46–120)

Walker,

What I think we're doing in these letters is philosophy. It's hard work to take an honest and searching look at our lives. It always has been, and people have always resisted it. Let's remember that our kind of philosophy involves deliberately making ourselves uncomfortable; it's exercise for the mind and spirit.

Think of what Socrates asked his fellow citizens to do: Examine your lives. Take a disciplined look at your actions. Test your beliefs. Ask the hard questions. Discover how much you don't know.

Socrates was a wily guy. Sometimes his questions were a bit unfair;

sometimes he twisted people's words. But he never held a knife to anyone's throat — he never *demanded* that anyone ask the hard questions. The people of Athens could have chosen to walk away. But his insistence that they question their beliefs was so discomforting, so exasperating, that they put Socrates on trial, condemned him to death, and made him drink poison.

He wasn't the last. Eight hundred years later, in the ancient city of Alexandria, lived the philosopher Hypatia. She was a master astronomer, the leader of a philosophical school, and one of the first recognized female mathematicians in history. But she was also a pagan and a freethinker at a time when Christianity was spreading rapidly. Hypatia never forced anyone to give up their religion. Not a word she said could make anyone's beliefs any more or less true. It didn't matter: finally fed up with an influential thinker who rejected their faith, an enraged mob seized her in the street and killed her.

She wasn't the last. Twelve hundred years later, the friar and astronomer Giordano Bruno shocked Rome with his radical beliefs about space and time. Not only did Bruno believe the Earth went around the Sun, he declared that the Sun was just another star in an infinite universe teeming with intelligent life. Of course, nothing Bruno wrote, no matter how persuasive, could change the actual shape of the universe. It didn't matter: for his heresies, he was burned at the stake. As he was led to execution, a wooden vise was tightened around his mouth to shut him up.

That last detail tells us something important. Socrates and Hypatia and Giordano Bruno had nothing but words — but some words, to some people, are so uncomfortable that they have to be silenced by any means necessary.

What if I'm living my life wrong?

What if my faith isn't true?

What if we aren't the center of the universe?

The deepest questions can also provoke the deepest discomfort, the deepest fear, the deepest rage. That often means they're working.

If philosophy doesn't make you uncomfortable sometimes, it's not doing its job. When we take a hard, honest look in the mirror, it's natural to be disturbed. When we discover things we don't like about ourselves — small ways we've been lying to ourselves, bad habits we've fallen into — it's natural to be angry.

Today, we don't burn people at the stake for asking uncomfortable questions. Usually we ignore them. Sometimes we ridicule them. But the impulse to run away from the hard questions hasn't really changed.

We have to learn to replace that impulse with a new one. Just as we can train ourselves to endure and even to seek the pain that sometimes comes from physical exercise, we can train ourselves to endure and to welcome the discomfort and fear that come when we do philosophy. Those feelings of discomfort are often proof that we're making progress.

— 2 —

Philosophy demands clear thinking, and a quest for clarity often leads to consistency. But if philosophy addresses real life, it will also address life's contradictions.

Consistency, like cleanliness, is usually good. But just as you can become obsessive-compulsive about cleanliness, you can become hypervigilant about consistency.

Some of the thinkers we most remember weren't afraid of inconsistency, because they were daring enough to face up to the mess of real life. (And many of the thinkers we forget made careers out of pointing out these inconsistencies.)

Poets like Walt Whitman got this. He wrote:

Do I contradict myself?
Very well then I contradict myself,
(I am large, I contain multitudes.)

When we were in BUD/S, I gave you a copy of Ralph Waldo Emerson's essays. Emerson had the same idea: "Speak what you think to-day in words as hard as cannon balls, and to-morrow speak what to-morrow thinks in hard words again, though it contradict every thing you said to-day."

Life isn't neat. Life isn't tidy. And philosophy needs to speak to life.

Philosophy is not, for me, a discipline about writing clever papers. It's a discipline about living well. The philosopher shouldn't offer a way of thinking, but a way of living.

Socrates spent his life in conversation, and served in his city's army in wartime, but he never wrote a word. Cato, the Stoic Roman who resisted Julius Caesar, was considered one of the greatest philosophers of his time because he died for his beliefs — but he never wrote a word either. The emperor Marcus Aurelius was called a philosopher because he radiated wisdom and dignity — even though he wrote philosophy only in secret, in his private diary.

These philosophers lived in the real world, Walker. They thought about life as it was lived in their time. Here's one of the thoughts Marcus Aurelius put down in his diary: "Do you get angry with someone for smelling like an old goat? Or for having foul breath? What's the use?"

This is the most powerful man in the world *and* the wisest philosopher of his day writing to himself about armpit stink. I point this out not to belittle what he did or thought, but to show that he was willing to live in the muck with the rest of us.

There is value in rigorously testing the logic underlying our thinking. But the difference between a philosophy fixated on the consistent use of words and a philosophy that speaks to life is akin to the difference between dissecting a horse and riding one. We'll measure the worth of our words by how they move us to live well.

— 3 —

The test of a first-rate intelligence is the ability to hold two
opposed ideas in the mind at the same time, and still retain
the ability to function.

— F. SCOTT FITZGERALD

Any serious person who digs into his or her mind will find a certain level of contradiction among strongly held thoughts and feelings, because those thoughts and feelings emerge in response to an imperfect world. A lot of superficial critics will take those moments of contradiction and pounce: "But before, you said . . ." You have to brush those critics off.

If you think deeply and you find that two important ideas seem to be in contradiction, what you should do first is celebrate: your discovery is evidence that you've had the courage to think deeply. You've become self-aware. You've discovered something about yourself that most people never have the courage to consider: that your own ideas, and your own life, might not fit into a tidy little package.

What do you do next? Press on. Maybe, as you think harder and live more, your contradiction will resolve itself. Maybe it won't.

Remember that the intention of philosophy isn't to help you live a logical life. It's to make you self-aware and help you live a good life.

Use logic, of course. But use it, don't serve it. Logic is a tool, not a master. The mysteries of life are such that it's unlikely that any set of propositions — no matter how rigorous, how structured, how measured — will ever be able to account for some of the most important things in our lives. Take beauty, for example. What would it be to live without moments of beauty?

In a similar way, Walker, if we're going to think well about our lives, we have to remember that some things can be true most of the time without being true all of the time.

Here's a well-known saying from a Supreme Court justice: "Hard cases make bad law." Extraordinary cases and extreme examples naturally pique our interest and invite our attention. And sometimes there's something to be learned about life in general when we look at a famous case in particular. But it's a mistake to root our thinking about rules for living in extreme examples. The tallest person in the world is over eight feet tall. That's fine to know, but we shouldn't expect it to guide the way houses and beds are built for the rest of us.

This is obvious. But it needs to be mentioned because as soon as you name a rule you think ought to guide conduct in general, like, "People who have strength should use that strength to protect people in need of protection," someone will say (and you told me you've really had to argue with people like this), "But what if there's a wolf attacking a man, and you've got a gun and you can protect the man, but the man is a child molester and a dictator who has tortured millions of people and, if the wolf doesn't kill him, he'll escape back to his country and starve his people? Should you protect him then?"

In that case your responsibility is pretty clear: use the gun to finish what the wolf leaves undone. This is obviously stupid, silly, and fantastic. What is real, though, is the tendency to give up on the search for principles that can guide our lives most of the time just because they fail to apply all of the time.

Fixating on extremes, like fixating on inconsistencies, can start to stand in the way of living well.

— 4 —

To recognize that good thinking involves confronting our own inconsistencies does not excuse us from doing serious thinking.

A serious philosophy doesn't have to be boring or complex. It can be engaging and straightforward. And to be guided by a serious philosophy means only that there is a relationship between thinking and action, in that order.

Too often, we dive into action and, in retrospect, discover that we should have thought first. Afterward, we try to explain ourselves to ourselves, but our thinking is more an exercise in justification than a search for insight.

We all do this. And there is no point in whipping ourselves for past failures to think. The danger, though, is that the explanation that justifies our past will become the philosophy that guides our future.

You've seen this a hundred times. And if you're like me, you've done it at least a few dozen times — well, OK, a few hundred. You do something stupid. Then you justify it. Then you start to believe your own justification. Then you start doing things to justify your justification.

Remember Baba, the Lithuanian Special Forces commando in our BUD/S class? As he was fond of saying: "This shit has to end. Now."

— 5 —

Zach, chances are good that, wherever you are right now, you're reading these words silently. In the ancient world, it was rare to find anyone who read silently. When words were read, they were usually read aloud, and often they were read to and with other people.

That was true of philosophy as well. It wasn't something you studied on your own; it was something you read out loud with others. Philosophy was a shared discipline, part of a shared effort to live well.

Plato wrote his philosophy in the form of dialogues — conversations. In his time, it's possible that they were performed aloud, like plays. Part of the message was that to live philosophically, you have to take turns listening and speaking; you have to look for truth with others.

Aristotle spent his time not as a solitary writer, but as a teacher living in a community of scholars and students. When you go to a bookstore and see a volume of Aristotle's *Nicomachean Ethics,* you're actually looking at a collection of his lecture notes. And when he taught ethics, he reminded his students that "the end of this science is not knowledge but action."

In Plato and Aristotle's world, traveling philosophers (like traveling preachers more recently) often drew huge, excited crowds to their talks. And in great cities like Athens, philosophy students lived together, ate together, studied together, talked together. Philosophy was something people did *together.* You talked, you listened, you argued, you agreed. You tried to see things from your friend's point of view. You tried to live up to your teacher's example. You pushed your friends when their effort slackened, and they pushed you.

America's founders understood philosophy in the same way. George Washington, as I mentioned a few letters ago, put on a play about the fall of the Roman Republic for his troops at Valley Forge. Benjamin Franklin, when he was just twenty-one, organized a club of friends called the Junto that met every week to discuss philosophy and public affairs. We still have a list of questions Franklin wrote to drive the discussions: "Have you lately heard of any citizen's thriving well, and by what means?" "Have you lately observed any encroachment on the just liberties of the people?" "Do you know of any fellow citizen who has lately done a worthy action, deserving praise and imitation? or who has committed an error proper for us to be warned against and avoid?"

If you want to live like a philosopher, do what Franklin did — seek out good conversation. Philosophy is, and has always been, a kind of conversation. It's only by engaging with others that we break out of the prison of our own prejudices, our own bad habits, our own fears. That's what we're trying to do together here.

If we recognize that our experience is limited, we should also recognize that our wisdom is limited.

There is something about soldiering, about living through a brush with death and being responsible for the lives of others, that the non-soldier will never fully understand.

There is something about starting and running a small business, about taking risks and being personally responsible for someone else's livelihood, that those who have never run a business will never quite grasp. There is something about being a parent, about love for a child, that a nonparent may never know. There is a certain kind of wisdom available to the soldier, the entrepreneur, the parent, and to people in a hundred other walks of life that you can't know unless you actually live those lives.

If we understand this — and if we also reflect on how minuscule our drop of experience is in the vast ocean of human experience — we should stand open to the wisdom that others have to offer. Philosophy is made to be practiced with others, because we all have a lot to learn from each other.

— 6 —

Zach, you've got your third kid on the way. I couldn't be happier for you.

I'm also grateful that we live in a world where we can look forward to childbirth with joy and not fear. Three thousand years ago, people celebrated the joy of a newborn child. But much more frequently than today, they also mourned the death of a stillborn child or a young woman who died giving birth. Three thousand years ago, people rejoiced when their warriors came home from battle. Much more frequently than today, they grieved when they heard the news that those they loved would never come home. Three thousand years ago, people gave thanks for the turning of the seasons with feasts and festivals. Much more frequently than today, they suffered famine, disaster, and disease.

To deal with this agony, they developed philosophies, the ideas and practices that built resilience into their lives.

Epictetus, a slave and a philosopher, lived in this ancient world of insecurity and uncertainty. Every time you kiss your child goodnight, he said, you should tell yourself, "Perhaps it will be dead in the morning."

The suggestion that you think of your child's imminent death every night seems alien and cruel to us. But in the ancient Roman world, more than a quarter of newborns died before their first birthday, and half of all children died before their tenth. Epictetus was not being needlessly harsh. Instead, he was reminding parents to be grateful for what they had in that moment, and to mentally prepare themselves for a hardship they might face any day.

Today, we're remarkably fortunate. We still worry about the death of an infant (how many times did you get up at night to check Shane's breathing in his first month at home?), but a young child's death is a tragedy far fewer of us have to face.

Before I joined the military, I'd seen the human suffering of ethnic cleansing and genocide in Bosnia and Rwanda. I'd seen children in Cambodia who were missing limbs taken by land mines. I saw the dead eyes of abandoned and drug-addicted kids on the streets of Bolivia. I have seen, as you have, blood spilled in battle.

There is still real hardship in our world, and we've both seen it. But we live in a world marked by great progress: food is more plentiful, disease rarer, early death less common, knowledge more accessible, people freer than at any time in history. Human beings exert a mastery over the physical world — traveling thousands of miles in several hours rather than several months, controlling air temperature with the twist of a dial, sharing ideas instantaneously across oceans — that would have seemed godlike to a person of Aeschylus's time.

But many of us lucky enough to take part in this ease and freedom have also lost touch with the wisdom about resilience built by men and women who lived in a harder world.

In our security and comfort, we slip quietly into the false expectation that life will afford us complete happiness. We believe that we will move only from pleasure to pleasure, from joy to joy. When tragedy strikes or hardship hits, too many of us feel ambushed by pain, betrayed by the present, despairing of the future.

— 7 —

Do you remember when we were in the first-phase classroom days after September 11, 2001, and the instructors were briefing us on the Taliban? They told us that the Taliban moved fast and light. Few supplies. Simple clothes. Rifle, ammo, minimal food. They sometimes walked in sandals made of rubber cut from tires. They were painting a picture of a rugged, mobile, lethal force.

One day you stood up in the middle of class and said something like, "Let's go! I'll wear tire shoes. I'll walk in the cold. I'll go light. I'm ready to fight." It was a great Walker moment. So let me use it to draw an analogy.

For most of history, our feet were hardened by walking on the rough ground. In our world, most people wear shoes. Shoes are good. They protect our feet. But we realize that it is possible to gain something very good and still lose something very real. What most of us have lost is the ability to walk barefoot over difficult ground.

Today, sheltered from the hardships of hunger, disease, heat, and cold that stalked human life for centuries, some people have lost their capacity to deal with real difficulty. Growing up in a protected palace of comfort, they have lost their ability to walk through pain.

— 8 —

Zach, the other day, you wrote to me about growing up in the woods:

About six months before I was born my folks traded a 1953 Willys pickup truck and $500 for that single-wide I would call home for the first nine years of my life. One day in winter, they hauled it up the skid trail, which would then become our driveway. I remember dad cutting in water bars with the dozer every winter to keep it from falling off the mountain.

The ranch was covered in Douglas firs and towering redwoods. A creek ran right through the middle of it and went a quarter mile down the driveway to spill into Austin Creek. My closest neighbor was a mile away.

My folks had about a quarter-acre garden with an eight-foot fence protecting the crops from deer and other wildlife. We had chickens and hogs and a couple of cows for butchering when the work got slim in the winter. My dad was a backhoe operator and mixer driver down at the end of the canyon where one of the town's three businesses was: a rock quarry and concrete plant. The other two businesses were a lumber mill and a logging and excavation outfit on the other side of the ranch.

One of his co-workers told me one time when I was about 20 years old, "I like your dad. He hates me, but the thing about your old man is that he hates everyone the same."

I've known you for more than a decade now, and I think growing up in the sticks has shaped the way you think, maybe even more than you know.

People who grow up like you did have a real connection to the earth. They grow up understanding that life has a reality — sun, moon, heat, frost, flood, drought — that is beyond human control, a reality we must accept, adjust to, and work with. When you were logging, each day was shaped by the burn of the sun, the speed of the wind, the snap of the cold. When the outdoors is a part of your life, it's hard not to be a realist.

But when people spend all of their time in a world shaped by human hands, they bring a different perspective to their lives. Those who grow up in or near cities often see the world as built by and for other people, and they tend to believe that if we continue to build it better, we can achieve perfection. Without openly acknowledging it, they often believe that the relentless pursuit of progress will eventually lead us to paradise. (A clue: ask them if there are any unsolvable problems. If they can't think of problems that won't ever be solved, they are most likely utopians, even if they aren't self-aware enough to see it.)

I'm painting with a very broad brush here, but this is a big idea with big consequences. The French Revolution was led mostly by urban-raised idealists who believed in the perfectibility of man. The American Revolution was led mostly by agrarian-raised realists who understood the imperfectibility of man.

The French Revolution led to a reign of terror and to dictatorship, as waves of utopians sought to kill anyone who stood in the way of the perfectly rational society. The American Revolution ultimately led to a constitution that divided power and set men against each other, lest any one person's failures destroy the entire country.

The French Revolution produced men like Maximilien Robespierre, who said things like this: "By sealing our work with our blood, we may see at last the bright dawn of universal happiness."

The American Revolution produced men like James Madison, who said things like this: "Ambition must be made to counteract ambition . . . This policy of supplying, by opposite and rival interests, the defect of better motives, might be traced through the whole system of human affairs, private as well as public."

I don't want to suggest that how you're raised or where you grow up seals the shape of your thinking for the rest of your life. (In fact, there are many counterexamples to what I've just suggested.) I do want to insist that realism — about the world we find ourselves in, about the imperfect communities we build, about our own natures—matters for resilience.

Resilient realists know that life—despite our highest ideals—is imperfect. You learned as a logger that you can't control the weather, and that the weather has real consequences for your work. You've learned, too, that you can't control the greed of others, and that greed has real consequences for your community. Human failings, like a gathering thunderstorm in the woods, are more dangerous if we close our eyes to them until it's too late.

Resilience is not a path to perfection. Instead, we seek to be resilient in the face of life's imperfect reality.

The political theorist Niccolò Machiavelli wrote: "The Romans saw when troubles were coming and always took counter-measures. They never, to avoid a war, allowed them to go unchecked, because they knew that there is no avoiding war; it can only be postponed to the advantage of others." In the SEAL teams, an instructor once said that WAR is an acronym: We Are Ready.

Readiness means confronting the reality that life's course is not completely under your control. Readiness is a form of humility, spurred by a recognition of how little we can know or control. Hardship is unavoidable. Resilient people recognize this reality. Then they prepare themselves for it, seeking to meet it as best they can, on their own terms.

Realism also teaches us humility about our limited ability to change others. The monk Thomas à Kempis understood this human limitation: "If you cannot make yourself what you would wish to be, how can you bend others to your will?"

Think about how hard it is to change your own behavior: to pull yourself out of a rut, to root out a bad habit. And all this difficulty comes when you try to change the single person over whom you have the most power—yourself. Reflect, then, on how much harder it is to change someone else.

We *can* have a profound influence on others. That's true. And I want you to serve because the world needs what you have to offer. At the same time, the most successful service begins with the recognition that people will make their own choices.

Imagine that human nature can be perfected, and the human failings all around you — others' and your own — will infuriate you. You might even find yourself tempted to think, like Robespierre, that people must be bullied or terrorized into goodness.

Recognize, as realists do, that life has a tragic character — that human beings are flawed, and that both the natural and the human world are beyond your power to control, and you'll have a better chance of serving effectively.

— 9 —

There are different kinds of simplicity. Some are better than others.

There is simplicity that comes from a lack of knowledge and experience. You told me that when you were a kid, you and your brother Ed were sitting on the porch one night and Ed asked your dad how all of the stars got up in the sky. You told him that God got up on a ladder and put 'em all there. That's a simple answer. Kids often have simple answers to explain the world. It's fun and sometimes beautiful. But if we live with a child's simplicity into adulthood, we often find ourselves ravaged by reality.

Think about how our understanding of good and evil changes, grows deeper and often more painful, as we grow older. Aleksandr Solzhenitsyn knew about evil: he was a writer who chronicled the Soviet gulag and served eight years in its forced-labor camps. He wrote: "If only there were evil people somewhere insidiously committing evil deeds, and it were necessary only to separate them from the rest of us and destroy them . . . But the line dividing good and evil cuts through the heart of every human being. And who is willing to destroy a piece of his own heart?"

The more we think, the more we study, the more we learn, the more likely it is that we will confront some of life's complications. As we begin to know more, we grasp details. We see nuances.

If we struggle with those details, nuances, and complications successfully, on the other side of them we achieve a different kind of simplicity.

I'm sure you've noticed that, in almost any endeavor, people who really know their stuff can explain it clearly. The master instructor knows the details but coaches with simple instructions: stand tall, breathe, and so on. The master teacher understands every word of her text but concentrates on the central idea. The ability to explain complicated things with clarity is a mark of mastery.

Unfortunately, it's sometimes those who have mastered the least who talk the most. When we practice philosophy, we strive to grow from the simplicity of the child to the clarity of the adult.

Simplicity is easy. Clarity is earned. We earn clarity by confronting complexity.

— 10 —

In philosophy we have to think about what it means to be good. This sounds like the ultimate philosophical abstraction: "What is the nature of the good?" Or, "What counts as being good?" But this also matters a lot to living a resilient life, and I'll explain why.

Broadly speaking, you will be faced with two ways of thinking about what counts as good in life: intentions or results.

When the genocide was happening in Rwanda in 1994, I remember that many people around the world were shocked and outraged. Many people wanted to help. I also remember that their wanting didn't matter.

There was a great dividing line between all of the speeches, protests, feelings, empathy, good wishes, and words in the world, and the one thing that could stop the violence: protecting people through the use of force or the threat of force. In situations like this, good intentions and heartfelt wishes were not enough. The great dividing line between words and results was courageous action. One of the greatest gulfs in life is between sounding good and doing good.

We are ultimately measured by our results, by the way our actions shape the world around us. Without results, all the kind intentions in the world are just a way of entertaining ourselves.

It may be helpful to think about the difference between intentions and results by looking at how the Greeks thought about right action.

The word that shows up again and again in their discussions of ethics is *arête*. As we've already discussed, *arête* doesn't really mean "virtue," though that's how it's often translated. When the Greeks used the word *arête,* it referred to excellence. They used the same word to describe the excellence of a vase, the excellence of a great runner, and the excellence of a person.

To be excellent is to be someone who produces excellence. There is no such thing as an excellent shoemaker who regularly turns out flimsy shoes. So think a bit about what the Greeks must have believed about having an excellent character. Your character was judged excellent not before you acted, but after. The judgment was based not on your intentions, but on your results.

When we think of virtue as an excellence, we don't ask, "What did I intend?" We ask, "What did I do?"

The "morality of intentions"—which would measure our goodness in terms of what we hope to accomplish rather than what we actually accomplish—tells us that our thoughts and feelings count for something in their own right. It's an appealing philosophy to those who exist, or want to exist, in a world of pure thought or feeling.

But it can also be a selfish kind of morality. It elevates the helper above the one who should be helped. It says, "What matters is the fact that I have the right opinions, not what good my opinions do in the world. What matters is what I hope or intend, not what you deserve or receive." In fact, a morality of intentions—even the best intentions—can distort your view of the world in a way that leads to great harm.

Think of it this way. It's nice that someone might want to help a child to read. It's nice if they show up every day to do so. But it's wrong to go to those lessons unprepared and incapable of doing real good. It wastes that child's time and stands in the way of the help she really needs. From the perspective of intentions, that volunteer might have reason to pat himself on the back. But from the perspective of results, that volunteer is making an active contribution to a child's illiteracy.

After the Rwandan genocide, the media flocked to stories of "desperate war orphans," and aid agencies set up orphanages across the border in Zaire for refugee children separated from their parents. The problem was that many of the children taken into these group homes weren't orphans. I talked with mothers who gave up their children—temporarily, they hoped—because they thought it was the only way to ensure their children's survival. It was a vicious cycle: money flowed into the centers to care for the growing number of children, and the increased resources led even more families to place their children in the centers. With little supervision, some children were abused; others were "fostered out" to "work" for unscrupulous people in the refugee camps. Sometimes these orphanages were moved back to Rwanda, and then children really were separated from their parents.

The orphanages grew from the best intentions, but they often harmed the very children they were intended to serve. The aid agencies could have directed their funds toward supporting caregivers and keeping families intact wherever possible; but, perversely, their actions helped to break families apart.

A morality of results doesn't demand that we succeed every time or else be judged bad people. It does tell us to put the well-being of others at the center of our judgments about right and wrong. Before I pronounce myself good, I have to point to something more than what I *wanted* to happen — I have to point to what I have done in the world.

A morality of intentions also fails to help us get better. If all that matters are our intentions, we don't have much of a reason to make ourselves better at doing good.

A morality of results is difficult precisely because it requires us to mold ourselves into wiser, tougher, more capable people who do good in a difficult world.

Many people shaped by the morality of intentions find that their abilities atrophy. They talk more and more and do less and less. With each disappointment with the world, they retreat further into themselves, convinced evermore of their own righteousness and the world's wickedness. People content with good intentions rarely make a difference.

It is hard to teach a six-year-old to read. It is hard to help a homeless woman find a job and break the cycle of poverty. But people accomplish this hard work every day. The people who accomplish such things regularly and with excellence are the ones who hold themselves accountable for results.

It's nice that you want to make a difference. But here's the hard truth: your wanting is irrelevant to the people who need your help. They don't need your wanting. They need your strength in action, and they need you to be open to discovering what actually works.

— 11 —

Remember the first day of BUD/S? It started with a four-mile run, in soft sand, at 0500. If you finished in 32 minutes flat, you got to sit. If you finished at 32:01, you got hammered. The instructors made the guys who failed run in and out of the 50-some-degree water of the Pacific again and again and again. They ran out of the ocean, dropped to the ground, and rolled on the beach until they were "wet and sandy."

I remember how the instructors circled around a man who'd failed the run and was now covered in salt water and sand. They were making him do pushups, and he had his hands buried in the sand and his butt in the air. His arms were shaking, failing him.

Drool hung from his lip as he tried to spit the sand out of his mouth. He must have said something like, "I'm trying," because the instructor exploded: "There is no *try*. We do not *try*. Your teammates do not need you to *try* to cover their backs. Your swim buddy does not need you to *try* to rescue him on a dive. Your platoon does not need you to *try* to shoot straight. There is no *try*. There is only *do*. *Do*, or *do not*. There is no *try*."

The fact that the instructor stole this line from Yoda in *The Empire Strikes Back* didn't make it any less true, or any less what we all needed to hear.

The lesson was this: If your best is not good enough, make your best better. If you tried hard and failed, then try harder, or find a new way to try until you succeed. Trying hard is trying hard. Success is success. There is a difference.

Despite an overwhelming amount of well-intentioned nonsense that we now teach our children, it actually is *not enough* to try hard. Yes, it's good to try hard. It is even better to try hard and — after suffering numerous setbacks and working through hardship and pain and temporary defeat — to achieve, to master. Trying hard builds character, but it is only the achievement that follows the effort that builds true confidence. We teach children that it doesn't matter whether they win or lose, it's how they play the game. But this lesson can be taught poorly or well.

Taught poorly, this lesson results in children who are careless of the outcome of their actions, who are more concerned with double- and triple-checking their inner state than with measuring themselves against the world. Taught well, though, this lesson makes clear that while the valiant might lose many, many times, the object of the valiant is to persevere until victory.

Intentions do matter. But they matter because they find expression in our actions and in our character. What ultimately matters is not what we intend, but who we become and what we leave behind us.

Those who live by a morality of results and responsibility are much more likely to be resilient, because what matters most to them is useful work. Because their effectiveness matters to them, they take seriously the lessons the world teaches them, including the lessons of disappointment. Because they don't allow themselves to retreat into the purity of their intentions, they learn to confront the facts of failure. This allows them to grow in humility and in the honesty with which they see themselves.

— 12 —

Certain ideas can be understood only when we contend with them in practice. The philosopher Martin Heidegger famously pointed out that you can't come to know a hammer by staring at it. You can't come to know a hammer by reading about one either. You have to use the hammer.

When you do, you hit your thumb. You bend the nail double when you whack it at the wrong angle, and then you have to undo your mistake. In time, you come to understand the hammer's weight in your hand, and you recognize the feel when you hit a nail square. Only by using the hammer do you come to know it.

Philosophy is meant to be *done,* not just studied. Only by using philosophy do you come to know it. It is a practice. It takes practice. So let's talk a bit about practice.

Practice

The fight is won or lost far away from witnesses . . .
in the gym, and out there on the road, long before I
dance under those lights.

— MUHAMMAD ALI

Zach,

You need to get into the game. At this point, it almost doesn't matter what you are doing — coaching baseball or football, working at the VA, starting your farm — it's just time to get to work.

Part of the joy of entertainment is that we can appreciate the fruits of someone's labor without having to do the work ourselves. We watch the dance, but we don't have to sweat. We watch the game, but we don't have to practice through injury. We watch the play, but we don't have to write, direct, act, light, or rehearse.

But if we're entertained too much and forget to practice ourselves, we'll lose sight of the work behind the beauty in front of us. We come to believe that dancers, players, and actors simply *have* talent, and we can forget that they have to struggle every day to develop it. We see the product, but forget the sweat that put it there. We forget that what looks effortless is usually the product of years of effort.

One benefit of pursuing excellence in your own life again is that it will shape the way you see the world around you. Whether it's a great game you watch, meal you eat, or story you read, you're more likely to see the sweat and care that went into it. Working hard yourself makes you more appreciative and respectful of the hard work of others.

— 2 —

Zach, this is going to read like a Zen koan, but I want you to practice practice. You must practice the art of practicing.

Let me explain. When most people practice, they think of themselves as practicing *how to do something*. What if, instead, you think of yourself as learning *how to practice something*? If you learn how to do something — change a tire, prepare a canvas, develop a photograph, pour concrete, make macaroni and cheese — then you've learned how to do one thing. If you learn how to practice, then you have learned how to learn anything.

It is only through practice that we attain excellence in any endeavor. And perhaps the greatest skill we can learn is the skill of practice itself.

We've already talked about some of the things that go into good practice: finding a model, thinking about identity, forming the right habits. The point I want to impress upon you now is:

You can practice more than you imagine.

You know that we can practice games and sports and instruments. But we can also practice, for example, gratitude. A daily practice of writing down things we are grateful for will, in time, make us grateful people. (In my experience, it will also make us happier.)

We can practice self-examination. Seneca recommended looking back over each day's actions before going to bed. He said that you should ask yourself: "What evils have you cured yourself of today? What vices have you fought? In what sense are you better? . . . When the torch has been taken away and my wife, already used to my habits, has fallen silent, I examine my entire day and measure what I have done and said. I hide nothing from myself."

We can practice prayer. We can practice compassion. We can practice courage and math and speaking with confidence and how to braid our daughter's hair. We can practice the habits of being a good father and husband and son. We can practice our vocation.

People who don't understand the possibilities inherent in practice often conclude that they "are" a certain way. When they fail or succeed they think, "I am stupid" or "I am smart" or "I am lazy" or "I am evil" or

"I am fat" or "I am funny." By concluding that they "are" a certain way, they fix their identity to the present and the past, and they often look to the future with fear and trepidation.

Those who practice practice use their experience to inform who they *can be*. "That happened, so next time I should . . ." or, "If that happens again, I'll . . ." or, "That was great, and to get even better, then next time I should practice . . ."

Several letters back, I wrote to you about how resilience is not about bouncing back but about moving through. Learning how to practice is essential to moving through, because it is the discipline of practice itself that allows you to take what happens to you, integrate it into your experience, and then act again. The more you see that life can be practiced, the more resilient you will become.

— 3 —

Almost everything can be practiced, but practicing anything starts with the will to work. When I was boxing at Oxford, my friend Ben was the captain of the university team. You'd like Ben. He grew up in South Dakota, spent a lot of time bow-hunting in the woods, worked as a hotshot on one of the fire crews out west. He's got a gaggle of great stories about being attacked by crocodiles while kayaking in Australia, or hunting wild boar with spears in the South Pacific.

I'll tell you a few of my favorite things about Ben. One, the man could not conceal an emotion to save his life. If someone was saying something that Ben thought was rude or stupid, Ben would look at the guy with a face of absolute disgust.

Two, a quick story. Ben was dating Angela at Oxford, and they're now married with three beautiful kids. Angela is black, and one day she was walking down the street and some hooligan yelled something racist at her. Then he yelled again. Angela walked a little faster, and the guy kept taunting her. When he walked away, Angela followed. Unfortunately for him, he went right past where Ben lived. Angela banged on Ben's window and told him what happened, so Ben jumped out of the window wearing socks and shorts and chased the guy for over a mile through the streets of Oxford. When Ben had him cornered, the man threatened to take a swing at him. Ben was never scared of taking a punch, and he leaned forward, offered his chin, and said, "Please, just give me an excuse." The man never took that swing; he stayed right there until the cops came.

Three, Ben tends to talk a lot when he's sitting down with his friends, but he's not much for public speeches. At the beginning of the boxing season, dozens of guys would come down to the gym wanting to try out for the Oxford boxing team. As they stood waiting for the first practice to begin, they expected to hear some words of welcome, some explanation of how the boxing team worked. Ben stood up, and this was his whole speech:

"We do two things here. We work hard. And we win. The reason we win is that we work hard. So really, we only do one thing here. If you don't want to work hard, don't waste my time."

Then practice started.

Look, Walker, you're a hard worker. You always have been. About that there's no doubt.

And you know that victories are won and excellence is achieved not on the field but in practice. You know that the gap between good performers and exceptional performers is not between those who know a lot and those who know a little, but between those who give some of themselves to their practice and those who give all of themselves.

You know that excellence comes wrapped in hard work. You know that the will to win is cheap and common, while the will to *train* is rare and noble.

With other people, you might worry about their will. That's not your problem. Your challenge right now is that since you've left the military, you can't see clearly what to train for, and you're struggling to figure it out: "How do I train for all of these other things that are happening in my life?"

— 4 —

When you coach the kids on your football team, you don't get to rewrite the standards of excellence, any more than you get to rewrite the rules of the game. In football, a good tackle starts from the leading shoulder and wraps up the ball carrier. In baseball, a good fastball arrives at a point between the batter's chest and knees.

There's no faking your way around these techniques: they are correct or they aren't. Athletic contests offer a clarity that's often missing from the rest of our lives. There are rules and points, time limits and victors. It's part of what makes watching sports enjoyable.

(It's also one of the reasons why the Greeks and the Romans put such a strong emphasis on physical training. They lived, of course, in a world that demanded physical strength, from farming to warfare. Yet they also understood that in order to train the spirit you had to train both mind and body, and that in training children to play games they had clear opportunities to train them in the virtues.)

Now, sports are also an extreme case: a good life is not nearly as simple as a home run or a touchdown. Life isn't a sport or a mission, but we can still create clarity in our own lives about what is good.

I recently spoke to a group of pipefitters and steelworkers. In these trades, the pipes fit or they don't. Water flows or it does not. Structures hold or fall. In short, there are clear standards for what is good.

The same can be said of other work. A carpenter has a level. A business has a bottom line. A team looks at the scoreboard. Some standards of the good are so easily measured that they can be understood by anyone. You place a level on a table and you look — is the table level?

Other standards are harder to formulate. Think of a social worker who is sent into a home with the charge of protecting a child from possible abuse. What constitutes excellence here? The social worker is operating with imperfect information in a web of new relationships. She wants to respect the parents' right to custody of their child, while aiming to protect the child from abuse, while also knowing that removing the child from a difficult home may end one hardship only to begin another.

In this case, coming to a shared and common standard about excellence is a much tougher task. One of the reasons why we talked about models before and in so much detail is that especially when things get messy, your models can provide you a standard for excellence in your work. When you don't know where to look for a standard, you can start by asking, "What would they do if they were here?"

— 5 —

Every few months we've been getting a group of veterans together, and at one of these meetings I wrote this equation in front of them:

$$\frac{\text{The magnitude}}{\text{of the challenge}} \times \frac{\text{the intensity}}{\text{of your attack}} = \frac{\text{your rate}}{\text{of growth}}$$

It's an idea, of course, not a real formula. But you do need big challenges in your life, and you need to bring intensity to those challenges if you aim to grow. I hate to use the BUD/S analogy so much, but here goes: it was the hardest military training in the world, multiplied by the intensity you brought to it. Now think about how much you changed. Think about who you'd be today if you'd never been a SEAL.

I don't know if this is the case for you right now or not, but what stunts a lot of people in their practice isn't that their goals are too big, but that their goals are too small. It's important to be able to break big challenges down into attackable pieces (and we'll talk more about how resilient people segment challenges later), but why work your heart out for a goal that's small?

— 6 —

Five variables go into training or practice of any kind: frequency, intensity, duration, recovery, and reflection.

Frequency is important because we learn through repetition. Our bodies and minds and spirits need to adapt between each practice.

Intensity is important because we grow only when we push ourselves beyond the boundaries of our past experiences.

Duration is important because we need to train as long as necessary for our bodies, minds, and spirits to adapt to our work.

Recovery is important because our bodies, minds, and spirits need time to adapt to what we have learned. When we sleep after exercise, we can grow stronger. When we sleep after studying, we can grow smarter. Even monks take breaks from prayer so that their spirits can grow.

Finally, reflection is important because we have to consider our performance against the standards we have set, adjust ourselves, and integrate what we've learned into our lives. Our times of practice will become isolated islands unless we reflect. Reflection is the bridge between what we practice and the way we live our lives.

— 7 —

A book — Aristotle's work on ethics, a good biography, or one of Aeschylus's plays — can teach you *about* resilience. But resilience *itself* can only be built by practice. To build resilience, we must practice it, not haphazardly, but deliberately.

And remember, Walker, in almost anything that you choose to practice — gratitude, your bench press, or making breakfast for your daughter — you are going to fail a time or two or two thousand. If you aren't failing from time to time, there are two possibilities. One, you're Superman. Or two, you aren't pushing yourself hard enough. Which do you think is more likely?

— 8 —

In ancient Greece, repetition was an expected and integral part of philosophy. People attended philosophy lectures in the way that, today, people might go to church every week or read a particular magazine every month. The Greeks understood that shaping human behavior requires repetition. This is as true of mental and spiritual training as it is of physical training.

We can lose focus. We take a day off, and then a week off. We forget what inspired us in the first place. And to prevent these things from happening — to prevent the slackening of effort that can come in any practice — we build structures of repetition into our lives.

In repetition, three things happen. First, we are reminded. Most of the important things in life need to be taught only once, but we need to be reminded of them often. Marcus Aurelius's practice of philosophy was really nothing more than an elaborate system of self-reminding. He recognized that "we need more often to be reminded than informed."

Second, as we change over time, the same message works on us in different ways. A message about mental toughness in the face of exhaustion will be heard differently by the young athlete than by the new parent.

Third, an idea is similar to a tool: for it to become part of who we are and how we think, we have to become familiar with it. We become familiar with ideas not only by reading about them or hearing about them, but by thinking about them, talking about them, writing about them, and *using* them in our lives.

Practice and purposeful repetition are what separate an idea that interests us for a moment from an idea that becomes a part of our character.

— 9 —

When I was in high school, I remember my English teacher Barbara Osburg telling me a story about a young couple. I can't remember if it was a true story about people she knew or a story about people she had read about in a book, but her mind was always full of wisdom gained from both, and I don't know that it makes much difference. Here's the story:

A young mother is holding a baby in her arms. At the same time, she is trying to cook dinner. Dinner is about to burn. Just as she needs to grab the pot from the stove, the phone begins to ring.

Meanwhile, her husband is upstairs writing. She calls to him for help, and he murmurs something about his writing. She walks upstairs and stands in the doorway of the room where he is typing. He does not look up. She gets his attention by saying, "I need you to listen to me," and asks, "If there were a fire right now, would you run through the house to save me and the baby?"

He says, "Yes, of course."

She replies, "There's never going to be a fire."

We talked about this before, Walker. People want to imagine that somehow, when "the moment" comes, they will be heroes. But there are rarely such moments in anyone's life, and when they do come, they last for mere minutes. What usually matters in your life is not the magical moment, but the quality of your daily practice. As the novelist Anthony Trollope wrote, "A small daily task, if it be really daily, will beat the labours of a spasmodic Hercules."

— 10 —

You've talked about helping your fellow veterans who've come back from the war. You'll be great at it. One of the reasons you'll be great is that you respect people enough to know — and your own struggles have shown you — that even smart people can make bad choices. And that will set you apart from a lot of the "smart" people who want to "change the world."

Many programs run by the professional improvers of society are built on education, not training — on delivering facts rather than strengthening practice. Knowledge matters. But our efforts too often stop at knowledge, because it's easier to measure what we've told people than it is to measure how we've changed people. It is easier to preach to people than to practice with them.

We're all complicated and difficult to improve, and each one of us is difficult in a different way from the next. Practice that actually improves us in meaningful ways takes huge amounts of dedicated time, skill, and attention — and even then, we can't be certain of success.

Is the problem really that people don't know enough? Or is it that they don't *do* enough of the right stuff? It's an important question to ask, because it helps us to get clear on the relationship between education and training.

We often assume that learning is enough, that once we know something is good or right or wise, we'll act on that knowledge. Only rarely is that true. We're adults. When we do things that are bad for us, we usually know they're bad for us. Our intentions and our actions never line up as perfectly as we'd like.

People have struggled with this disconnect between intentions and actions for thousands of years. Saint Paul grappled with it: "I do not understand what I am doing, because I do not practice what I want to do, but I do what I hate."

Here was a man who knew what the right thing was and still did what he knew was the wrong thing, again and again. And those were the words of someone disciplined enough, energetic enough, and passionate enough to accomplish what Paul did. Do we expect to do any better?

I don't know if you ever watched GI Joe cartoons growing up, but at the end of most of the shows, they'd run a public service announcement — what to do if there's a fire in your house, what to do if you're lost, why you should always wear a life jacket and obey railroad crossing signs. Every message would end with one of the characters saying, "Now you know. And knowing is half the battle."

Maybe. Maybe it's half. But it's half at most. Knowing is usually the easy part. Doing is much harder.

In any endeavor to change practice, you have to ask: Why would smart people do something that seems to be bad for them? You can usually answer that question only by getting to know people.

It's helpful to know something about resilience, but to *be* resilient you have to practice, to train in resilience. Education is different from training. Education aims to change what you know. Training aims to change who you are. Practicing practice will enable you to — in the words of the old Army commercial — be all that you can be.

Pain

Walker,

You told me you broke three ribs when you were sixteen, in your first summer as a logger. I've broken bones too; it's painful.

The first time I broke a bone, I was a teenager playing soccer. I fell backward and landed funny on my left hand. It hurt the moment it happened, but not badly, and I didn't realize I had a fracture until I was on the sideline and it started to swell. Later, in college, I broke my leg playing a pickup football game; that one hurt much worse. Most recently, a few months ago, I was fighting in a tae kwon do match, and when I walked off the mat, I saw that my foot had swelled and I knew — broken.

Every broken bone offers a different kind of pain. The ones that crack really hurt — there's that flood of adrenaline, the rush of blood, and then the dull throbbing punctuated by sharp spikes of pain.

But the pain of a broken bone has little in common with the pain that comes from being unable to find work: the monotony and self-doubt, the slow drain of energy from your mind and your body, the hopelessness that sets in as you wake up and remember that you have nowhere to be that day. And that pain, of course, is different from the pain you feel when someone you love dies and you catch yourself thinking about her as if she were still alive.

If you begin to think about all of the kinds of pain in the world, it doesn't take much imagination to make a daylong list. These many kinds of pain often have little in common except the word that barely ties them together. So when we refer to pain, it's important to remember that there is not one kind, but many. (Fortunately, there is also not just one kind of joy, but many.)

— 2 —

How do you begin to analyze pain, to understand it? Let me suggest this. Though there are many kinds of pain, all of them can be divided into two camps.

There is the pain we seek. And then there is the pain that seeks us.

The pain that comes from study, from training, from pushing ourselves — all of that, as unpleasant as it might be to bear — is pain we seek. Because we have brought it into our lives, it is easier to understand, plan for, and work through.

But there is also the pain that seeks us. In its milder forms, this pain is just the unfortunate and bad stuff that happens in a normal day. But in its most virulent form, this pain is the stuff of tragedy. This is losing your brother, your wife, your husband, your child. This is the pain that comes from fire, flood, famine. This is the pain that follows when the doctor calls you and asks you to come in, sits down next to you, and says there's bad news — and you know then what is going to kill you. This is a different kind of pain, and philosophers and theologians and counselors and pastors and priests and poets have all tried to explain where it comes from and what it means.

Philosophers have tied this kind of pain to the idea of *fortuna*, from which we derive the concept of "fortune," or the pain of chance. Unlike a pain we might seek when we set out to accomplish a goal, the pain of *fortuna* hits us without regard to our desires and often without warning. *Fortuna* suggests that certain things are written into our lives, certain events are beyond our control.

There is no easy answer for this pain. There is no pill to take, no prayer to make that lets us wake the next day without pain. At some point, we all have to wrestle with the pain of fortune. All that can really be said about this kind of pain was summed up by Seneca: "Fate guides the willing but drags the unwilling."

Led or dragged, there are some places we have no choice but to go.

— 3 —

The pain brought by fortune is, of course, as old as our species. But profound thinkers have developed strategies to confront this pain, to understand it, and to find a measure of serenity even when everything is crumbling around us.

The Stoics taught that our response to the world, our choice to accept or reject what we cannot control, is the only thing completely within our power. We can make ourselves miserable by railing against what has already happened, or we can accept our place in a universe greater and more complex than we can possibly imagine.

We've talked a bit about Epictetus, who lived no one's idea of a comfortable life. His advice to his students was simple: "Do not try to make things happen the way you want, but want what happens to happen the way it happens, and you will be happy."

To be sure, that's a lot easier said than done, and in some cases giving this advice would sound cruel. When our fellow SEALs Axe and Suh were killed in Afghanistan, should we have wanted that? Would it have made us happy to want that? Of course not.

The Stoics knew this. But the Stoics also realized that building an attitude of acceptance — an attitude grateful for what we have, but not so attached to what we have that we can't imagine it being taken away — takes disciplined practice.

One practice they recommended was called the "premeditation of evils." We imagine the worst that can happen, not in a fit of worry, but in a controlled examination. When we do this, we find that many evils are hugely inflated by our fear. When we really think about them, we realize that we can face and defeat them. And more important, we grow prepared. When evils do meet us, we meet them not in a state of shock, but with practiced readiness.

Still, we recognize that even this discipline (and later we'll talk more about how people really do this in practice) can break down in the face of pain, because we are human.

I've written to you a bit about Cato — tough and Stoic, he ate simple food, walked when others rode, and always went barefoot. But when his half brother, the relative he loved more than anyone in the world, grew sick and died before Cato could make it to his deathbed, none of Cato's Stoic training could protect him from grief. Cato's friends were shocked to see him break down and embrace the body with tears streaming down his face.

Cato's enemies called it a massive show of hypocrisy. But with more sympathy, I think we can find a lesson for us. We can and should pre-

pare for pain. But we do so knowing that sometimes even the best prep-
arations fail, because we are human.

—— 4 ——

Machiavelli also wrestled with the pain of fortune. Most people think
of Machiavelli as a political philosopher, but he wrote his most famous
advice to his prince only after his life took a disastrous turn.

On November 6, 1512, Machiavelli was a powerful official in Florence, trusted to manage the city-state's militia and diplomacy. On
November 7, after a change of government, he was fired; within
months, he was also arrested on false charges, imprisoned, and
hung by the wrists until his shoulders dislocated. Then he was ex-
iled.

So thinking about fortune was not something Machiavelli did for
fun. It was something he had to do to make sense of his own life. Here's
the conclusion he came to:

> I think it may be true that fortune determines one half of our actions,
> but that, even so, she leaves us to control the other half, or thereabouts.
>
> And I compare her to one of those torrential rivers that, when they
> get angry, break their banks, knock down trees and buildings, strip the
> soil from one place and deposit it somewhere else. Everyone flees before
> them, everyone gives way in the face of their onrush, nobody can resist
> them at any point. But although they are so powerful, this does not mean
> men, when the waters recede, cannot make repairs and build banks and
> barriers so that, if the waters rise again, either they will be safely kept
> within the sluices or at least their onrush will not be so unregulated and
> destructive.
>
> The same thing happens with fortune: She demonstrates her power
> where precautions have not been taken to resist her; she directs her at-
> tacks where she knows banks and barriers have not been built to hold
> her.

Fortune is a river that can carry away everything in its path. Machiavelli knew that from experience. But we can be strong too, and smart,
and we know that rivers flood and that pain will come. We can build
defenses and virtues, dams and friendships, canals and character. We
can plan, anticipate, adapt.

Fortune is powerful but not omnipotent; we are vulnerable but not helpless.

— 5 —

When some people see a world full of suffering and joy, pain and wisdom, they wish for more of the good stuff (joy, delight, rest, ecstasy, courage, compassion, love) and less of the bad (hardship, struggle, weariness, pain). Plenty of false prophets of "success" and "happiness" play on this hope. They promise that pills can change you, that tricks can save you from hard work, that achievement and fulfillment can be yours if you simply think enough happy thoughts.

Yet there is wisdom much older than their cheap promises that is likely to outlast them. Most of our enduring religious stories, our great works of literature, and our most compelling philosophies have a different answer to the question of pain. They tell us that there is no shortcut around it.

Jacob is not freely blessed by the angel. He must wrestle it through the night.

The Buddha taught that the first step to wisdom comes when we realize that living means suffering.

Dante can begin his journey through hell and heaven only when he loses his way in a "dark wood."

For all of us, the path to wisdom runs through the dark wood of pain. And we can never begin to master pain unless we look it in the face — unless we begin to understand it.

The other day, I reread some of Grimm's fairy tales. Man, Walker, those are some tough tales for kids. In the original "Cinderella," the wicked stepsisters cut their toes and heels off trying to fit into the glass slipper. In the original "Snow White," the evil queen is forced to put on red-hot iron shoes and dance until she dies.

But even as recently as two hundred years ago, when the Grimm brothers' tales were first published, people understood that kids could handle the tough stuff. And it's no accident that kids start getting interested in fairy tales right around the time they start to realize that there are real things to be afraid of. There's a reason why kids have been drawn to tales like these, and why children can often handle much more difficult material than adults give them credit for. We can teach them that the way to deal with pain is not to imagine a magical land where pain doesn't exist, but to find a way to face it with courage.

— 6 —

There is a time to be unhappy. Because of what fortune brings, sometimes we *should* be depressed. In fact, if you are paying any attention to what is happening around you, you should be depressed and angry and sad at times.

Unhappiness in the face of terrible loss is not evidence of a disease, and it's not a mental disorder. There are entire industries designed to persuade you otherwise, Walker, but if you are not depressed by some of what life throws at you, then you are not seeing or hearing or feeling all of the world around you.

Many of the most resilient leaders — Abraham Lincoln, Winston Churchill, Gandhi — saw the tragic nature of life. All suffered through episodes of depression. They were also people who endured with courage when entire nations were counting on their strength. And in their pain, they built a depth of wisdom that few of their contemporaries could match.

"With Lincoln," writes Joshua Wolf Shenk, the author of *Lincoln's Melancholy*, "we have a man whose depression spurred him, painfully, to examine the core of his soul; whose hard work to stay alive helped him develop crucial skills and capacities, even as his depression lingered hauntingly; and whose inimitable character took great strength from the piercing insights of depression, the creative responses to it, and a spirit of humble determination forged over decades of deep suffering and earnest longing."

It would be wrong to say that Lincoln ever overcame his depression: "Whatever greatness Lincoln achieved cannot be explained as a triumph over personal suffering. Rather, it must be accounted an outgrowth of the same system that produced that suffering. This is a story not of transformation but of integration. Lincoln didn't do great work because he solved the problem of his melancholy; the problem of his melancholy was all the more fuel for the fire of his great work."

Shenk adds that a man like Lincoln would most likely be disqualified from holding public office today. His depression would be seen as a failing of character.

An unwillingness to endure the hardship of a depressed time keeps us from the possibility of capturing the wisdom and strength and joy that can exist on the other side. There is a season to be sad. Painful things hurt. Allow yourself to be hurt.

— 7 —

It seems counterintuitive to apply pain to someone already in pain. But to change people, you usually have to challenge them. I've worked with many veterans who are carrying real pain. They have experienced a life in combat that 99 percent of Americans will never know. They have held friends in their arms as they bled to death, or watched them splattered across a dirt road in Iraq. Some have had death knock at their doorstep, and in the process they've lost arms and legs, eyesight and hearing. Too many have anesthetized this pain with a bottle of alcohol, whittled their lives away staring at the TV, let days go by without ever speaking to another human being.

In our work, we don't give things to veterans to ease their pain; we put a challenge in front of them to rebuild their purpose. The challenge is to begin to serve again in their community. We ask them to take on a new kind of work — tutoring a kid in reading, or building a house, or helping a person who's homeless — with all the fear an unfamiliar task can bring with it.

Let me tell you how this works in practice. Tim Smith was one of the first veterans I worked with when I came home. Tim deployed with the 1st Armored Division into Iraq. They fought hard, and Tim saw friends carried off the battlefield wounded. But he had an important mission and a great team. One day, Tim and his close friend Doc went on a supply run. They were at one of those little PX stores, and Doc bought a cell phone to talk with his wife and two young kids. The next day, as Tim was coming off guard duty, a friend told him, "Smitty, I've got some bad news." Eight of Tim's friends had been killed in an explosion. Doc was one of them.

When Tim came home, he tried to get things together. His first six months were the hardest. He had a lot of time to think and not a lot to do. Eventually he went back to school to finish his degree and found a job working the night shift at the post office. When I met Tim, he had one young son. Another would come soon. He was still waking up in the middle of the night to check for his rifle under his bed. Tim had a supportive wife, but as he struggled to wrestle his life together, he wondered if he was being a good husband.

It was clear to everyone that Tim was in pain. When we sat down, what I said to him was pretty simple: "How are you going to continue to serve?" He knew that his family needed him to be strong, and I told him that we, his community, his country, needed his strength too. Now keep in mind, Tim was already working. He had a family to take care of. He was dealing with a few injuries, both psychological and physical. And I'm asking him to do more, not less. I'm asking him to push himself, to serve again.

Tim said that it was the first time since he'd been home that someone had asked something of him. It was the first time since he'd been home that someone had respected him enough to challenge him.

Tim rose to the challenge. We traveled together around St. Louis to find a good place where Tim might serve. Before long we found a volunteer position with the VA. Tim later turned that volunteer position into a full-time job.

When you come to St. Louis, Walker, we'll have dinner with Tim. When you think about models, Tim could be one for you. He eventually finished his master's degree. Then, after a few more years of solid work, he left his job and started his own business, Patriot Commercial Cleaning. Tim now employs other veterans, who go to school during the day and work at night. He's now got nineteen veterans working for him on thirty-four contracts all over Missouri and Illinois.

Sometimes — not always, but sometimes — you fight fire with fire. You meet pain with pain. You give a challenge to someone who's challenged, and he grows stronger.

— 8 —

The other day, I was talking with a friend who had a job many of us would envy: it paid well and provided steady work that would likely support him for the rest of his life. His problem? He was bored. And it was boredom of the most painful sort: he was bored with himself. He felt no urgency in his life, no sense of meaning. The prospect of leaving his job, however, would mean uncertainty and financial insecurity for his family. Either path would lead to pain — one of boredom, one of uncertainty.

Life rarely presents us with painless choices.

But if the choice is understood as one between two types of pain, then the questions to ask are: Which kind will make you better? Which kind of pain can you confront productively?

My brother once helped me to think through this. I had been back from Iraq for a few months. I had started to work with veterans as a volunteer and begun my own business to support myself. Though I worked hard from early-morning alarm to late-night crash, I still couldn't get everything done. I needed help and wanted to hire someone, but had little money.

My brother said, "Look, you have two choices. If you're working hard on the right things and there's still too much to do, that's pressure you can't do much about. On the other hand, if you hire someone, you're looking at being dead broke sooner, which will put pressure on you to make money. But that's something you can do something about. So," he said, "pick the pain you can confront most productively."

I hired someone. I still struggled, but eventually we made it work. It was the right kind of pain.

— 9 —

C. S. Lewis called pain God's "megaphone to rouse a deaf world." He's right that pain grabs hold of our attention like nothing else, but through the megaphone of pain we rarely hear instructions. Whether we feel a dull ache or a piercing, shooting pain, we find that pain is usually dumb. Pain gets our attention, but it does not instruct. It can tell us to look up, but rarely tells us where to go.

While it's important to recognize what pain has to offer, it's not enough to simply experience it. It has no value on its own. For pain to be valuable, it has to lead to the right kind of understanding.

— 10 —

With pain, as with people, we can find ourselves frozen in an unhealthy relationship. Over time, our reactions to pain get stacked one on top of the other, and we find that we've built a habitual relationship to pain.

When we see people who are stuck in pain, we see people whose relationship with pain remains unhealthy and unchanged. And the reasons for staying in an unhealthy relationship — because of habit, because of familiarity, because we can't imagine alternatives, because we're following bad models, because we are embarrassed, because we are afraid — go on and on.

People frequently hold on to an unhealthy pain precisely because that relationship is comfortable. Of course pain hurts, but the pain you know can seem easier, more manageable, than the unknown pain you might encounter if you took a different path.

— 11 —

Marcus Aurelius, the Stoic emperor, often wrote in his diary about his relationship with pain: "It is in the power of the soul to maintain its own serenity and tranquillity, and not to think that pain is an evil. For every judgment and movement and desire and aversion is within, and no evil ascends so high."

He didn't believe that pain was made up. He knew that pain is real. He did, however, recognize that we can choose how we respond to pain. We choose our relationship to pain.

Pain is rarely constant. Pain waxes and wanes, ebbs and flows. And so, too, does our relationship with it. To work through pain is not to put an end to pain, but to change how we relate to it. Some pain never goes away. The pain of losing a child is never overcome. The pain of a terminal illness may increase as time passes. The pain of Lincoln's depression never lifted.

To work through pain is not to make it disappear, but to make it mean something different for us — to turn it into wisdom.

Now let's be clear, Walker: "Unnecessary suffering is masochistic rather than heroic." If you can avoid unnecessary pain, avoid it. If you can't avoid it, then you have to choose your attitude toward it.

Some pain is good and necessary. A lot of people in the modern world tend to misunderstand this: they believe that the ideal life is the painless life.

Viktor Frankl thought differently. Frankl was no armchair student of suffering; he was a psychiatrist who survived slave labor in Auschwitz and lost his parents, his brother, and his wife in the concentration camps. As Frankl was hauled away, the Nazis confiscated the only manuscript of a book he was set to publish, destroying years of his work. But on each scrap of paper he came across, he jotted down the notes that would help him rewrite his book should he survive. "I am sure," he wrote, "that this reconstruction of my lost manuscript in the dark barracks . . . assisted me in overcoming the danger of cardiovascular collapse."

Frankl came to see that his unfinished work kept him sane: "Mental health is based on a certain degree of tension, the tension between what one has already achieved and what one still ought to accomplish, or the gap between what one is and what one should become. Such tension is inherent in the human being and therefore is indispensable . . . What man actually needs is not a tensionless state but rather the striving and struggling for a worthwhile goal, a freely chosen task."

If there is tension in your life, if there is some deep worry about living a worthy life, then . . . good. That tension and worry is part of a well-lived life.

Mastering Pain

Walker,

Think about the people who greeted you when you joined the military. I remember my drill instructor. He made it very clear that my pain was of little concern to him: "I do not want to hear your bellyaching about being hungry, being tired, being cold."

He was also the man who taught me to stand at attention. Remember learning that? It seems simple now. You stand with your body straight, your chest up, heels touching, hands at your sides, your gaze fixed forward. And — this is surprisingly hard for the novice — you do all of this even when you have a bead of sweat running down your face.

The sweat is a nuisance. But — and we learned this fast — you *do not* address that nuisance by wiping the sweat away. You *do not* raise your hand and say, "Hey, sir, I've got a bead of sweat running down my face. It's making me kinda uncomfortable. Can we talk about it?" You stand at attention and ignore the sweat.

Many of life's annoyances just have to be ignored. That doesn't mean that we suppress, ignore, or deny every pain. Serious pain has to be confronted. But one mark of resilience is learning to tell which pain deserves our attention. Paying attention to every pain, all the time, doesn't lead to resilience. It usually just leads to whining.

So which pain matters?

Start with this: not *all* pain matters.

There are people whose attention is consistently drawn away from their purpose and toward their pain, like a moth to a light. Such people, who pay attention to every annoyance and obstacle in their way, are usually unsuccessful in their endeavors. In extreme cases they are mentally ill. A healthy person, a flourishing person, learns to move past a lot of annoyance and a good deal of pain.

— 2 —

The soldier standing at attention must learn to ignore the bead of sweat running down his face. That is true. For 9,999 out of every 10,000 people who practice a discipline in its early stages, that is the right thing to do, and it's a fine way to explain what must be done. But to achieve mastery at the outer edges of excellence, and to achieve precision in our thinking, we have to unpack the word "ignore."

If I am ignoring something, I am aware of it. I am aware of it as an annoyance or perhaps as an irrelevance. Yet in order for me to ignore something, I am both aware and *choosing* not to focus my mind and my time on what I am ignoring.

This is a good, important initial step. If we can learn to ignore things that don't matter much, we have made a lot of progress. But we often trip up when we think about the next steps.

Truly great performers will often tell you that they "don't even notice" the pain. You probably know from experience that this happens sometimes. Adrenaline is a great gift. Adrenaline blasts, blood pumps, our focus narrows, and we literally don't notice things that ail us.

But at the outer edges of excellence, we develop a more finely tuned awareness. At the outer edges of excellence, the trained soldier is "aware" of the bead of sweat, just as the athlete is "aware" of pain, because they *are* the pain. This sounds abstract and almost spiritual, because, well, it is.

In true mastery there is a transcendence at work: you actually are your pain. Your pain is not something separate from yourself, something you overcome or ignore or fail to notice. It is a part of who you are. And even this is not quite right — it *is* who you are, as much as your own thoughts and your breathing. Your pain is no longer outside of you. It *is you,* and you are it.

And here we've bumped up against the limits of language. Many people have tried to describe this well, and I encourage you to read their words, which may serve you better than mine do here. But at the end of the day, you cannot know this by virtue of anyone's explanation. This is not the kind of knowledge that you can achieve by reading about it. You'll have to do it, and then *be* it.

— 3 —

Do you remember when we were at U.S. Army Jump School at Fort Benning? After BUD/S, learning to jump from a plane felt like a vacation. I think somebody called it three days of instruction crammed into three weeks. We felt there was a ton of wasted time.

One day we jocked up and then sat in the hangar, strapped into our parachutes, for hours . . . and hours . . . and hours. I can't quite remember why. I remember that Eddie said they did it for motivation: after sitting and waiting for that long in that much uncomfortable gear, surrounded by that many stinking guys, you'd jump from the plane *without* a chute.

At the end of an eight-hour day that seemed mostly like nonsense, you and I went to the gym and worked out. While we were lifting, we decided that we were ready to try a new max. So we both put more weight on the bar than we'd ever lifted before.

But let's be more precise. We put on a little more weight — two and a half pounds more — than we'd lifted before. We pushed ourselves, but we weren't stupid about it. And there's a more general lesson here.

You don't have to push yourself to a new max every day. That's a recipe for injury. But you do have to push yourself. You do have to step beyond the boundary of your past experience. You do have to regularly and consistently pursue excellence at the edge. And you especially have to do it when you find that the world is giving you excuses to sit and do nothing.

At the same time, there's a right way and a wrong way to push yourself. If you load a bar with a lot more weight than you've ever handled, you're going to hurt yourself. When you wake up and decide to do something crazy, you often end up in the hospital, or at least in a state of exhaustion and discouragement. Resilient people take risks. They might take big risks. But, as ever, there's a line between courage and stupidity. It's easy to do something crazy and hurt yourself. That's plain dumb. It's much harder, and also more valuable, to train and practice and prepare, and then push yourself just enough.

Several ancient authors make analogies to wind and fire and wood. A small flame grows with a whisper of air but is extinguished by a strong wind. A wheelbarrow of wood will smother a flicker but feed a raging fire. You fuel your excellence with challenges made to match you in the moment.

* * *

When we exercise vigorously, some physiologists believe that we actually tear our muscles at a microscopic level. When we rest and nourish and heal, our bodies repair the tears and we become stronger. If the muscles are torn too much, we are injured. If they do not tear enough, there is no growth. If they tear the right amount, and then we recover in the right way, we find that we've become stronger.

Just as the athlete moves through muscular pain to become stronger, we can move through emotional and psychological pain to become stronger and grow wiser.

But — and I want to emphasize this — we do not grow *because* of the pain. We grow when we recover from the right pain in the right way.

To recognize the value in hardship, or to appreciate that any kind of achievement requires suffering, is different from praising pain for its own sake. A boxer doesn't just take punishment in the ring. He tries to take as little as possible. Think about the phrase "roll with the punches." People who don't know boxing think that the phrase means something like: you get punched and you keep going. In fact, to roll with the punches means to twist your body — maybe even to slide slightly — so that the blow doesn't catch you full force. That's the idea of rolling with the punches: there is no virtue in taking punishment for the sake of punishment.

I try to remind myself: Push yourself, but don't be an idiot.

— 4 —

There's a difference between pain and suffering. You often don't have a choice when it comes to feeling pain. You often *do* have a choice about whether you suffer, because suffering is created by your perception of, and relationship to, pain.

Walker, think back to when you dived for abalone as a kid. Each time you broke the surface, your muscles were sore, your lungs burned, you panted for breath. Physically speaking, you were in pain. But were you suffering? No — it's one of your happiest memories.

Consider this: one of the quickest ways for a medic to snap somebody out of her suffering is to ask her to describe her pain. You've done this with your kids when they're screaming. You ask them to tell you what's hurting them, and the mere act of having to breathe in order to speak slows their screaming. Then, describing what hurts forces them to step outside their pain and look at it. They might still be hurting, but they're calmer now.

What happens is simple. And it works in most situations. To describe your pain, you have to (metaphorically) step outside of it. You have to look at it, analyze it. Instead of being *in pain*, you are now thinking about what the pain is doing to you. What's happened, at the most basic level, is that you've changed your relationship to pain.

The pain might still be piercing. But by describing it, we *see* our pain. What happens — and this is true whether the pain we feel is from a knife wound, hunger, or a dearly loved relative's death — is that deliberate attention to pain helps us separate the physical sensation from the suffering we mentally attach to that sensation.

What's true about pain in this sense is similar to what's true about fear. It does its worst work when it's hidden. The minute we write down what we are afraid of, or take objective stock of what's hurting us, we begin to gain control.

There is a difference between recognizing that pain is real and believing that pain must always be devastating. Losing a friend in battle is always bad. Losing a brother in an accident is always bad. Losing a child to disease is always bad. To be abused as a child is always bad. But when we approach people who have been hurt with the belief that they will necessarily be broken, we do them a double injury.

Many people *will* be hurt for some time. Many people *will* be traumatized. Some scars *will* be carried for a lifetime. But not everyone who's been beaten will be broken. And usually, no matter how harsh the hardship, there is the possibility of light on the other side.

To recognize that it's possible for people to endure abuse, violence, or the untimely death of someone they love isn't to deny the tragedy of what they have experienced (which would be unhealthy or impossible for them to do in any case). It is, in fact, to offer them the one thing they may most need when the world looks as if it's all a catastrophe: hope rooted in reality.

When I was in Iraq, one of the SEALs I shared desk duty with was a Tier One sniper. He was recovering from an injury and reading Thich Nhat Hanh at the time. (I know — a sniper reading a Zen Buddhist. It was one of the things I enjoyed about the SEAL teams. It reminds me of a quotation about the Greeks from Edith Hamilton: that they were "lovers of beauty without having lost the taste for simplicity, and lovers of wisdom without loss of manly vigor.") Thich Nhat Hanh writes that suffering is something we create through our attachments: what makes people suffer is not so much the physical sensation they experience, but the *meaning* they attach to their losses.

I believe that you can't live a flourishing life without attachments to people and purposeful work. But there is wisdom in recognizing that certain attachments can be unhealthy and cause us pain. And part of the art of living is knowing the who, what, when, where, how, and why of being attached.

You've known people who choose to suffer even when they're not in much pain, obsessing over every little ache. You've also known people who choose not to suffer even when they are in great pain. They show us that we can recreate our relationship with pain.

I know that sounds a bit abstract when you read it. But it's real when you live it. Seneca was a chronically ill man for much of his life; it didn't stop him from writing many letters on the good life that still make me sit up and pay attention. Epictetus, one of the most revered philosophy teachers of his day, was disabled from childhood in a world without wheelchairs, handicap ramps, and effective painkillers.

My point is not that Seneca and Epictetus were legendary tough guys. They weren't. But they found ways to work with pain without letting it consume them. In their writings and their examples they left us clues. They remind us that none of us need to be trapped in our suffering.

Most profoundly, we can shape our relationship with pain by choosing the meaning we give to pain. At the extreme, consider martyrs tortured for their beliefs who experienced their pain as a profound religious experience. That doesn't justify their torture or make their pain any less. But the sufferer who sees himself as a martyr has found a way to give meaning to pain.

— 5 —

My boxing coach Earl used to say, "You can't get better fighting someone who's worse than you."

The painting *Dempsey and Firpo,* by George Bellows, hangs above my desk. In 1950, the Associated Press polled the leading sports editors

in America to find out what they considered the greatest sports moment of the first half of the twentieth century. They selected this punch,
this moment from that fight, over all others.

Largely forgotten today, that punch was thrown in 1923. Boxing was
the dominant sport of the day. A crowd of eighty thousand had come
to New York's Polo Grounds to witness the contest for the heavyweight
championship of the world. See the man falling through the ropes?
That's Jack Dempsey. He won.

Dempsey was boxing's superstar. The "Manassa Mauler" earned his
nickname with crushing punches. That evening, Dempsey fought the
towering Luis Ángel Firpo, "the Wild Bull of the Pampas," the first Ar-
gentinean ever to contend for the heavyweight crown.

Toward the end of the first round, Firpo managed to pin Dempsey
against the ropes. With a combination of vicious punches, he knocked
Dempsey out of the ring. As Dempsey landed, the back of his head hit
a reporter's typewriter, opening a serious gash.

The ringside reporters shoved Dempsey back onto the canvas in
time to beat the count. As Dempsey got his legs under him, Firpo

quickly pounced, delivering another barrage of punches. Still wobbly, Dempsey was just able to fend Firpo off when the bell sounded to end the round.

Dempsey had suffered the most dramatic knockdown of his career. Yet he came out of his corner furious to start the second round. In fifty-seven seconds, he knocked Firpo out with a blow to the jaw. "And then," as one writer put it, "in a moment of almost heartbreaking pathos, the tiger of just seconds before turned into a lamb, stooping down to help up his bloody, beaten foe as the more than 80,000 in attendance at the Polo Grounds roared their approval."

Before that night, Dempsey had been one of the sport's least popular champions. More often than not, spectators shouted for him to be knocked out. But that changed when the crowd saw him humbled, pushed to the limit of his ability, and still triumphant. It was Dempsey who defeated Firpo, but it was Firpo who made Dempsey an unforgettable champion.

Dempsey became a legend not despite Firpo, but because of him — just as Ali was great because of Frazier, Shakespeare was great because of Marlowe, and Raphael and Michelangelo pushed each other to new heights. We don't know what greatness we're capable of until we're tested.

In boxing, we're challenged by an opponent. In life, we're more often challenged by a condition or a cause. When Mother Teresa started a school for the poor in a slum of India, she had no supplies and no classroom. "She simply saw that there was need for a school. The fact that there was no building, no chairs or tables, did not deter her. On a small open patch among the shanties, she began to scratch the Bengali alphabet with a stick on the ground. A few more children appeared and with each passing day, more and more children joined. In a spirit of community participation someone donated a chair or two, a bench and a blackboard. Within a few days, the little school had become a reality."

From these humble beginnings, Mother Teresa eventually made it possible for hundreds of thousands of the poor and uncared-for in India to die with dignity.

Walker, you won't be in a ring or on the streets of Calcutta, but you will need a worthy adversary.

— 6 —

We all talk to ourselves. You may not speak your thoughts out loud or share them with others, but there is always a conversation in your head about your environment, the people around you, and, most important, about yourself.

You can't shut this conversation off. The best you can do is turn it in your favor.

There are times when our self-talk becomes destructive.

I screwed up.

I'm stupid.

I don't deserve to be here.

Everyone thinks like this occasionally, but repetitive negative inner monologues can be destructive.

There are any number of strategies for stopping these destructive ideas from rattling around inside your head. You can argue with your self-talk: "No, you're not a horrible brother because you forgot a birthday." You can argue with friends as they replay your self-talk to you. They might say, "You didn't win the contract; your business is going to fail." You say, "I'm glad I applied. Tomorrow is another day. I've got a great business, I provide great service, and I'm going to win a contract soon." The second method is more effective, but it takes a good and patient friend to do this well. Some people snap a rubber band on their wrist every time they catch themselves putting themselves down, while others jump up and down while smiling (it sounds nuts, but you *do* feel better).

There are lots of ways to do this, but all of the strategies have two features in common. One, they make you aware of your self-talk. Two, you start to change the voice in your head. (This, again, is hard. It takes a lot of mental effort and attention, and many people simply aren't willing to do the work.)

Once you're aware of the habit of destructive self-talk, you can — as with any habit — replace it with a new one.

Talking positively to yourself will feel different at first: maybe it will come as a relief, or maybe it will just feel fake. But remember that changing the tone of your self-talk won't work if you try it only once.

If you want to get in shape, you don't go for a run once or lift a weight once. You have to turn these activities into habits, until the day comes when you feel odd *not* doing them. Positive self-talk is the same: if you make it a practice, it works. Ultimately, you'll discover that, in tough moments, you've got a voice in your head that recognizes difficulty but still helps you to see possibility; it will become a part of who you are.

And please, Walker, don't think you need to give yourself the Gettysburg Address. Don't think you need to fill your mind with happy-clappy nonsense. Effective self-talk is usually simple. It's usually brief, even dull. A phrase is often better than a sentence, and a word will sometimes do just fine. Here are some examples researchers have collected from successful athletes:

Good job, do it again.
Concentrate. Breathe.
Stay tough.

There is a difference between self-talk that is aspirational and self-talk that is delusional. The difference is not in the words. The difference lies in practice. You can try to talk yourself up before a big contest, but if you haven't done the training, you won't believe your own talk. Self-talk tied to disciplined practice enhances your power. Self-talk divorced from practice is just self-delusion.

— 7 —

Master Chief Will Guild talked about "getting to your dot" to master pain. Remember that the instructors had those frog feet "dots" painted on the grinder, where we'd line up for physical training? We'd start PT standing on our designated dot.

Well, the instructors found that most of the guys who quit BUD/S didn't quit *during* training. They quit when they started to think about all of the training *ahead*. The lesson of "getting to your dot" is that you don't need to do all of your training at once. All you need to do at breakfast is eat breakfast. (And that's a real task. Eat well, get down good calories, because you're going to need the energy.) All you need to do after breakfast is to get to your dot—to jog to your spot on the grinder. Once people made it to the dot, they usually found the strength to make it through that PT session.

* * *

The process of taking a large goal and breaking it down into smaller parts is called segmenting. It's a simple technique, but it can make seemingly impossible hardship more manageable. We break hard things down into smaller and smaller steps until each step is easy.

We make the large thing small, and the small thing smaller, and the smaller thing smaller still, until the next thing is the only thing, and that next thing happens now.

For example, a person with severe depression might find it overwhelming to get out of bed in the morning. So, don't do it. You don't have to. You don't have to get out of bed if it's overwhelming.

But you do have to learn to ask yourself, Can I move my toes? Yes. Then do it. Can I move my fingers? Yes. Then do it. Can I open my eyes? Yes. Can I take in a deeper breath? Yes. Can I put one leg over the side of the bed? Yes. Can I put another leg over the side of the bed? Can I put some weight into my heels? You're out of bed.

Remember the second night of Hell Week, Walker? We'd already been up for twenty hours. We'd been running with boats on our heads, swimming in the ocean, running through the obstacle course, carrying logs. It was miserable. We were frozen and pained, but our adrenaline had carried us through the first night and carried us through the next day. Then we arrived at the beginning of the second night. We're thinking to ourselves: I'm more tired and more exhausted and more beaten than I've ever been in my life. And it was then, at the beginning of the second night, that the instructors ran us out to the beach. We stood there in a line, and as we watched the sun drift down, they came out with their bullhorns to get inside our minds.

"Say goodnight to the sun, gentlemen. Say goodnight to the sun."

"Tonight is going to be a very, very long night, gentlemen."

They reminded us that tonight was going to be our first full night of Hell Week.

"And you men have many, many more nights to go."

We watched the sun slip lower and make contact with the ocean.

As the sun slipped beneath the waves, something broke in our class. Out of the corner of my right eye, I saw men running for the bell. First two men ran, then two more, and then another. The instructors had carried the bell out with us to the beach. To quit, you rang the bell three times. I could hear it ringing:

Ding, ding, ding.
Ding, ding, ding.
Ding, ding, ding.

A pack of men quit together. Weeks earlier, we had started our indoctrination phase with more than 220 students. Only 21 originals from class 237 would ultimately graduate with our class. We had more men quit at that moment than at any other time in BUD/S training.

Who would have thought, after having to swim fifty meters underwater, endure drown-proofing and surf torture and the obstacle course and four-mile runs in the sand and two-mile swims in the ocean and log PT and countless sit-ups and flutter kicks and pushups and hours in the cold and the sand, that the hardest thing to do in all of BUD/S training would be to stand on the beach and watch the sun set?

It was the darkest moment for so many because they weren't thinking about what was right in front of us. They were thinking about everything that was to come. And in their minds, what they hadn't yet seen or touched or tasted turned monstrous.

We went from more than 220 down to 21. I can count on one hand the number of people who quit when they were actually doing something. People quit when they started to think about how hard something was *going* to be.

When things feel too big to handle, break 'em down. It worked for you then. It'll work for you now.

— 8 —

You got through Hell Week by staying focused on the reality in front of you, not the phantoms your imagination conjured up or the fear the instructors tried to put into your head. And that's not just a lesson for the SEAL teams. That's how we can make it through any difficult part of our lives.

Ernest Hemingway argued that "cowardice . . . is almost always simply a lack of ability to suspend the functioning of the imagination." When we make a mistake, we often have to face a tough reality. That's even harder to do when it's accompanied by a tortured imagination. Many of us lose control of our imaginations without noticing. We start with a failure and then pass judgment on our entire lives, our futures, our character.

We don't learn from failure by mentally turning it into a catastrophe. We learn from failure by facing it and seeing it for what it is—no more, no less. Face reality. Isolate what happened. Separate what just happened from what might happen in the future. If it helps you, write it down. And once you've looked at reality, focus your energy on the task you can control that's right in front of you.

When I was a kid, my dad showed me how to hold a magnifying glass, focus the rays of the sun on a fallen leaf, and draw out a curling wisp of smoke as the leaf caught fire.

There is a power in focus. A laser is just focused light, but it can cut through steel. In the midst of hardship and fear, suffering and difficulty, the person who's built the habit of focus harnesses tremendous power.

— 9 —

You're standing at the edge of the pool with your boat crew behind you. It's early in the day, and the air still runs with a chill; a few of the instructors in wetsuits and fins are floating in the pool; you close your eyes and roll your neck and relax your shoulders; you breathe in and out and then in, long long long, and out, slow slow slow. As you slow your breathing, your heart rate drops. You open your eyes and wait for the signal from the instructors. As they give the word, you suck in air deep down in your belly, and you keep filling and filling and filling until you feel that every last corner, every crevice of your lungs, is packed with oxygen. As you do so, you see other men jump into the pool. You stay calm; this is not a race. You've planned your dive and now you are going to dive your plan. You may be the last man standing on the pool deck, or you may be the first to go. But you jump when you're ready. You jump as far into the pool as a good leap will take you, and on impact you keep your body relaxed so that your feet and then your hips and then your shoulders and then your head cut under quickly, and you let yourself sink one foot, two feet, three feet, and then you flex your core and swing forward at the hips into a tight ball as you do a front flip underwater. Then you swim for the bottom of the pool, and with each stroke . . .

Walker, you recognize this as mental practice for the fifty-meter underwater swim. Mental visualization is no substitute for physical practice. In fact, we knew how to visualize only because we had actually swum across the pool—ten meters, then fifteen, then twenty, then twenty-five, then thirty—so many times before. But practice makes you better. Resilient people learn how to mentally prepare themselves for difficult endeavors.

To prepare for that swim, you practice in the pool—and, just as important, you can practice in your mind. You can practice what it will feel like when you get to the end of the pool, turn, and push off the wall, when you are absolutely out of oxygen and can't even see the other side yet. You can imagine telling yourself "Stay" as you pull your hands through the water, kick, and feel your body shoot forward, then "Relaxed." You can imagine swimming deep, a few inches above the bottom, and keeping your eyes open and your face relaxed.

In the moment, you aren't going to remember that the partial pressure of oxygen is higher at depth; you won't remember that your rate of oxygen consumption is tied to your heart rate; you won't remember that tension in your body uses strength and burns oxygen. You won't remember any of this, but you won't need to think through what you are doing then, because you'll have practiced it so many times before.

Mental visualization, or mental rehearsal, is one of the most powerful ways that we have to master pain, fear, and difficulty. Resilient people know that life is going to be hard, so they prepare themselves for hardship. You remember how the Stoics practiced the premeditation of evils? In some ways, it's the same thing. For Seneca, it was the difference between carrying on and breaking down: "Everyone approaches a danger with more courage if he has prepared in advance how to confront it. Anyone can endure difficulties better if he has previously practiced how to deal with them. People who are unprepared can be unhinged by even the smallest of things."

So you imagine bad things that might happen—being out of oxygen thirty meters into a fifty-meter swim, realizing that you've misplaced your notes when you stand up to speak in public, being told that you've lost your job. Then you imagine how you'll make it through: "Stay" . . . "Relaxed."

Will Guild taught us that when you are ambushed by hardship, when everything is new and difficult, you can easily be overcome by events.

Mental rehearsal allows your mind to be in a place where your body cannot be. Mental rehearsal, practiced properly, is simply productive preparation.

The Stoics recognized something very basic about human beings: we worry. Today, people tell you, "Don't worry." That's usually friendly advice — and also unhelpful. People do worry. You worry. I worry. You can try to push fear out of your mind, but you'll find that one day it seeps back in, like rainwater working its way into the soil.

It's better to tell people, "Worry productively." If you're going to spend time thinking about bad things that might happen, then use that energy for a purpose. Go ahead and visualize the worst that can happen. But instead of wallowing in your worries, imagine how you'll respond to them. Practice. Mentally rehearse what you'll do. Imagine and envision yourself making it through hardship.

— 10 —

When you mentally rehearse, don't imagine success falling into your lap. Imagine everything: the tingling at the back of your neck, the fear in the pit of your stomach.

Your mind is built to prepare for problems. That's more than OK — it's good. The goal of mental rehearsal isn't to fill your head with happy thoughts about the future, but to prepare yourself to succeed in the real world. And one of the ways you succeed in the real world is by anticipating obstacles, including your own fear. When you do that, you tap into a survival mechanism hard-wired into the human brain.

Imagine a man five thousand years ago who wakes up and says, "I think I'll take a walk and look for berries. I bet I'll find an enormous patch next to a stream of fresh, flowing water. Let's go!" Then imagine his neighbor, who wakes up and says, "When I go looking for berries today, I might not find any food at all. I'd better take some with me. It could be a dry day without water, so I'd better carry some with me. There might be a tiger on the path, so I should walk with friends and carry my spear. Let's prepare."

Walker, you and I are here only because the second man prepared and survived. Preparing, mentally and physically, means imagining what might go wrong. It also means imagining how you will react to, cope with, and overcome potential hardship.

Don't imagine yourself stuck in your worst-case scenario, panicking and flailing in an endless loop of disaster. Imagine real hardship. Then imagine how you are going to make it *through* that hardship.

Both a panicked mind and a resilient mind will engage with fearful, anxious thoughts. What makes the resilient mind different is its ability to direct those thoughts productively.

In the SEAL teams we called it contingency planning. Other people might call it worst-case-scenario thinking.

What if we're shot at as we leave the compound? What if the room is booby-trapped? What if she is wearing a suicide vest?

The naïve mind imagines effortless success. The cowardly mind imagines hardship and freezes. The resilient mind imagines hardship and prepares.

— 11 —

He who fears he shall suffer, already suffers what he fears.

— MONTAIGNE

It's hard to wrestle with a ghost.

You either own your fears or they own you. Fears do their worst work when they knock around in your mind. You can't fight your fears until you put them in front of you. Write your fears down. Make them face you. The minute you do this, your fears will shrink, and you will grow.

When you acknowledge pain and allow yourself to feel it, you see it for what it is — and then you are wrestling with something solid.

Walker, I've written to you before about Marcus Aurelius. He was the most powerful man in the world while he was alive — and yet, like nearly all of us, he was afraid of death.

At least that's what I think when I read his *Meditations*. The book was his private diary, written at night in army camps and field tents, discovered only after he was gone. In it he wrote, for an audience of one, his fears, his worries, his stresses, his reflections, and his maxims for living.

He was afraid of being corrupted by power: "Don't be a Caesar drunk with power and self-importance: it happens all too easily. Keep yourself simple, good, pure."

He was afraid of his own death: "See how quick and coarse the drama of human life runs: yesterday a mucous membrane; tomorrow an embalmed corpse or a heap of ash."

He was afraid of the death of people he loved: "One man prays: 'How I may not lose my little child,' but you must pray: How I may not be afraid to lose him.'"

Did writing this diary of fears make Marcus Aurelius a better man? We can't know for certain. But we are certain that most everyone recognized him as the wisest, most dignified man they had ever met, and that people still recognize his wisdom today. He spent his life wrestling with fears and doubts little different, at bottom, from yours.

— 12 —

I knew a boxing coach who had once been a trainer to one of the heavyweight champions of the world. The heavyweight called him one day, and the trainer could hear fear in his voice. "Hey man," the champ said, "I need your help."

"OK," the trainer said. "What do you need?"

"I need you to take care of something for me."

"What do you need me to do?"

"Well, there's this guy," the champ said, "he's in the other room, and I'm gonna take the phone in and I want you to talk to him."

"Who is it you want me to talk to?"

"He's my gardener."

"Your gardener?"

"Yeah, yeah, he's in the other room and he's got this bill and he's trying to overcharge me."

The trainer realized at that moment that the heavyweight champion of the world was afraid to confront his gardener over a bill. And that, he explained, was one of the reasons why so many of these men are taken advantage of once they become champions. For all their physical courage, they had never learned how to confront someone over a social issue, an emotional issue, a financial issue. When they became champions, they had to deal with all of these issues at once, and they were filled with fear.

* * *

Everyone, Walker, has uneven courage.

We build courage through the practice of facing fear, and while we may learn to face fear comfortably in one context, we may still act cowardly in another.

Walker, you are not alone in this. There are veterans who strapped on body armor, checked their radios, loaded their rifles, stepped into Humvees, drove into the streets of places like Fallujah, kicked down doors with armed terrorists behind them — and yet, because their faces have been burned, they're sometimes afraid to go to the mall when they first come home, because of what kids might say.

Eric Hoffer talked about this. Before he started his career as a longshoreman, Hoffer was a migrant farmworker, following the ripening peas northward in inland California. From January to June of 1936, he picked five hundred miles' worth of peas. String bean season came next, and on the morning it was time to switch over to the new crop, he remembered how "hesitant and anxious" he felt. "Would I be able to pick string beans? Even the change from peas to string beans had in it elements of fear."

Hoffer was a student of human psychology, and he recognized in himself that even this small change from peas to string beans left him frightened. You will be — as we all are — hesitant, anxious, fearful, and sometimes terrified as you make changes in your life. This is natural, even for someone who has been as courageous as you have in other endeavors.

It is natural to have uneven courage. It is necessary that you understand this about yourself.

We all have pain we've mastered and pain we've run from.

We also all have a choice to make: stop running and build a new kind of courage.

— 13 —

In the Bible, the ideas of breath and life are the same thing. I'm sure you've heard this line from Genesis: "The spirit of God moved upon the face of the waters." The Hebrew word used for "spirit" is *ruach*, which also means "breath." In Genesis, it's the same breath that is breathed into creation to give humans life.

Breathing is one of the first and simplest things we do. It's also the easiest thing to forget about. Yet people have been consciously thinking about breath — and the way it seems to link our bodies to our spirits — for thousands of years. Becoming aware of our breathing and taking control of it when we need to is one of the most powerful ways to take control of ourselves, especially when we're afraid.

We can begin to control the involuntary processes inside our bodies by controlling our breath. The hormones your body releases during periods of stress are the source of your fight-or-flight response: your heart beats faster, your pupils dilate, your breathing grows quicker. You may even get tunnel vision or tunnel hearing: your senses focus solely on the danger in front of you, blocking out the rest of the world. And this works great: it's perfect for fighting or fleeing. If you have to sprint from or fight off a predator, you *want* your blood pumping, your lungs taking in extra oxygen, your senses blocking out everything that doesn't have to do with saving your ass.

But here's the problem with fight-or-flight: we've invented all kinds of new, modern ways to be scared. And in many of these situations, our body's natural response to fear is useless at best and often harmful. How about the fear of public speaking? Your heart starts pounding, but it's not going to work well if you run out of the room or try to fight the audience.

It turns out, though, that your body also produces antidotes to this condition, and their release is triggered by deep, controlled breathing. This means that the relaxing effect of deep breathing isn't in your imagination; it has a physical reality. And it means that you have access to a powerful calming path whenever you hit your body's "manual override" switch. That switch is controlled breathing.

Try this: inhale through your nose while slow-counting to four, hold your breath, then exhale through your mouth while slow-counting to four. Try this for just four minutes.

You can use your breath to gain hold of your anger. You can use your breath to quiet an attack of panic. You can use your breath to bear pain. (There's a reason why, in childbirth, doctors and midwives often tell laboring women to take powerful and rhythmic breaths.) You can use your breath to create awareness. (There's a reason why meditation often begins with a focus on the breath.) You can use your breath to direct power. (There's a reason why boxers and martial artists exhale when they strike.)

Controlling your breathing won't erase your fears or eliminate your pain. But to be resilient, you have to learn how to exercise control over what you can control. At the most basic level, you can almost always control how you breathe. And controlling how you breathe will almost always shape how you feel, how you think, and how you react.

And let me mention one funny thing here, Walker. People often grasp for the complicated instead of embracing the simple. They'll spend two hours writing about their fears, but won't spend two minutes focusing on how to breathe. They'll track down and read an ancient book on character, but won't spend two minutes focusing on how to breathe.

There are a few reasons for this that are worth considering. The first is that simple tasks offer fewer excuses. The more complicated you make something, the more excuses you create for yourself.

The second is that beginning something new, even when it's simple, is hard. It makes us afraid. People introduce complication as a way to avoid beginning.

The third is that people who give advice or help, or who coach or teach, often feel that if what they tell people to do is simple, then they won't be considered experts.

Some experts like to pretend that they have some kind of special, even sacred knowledge. This is one of the reasons why doctors will prescribe antipsychotic medications, antidepressant medications, antianxiety medications, and psychotherapy regimens, but they won't insist that their patients engage in simple, vigorous, regular exercise.

Of course, people who will not make the effort to control how they breathe have little hope of taking control of larger things. If you won't exercise enough discipline to slightly alter just once in a while the thing that you do thousands of times a day, then you will not have the discipline to change the course of your life.

But if you do learn to control your breathing, you will have gained experience in how to control what you can control. If you do learn to bring awareness to how you breathe, you are likely to bring awareness to how you live.

And there's a bigger point here, Walker. Resilience isn't just in your mind. It's in your body too. We're all physical beings. Sleep matters. Exercise matters. What you eat matters. You'll be happier if you are healthier. You'll be more resilient if you're better rested. Your physical strength is part of your mental strength. You know all of this, Walker. Most people do. It's not a problem of knowledge, but one of action. So do this:

Just breathe. If for no other reason than to remember that you have control over how you feel. You have control over yourself.

— 14 —

Suffering isn't only in what we experience. It's in how we process what we experience — the perspective we bring to pain.

From the perspective of SEAL candidates at the start of Hell Week, a sunset on the beach can signify impending torture. From the perspective of a tourist a few miles up the coast, that same sunset can be beautiful.

Sometimes our perspective is simply a question of who we are and where we are. Other times, we can change our perspective. In those moments, we realize that what looks like a crisis or a tragedy doesn't have to be.

Part of what makes many people miserable is simply a lack of perspective. I remember one day when I was living in Southern California, my girlfriend at the time invited me to go with her to Tijuana. She'd spent a few summers working there in what she called "the dump." The dump sounded like an awful name for any place where people live, but when I got there, I found out that was exactly what it was. She'd worked in a summer program for the children of families who lived near the trash dump. The dump was a giant mound of rotting garbage, and families squatted in shelters made of wood and mud and corrugated metal in the shadow of the dump.

We started our trip to Tijuana in the morning, and on the way we stopped at Coronado. You remember Coronado: a beautiful little island of wealth and luxury. I thought it was a fun community. But like every place that pops with wealth, you found people who were spoiled and unhappy. As we walked out of a bagel shop — I don't remember exactly what caused this incident — we saw a woman in an expensive suit, covered in jewelry, screaming at a man as she got into her luxury car, slammed the door, stomped on the gas, and drove away.

At the dump in Tijuana, my girlfriend caught up with a fifteen-year-old girl who'd been in her program. The girl had had her quinceañera a few weeks before, and she was telling us all about it. Her friends stopped by, her mom came out — everyone was smiling. It was clear that the family had few possessions, but they had a lot of happiness.

Now, all this sounds very clichéd, Walker. The poor happy family. The rich unhappy bitch. The reality is that most people's level of happiness and life satisfaction gains markedly as they rise from destitution, and — some nuns and monks excepted — it's usually only rich fools who praise the virtue of abject poverty. My point here is that, trapped in a pocket of wealth on the island of Coronado, it seemed to me that the woman I saw had lost perspective.

This doesn't mean that every time you shrink your shirt in the wash or burn dinner you should say, "Well, thank God I'm not a destitute child in Cambodia whose legs were blown off by a land mine." But you can probably make time for gratitude once a day. The practice of perspective can keep us balanced in moments of hardship.

Sometimes — more times than we'd like — we're powerless over pain. But we always have the power to put pain in perspective: the perspective of whatever good fortune we're still blessed to have, or the perspective of our purpose. When we do that, we start to find ways to bear pain with strength.

And at this point, Walker, you're probably beginning to grasp that while I called this letter "Mastering Pain," it's really about different ways to master yourself. Very often the world is what it is and will be what it will be. Despite all of our desire and effort, we'll never eliminate unfairness or do away with tragedy. And we'll never really "master" pain. But we can gain some mastery over ourselves.

— 15 —

A few days ago, you wrote me about a major milestone in your life: "Last Sunday I went past my 90 days of sobriety. My eyes are clear and open wide. The gratitude I feel for clarity forces me to drop my pride and give credit where it's due. The credit belongs with other people and the examples they've been to me. I owe my community."

I've noticed how often the word "gratitude" has been coming up in your letters, Walker. I think that building this habit of giving thanks is one of the best things we can do to grow in resilience.

There's been a lot of research on gratitude in recent years, and nearly all of it backs up what Cicero said two thousand years ago: it's "the parent of all the other virtues."

People who practice gratitude are less stressed and less depressed than those who don't. They're less likely to be overwhelmed by bad fortune. They even sleep better at night. One finding stands out: of all the personality traits psychologists studied, nothing did more than a sense of gratitude to promote happiness.

That's why it's such a big deal that, even in the middle of a difficult time, you've found ways to give thanks. A moment of eye contact when we say "thank you," a list of the good fortune we've had this week or this year, a visit to a teacher or a friend or a relative who was there for us at a difficult time — these things make us happier, kinder, stronger.

We could spend a lot of time thinking about why gratitude works, but I think it's pretty simple. When we express thanks for something, we call our attention to the good things in our lives. We remember those things that we might otherwise overlook, take for granted, or forget. And when we offer thanks — when we express our thanks *to* someone or something — we're reminded that we're not alone.

— 16 —

What keeps you holding on to your pain?

Often, when it's pain caused by someone else, you hold on to your pain out of anger. You hold on to your pain out of a sense of justice —"he needs to come and apologize first." You hold on to your pain because part of you would rather be right than happy.

But as much as you think your anger is hurting the other guy, part of you also knows that refusing to forgive hurts you more than anyone. The other guy couldn't care less about your anger. There's a great image in the Talmud of the self-inflicted stupidity of this mindset: "He who bears a grudge acts like one who, having cut one hand while handling a knife, avenges himself by stabbing the other hand."

I love that image. When you're hurt, you really are cut and there's no wishing the pain away. But when you hold on to the pain longer than you need to, it's like cutting yourself over and over again.

So you can look at forgiveness in the same way you can look at gratitude: it's an attitude directed outward. But the person to whom you owe the practice is really yourself. It's been said that to forgive "is to give up all hope for a better past." In other words, to forgive means to give up your desire for power over what you can't control. Resilient people know how to focus their power. And although the past is outside your power, how you live today and how you live tomorrow are still yours to control.

– 17 –

People who are suffering a great hardship often turn to prayer. They are looking for strength, guidance, and perspective. They're looking for solace, for hope. They're not always seeking a promise that everything is going to be all right, but "the certainty that something makes sense, regardless of how it turns out." The certainty that we can find purpose even in our pain.

Prayer brings together many of the tools of resilience we've been thinking about: gratitude, perspective, an acknowledgment of limits, a reminder of purpose.

When things get really hard, people pray. Sometimes people are slightly ashamed of this. They feel oddly guilty, and believe that if they were truly faithful, they'd pray all the time. And they sometimes feel that if they don't pray all the time, they don't "deserve" to pray when times are tough.

I can't tell anyone else how to pray, but I find myself praying more when things are harder. I also find myself drinking water more when I am thirsty, and eating more when I am hungry, and sleeping more when I am tired. And I've finally begun to accept that if I pray more when I am troubled, that's just as natural.

My point isn't to recommend that everybody pray. What has worked for me and for you, Walker, might not work for everyone. But I would suggest that what many of us do in prayer is valuable if you want to build resilience. It's valuable to step outside yourself in a moment of reflection. It's valuable to still your mind and calm your breathing. It's valuable to ask questions, think back on where you've been, and search for ways to move forward.

Walker, you told me you pray. The next time, maybe you can think about this: "Prayer cannot bring water to parched fields, or mend a broken bridge, or rebuild a ruined city; but prayer can water an arid soul, mend a broken heart and rebuild a weakened will."

Reflection

✳

Zach,

Matthew Crawford is a motorcycle mechanic with a PhD in philosophy. You'd like his book, *Shop Class as Soulcraft,* which explains why he gave up a job at a think tank for a life running a repair shop.

Deep and productive reflection, he writes, often starts when we get our hands dirty. In science, many pivotal theories about the world began not with theorists at blackboards, but with skilled craftsmen in workshops. In the early nineteenth century, at a time when physicists were chasing mistaken theories of heat down blind alleys, mechanics were busy perfecting the steam engine. By trial and error, they figured out how heat, power, and pressurized air interacted in the belly of an engine, which led to the thermodynamic theory of heat, still taught in schools today.

Crawford's point is this: when you get your hands dirty, you often develop valuable ideas about how the wider world works.

— 2 —

Everyone has theories about how the world works. If we're open to the possibility that we might be wrong, and we adjust our thinking based on what we learn, then over time our theories become stronger and we can have more justified confidence in our ideas.

The right way to reflect on our lives isn't too different from the scientific method. Start with a hypothesis, and then — no matter how good it makes you feel, no matter how commonsensical it sounds, no matter whose authority you have to back it up—test it. Test it honestly. Test it ruthlessly. See how it stands up to the facts of the world.

Then let the results of that test—whether they affirm or contradict your hunch—shape your understanding.

We can learn a lot about building strong ideas if we think a bit about the history of science. Sciences in their early stages are often riddled with errors. (What's difficult about this is that they are riddled with errors that are—in their time—supported by most of the scientists working in the field.) And this is as true of theoretical as it is of applied sciences.

For hundreds of years, surgeons' single most common treatment was bloodletting. It was believed to cure everything from fever to insanity to acne. George Washington might have enjoyed more than a two-year retirement if three doctors hadn't contributed to killing him by draining too much of his blood to cure a sore throat.

When the science of the brain was still in its infancy, doctors believed they could discover your personality by feeling the shape of your skull. You can still find nineteenth-century brain maps that chart a different personality trait for each bump on your head: "benevolence" near your forehead, "acquisitiveness" just above your ear, "philoprogenitiveness" (the bump that determines if you want to have a lot of children) toward the back. Today, scientists map the brain with more advanced tools, but we're still a long way from understanding the links between the physical structure of the brain and the character of the person who carries it in her head.

Artillery, as you know, is something of a science, but in its early days it was often a deadly game of chance, full of primitive cannons exploding without warning. King James II of Scotland was killed when he tried to fire a new cannon called the Lion: "His thigh bone was dug in two with a piece of a misframed gun that brake in shooting, by the which he was stricken to the ground and died hastily."

New sciences still feel growing pains. The study of nutrition, for example, is still in its infancy. My guess is that we may understand only a little more about nutrition today than the doctors who killed George Washington understood about blood. It used to be that scientists thought that eating fat led people to get fat. For many years it was nutritional dogma that "a calorie is a calorie is a calorie." (Following the old logic, my brother-in-law once bet a guy in his office that he could live for a week on nothing but Oreos.) We still have a limited understanding of how hormones, exercise, and food interact. Seemingly every other week, some new study announces that cherry juice is the key to decreasing inflammation, or that the cabbage soup diet is the way to go.

Young sciences — like brain science in the nineteenth century, or the medieval science of artillery, or nutrition science today — get things wrong all the time. One of the reasons is that a science often starts its life heavy on theory, speculation, and elegant models, but light on hard data.

As long as scientists stay open to new experiences, inconvenient facts, and new ideas that explain those facts, over time our scientific understanding will get closer to the truth. Scientists turn their attention away from the way the world *should* behave, according to theory, and toward the messiness of reality. Over time, a science grows up.

There's no shame in starting wrong; if you had all of the answers, there'd be no need to live an examined life. But there *is* shame in staying wrong.

— 3 —

Without [action], thought can never ripen into truth.

— RALPH WALDO EMERSON

You're still figuring things out, Walker. So am I. We all are. And like a scientist, if you have theories but never test them, two things will happen. One, you'll have bad ideas. That's not so bad. But two — this is the bad part — you'll act on those ideas. It's the personal equivalent of bleeding yourself to cure disease or blowing your leg off firing a poorly made cannon.

Just as scientists build sound theories through experimentation, you can use your experience to build principles and ideas to shape your life. But to do this, you need to do more than just hypothesize and more than just act. You have to *reflect* on your experience.

And it's here, in reflection, where our culture is perhaps at its weakest relative to the ancients. Compared to the ancients, we live lives that are glutted with opportunities for distraction.

Think about travel. For most of history, travel meant walking or, if you were extremely lucky, riding on a horse or in a boat. Without radio or phones or the Internet, you were alone with your thoughts — one foot in front of the other, mile after mile.

Now, it's not as if everyone in the past who took a long, undistracted walk spent it pondering the meaning of life or the existence of God. But it did mean that there simply wasn't much else to do other than think.

Reflection wasn't something you had to set aside time for; it was a natural part of every day. What would you reflect on if you had hours to fill with nothing but your thoughts? Mostly, I'd guess, practical things: business to pursue, a piece of advice to give your child, memories and stories to pass the time. But somewhere in the course of those hours — maybe by accident, maybe by design — you'd have occasion to think about times when you've lived well or badly; you might consider the times of pleasure and pain in your life; you might come across thoughts about the mistakes, achievements, and joys of others. Whether or not you had a word for it, you'd find yourself reflecting on how to live.

And if you found these kinds of thoughts especially valuable, you might think about how to deliberately make reflection a habit of your life.

In third grade, I got my first job working for Roger Richardson. Roger and his wife, Anne, were neighbors whom I'd known my whole life. Anne had been my kindergarten teacher, and Roger hired me to help him with his yard. Eventually I took over mowing his lawn, and soon I started a little business mowing lawns around the neighborhood. In the winter, I'd shovel snow.

I remember coming to enjoy the work for a lot of reasons: the pay, of course, and the sense of satisfaction that came from a freshly cut lawn or a clear driveway, but I also came to enjoy the time I had to think. It didn't take a lot of mental effort to push a lawnmower or shovel snow, so while my body went back and forth across the lawn or up and down the driveway, my mind could go wherever it wanted. I often found that I thought cleaner and more deeply when I was working than I did at any other time.

Action in the world, and reflection on it, go hand in hand. You can't just sit down in a room and puzzle out your life. To reflect well, you need something to reflect on. There's a famous story about the Buddha that gets at this point. The Buddha began life as a sheltered prince, protected behind the high walls of a palace and sealed off from the suffering of the world. It was only when he escaped the palace walls and saw, for the first time, an old man, a sick man, and a dead man that he decided to set out on the path that led him to wisdom.

The Buddha's insights didn't come from his time of comfort and isolation. They came from his engagement with the hard facts of the world.

— 4 —

We're often taught that "thinking" and "reflection" are synonymous. They aren't. We don't need to draw too fine a distinction here — this is a point about life rather than semantics — but generally speaking, when we reflect, we are processing the meaning of something that we have learned or experienced. Often our reflections then guide our future actions.

Reflection is the kind of thinking that demands far more than intelligence. It demands, for instance, a certain kind of humility and courage. It requires the humility to recognize that you might have been wrong in the past, that you might be wrong today, and that you are certainly going to be wrong in the future. It takes the courage to be attentive to and honest about your own faults. And it takes a mind orderly enough and undistracted enough to enjoy its own company. To reflect well requires some virtue.

Walker, you've already been reflecting. You've been reflecting in your letters and in our conversations. The other day you wrote to me, "I've learned more about myself in the last two months than I have in the last ten years."

When we talked you said:

I realized the other day, when I was thinking about the fact that I couldn't lose weight — I had the sciatica issue, I wasn't motivated when I was injured — I got going good on my diet, then I got sick. I fell off. But then I got remotivated when I started to think about my identity. Who am I? How do I identify myself? Now I've got a picture in my mind's eye of who I want to be, and I can feel the strength coming back . . .

I am now becoming a complete man, a new individual. I was in one of my AA meetings, and I was sitting there and it was like I was watching myself from the outside. And it's powerful, I'm surprising myself, because I feel like the wisdom is coming out—I don't even really know how to explain it—but it's working. I can tell when I'm talking that it's getting through to other people too. Not only is what I'm saying helping me, but I can tell that what I'm saying is accepted and understood and beneficial to the people around me and right across from me.

Walker, watching yourself from the outside is reflection. And here's the thing: most people can do this. Most people can do this very well. But too few of us actually start.

—5—

A lot of people talk too much. Especially when they are trying to learn, they ask too many questions.

I was once training a young kid in boxing—I was a young kid myself—and after every punch he wanted to stop, put his fists on his hips, and ask me a question. Finally he asked me something about sparring, and I just said, "The answer to your question is in the heavy bag."

A lot of people need more work and less talk. More action, less complaining. We need to hear less about their feelings and see more of their effort.

That's not your problem, Walker. You are a person of intensity in almost everything you do, and, if anything, you could use some structured, healthy reflection to guide your actions.

Even as I write this, I realize that "guide your actions" is almost equivalent to writing "guide a tornado." But just as talk minus action equals nothing, action minus thought can lead to disaster. And that —disaster—is how you've described where you were a few months ago, so let's think about how to reflect well.

—6—

Where do you start when reflecting on your experience?

Let's make it simple. You can start with this question: Who do I want to be?

If you have an answer to that question, everything flows from it. If you have a sense of the person you are trying to create, then you will know better, in any given situation, what to do.

But let's not pretend that question has an easy answer. It takes a lot of hard thinking to work toward an answer, and you can't put your entire life on hold while you're trying to figure it out.

So make it simpler still. Ask yourself: What am I aiming to do? What do I want to make happen? If you want to use military language, ask yourself: What is my mission in this moment?

It's often hard to know exactly what you're aiming at. It's hard to define your mission. It's even hard to know what you want to make happen in the world. That's OK. In fact, that's kind of the point — that is where the *work* of reflection takes place. You have to work to figure these things out as best you can.

Remember when we were talking about beginning? We said that you don't have to know what perfect looks like, but you do have to know what better looks like. If you know better from worse, then you've laid the groundwork for quality reflection.

We can keep this straightforward. You ask: What was I aiming at? How did I do? What do I need to do differently next time?

The other day, you wrote me about your first summer in the woods as a logger:

> *Everyone heard the story about Kern's toes getting smashed by a tree he felled and the time Jim had that log roll on him in the landing. Steve told me about the time he had a mighty redwood unwrap and splinter on him like confetti. He wound up pinned to the mountain by a 16-foot redwood splinter that stabbed directly through his left forearm busting the artery and shattering his radius. Everyone knew the woods were dangerous and unpredictable. And at one point or another, everyone worked in the woods. It was something we grew up knowing we would do and I chomped on the bit.*
>
> *The day I turned 16, I started in the brush setting chokers. Within a few weeks I was running a chainsaw and playing around on the loader a little bit. I remember where I was when I saw my first 6-foot redwood butt cut being skidded into the landing. With a foot of bark wrapping the entire thing it was almost 8 feet tall. When the loader grabbed a hold of it and*

tried to lift it off the ground the back tires lifted instead. The front tires of
the loader started going flat as it barely skipped the log around the landing.
We had to dig a hole in the ground, drive a log truck down into it, drop
the stakes off the trailer and roll the log onto the truck to get it to the mill.
That's big timber logging right there.

I learned how to file a chain to keep it sharp and when to gas and oil the
saw to keep it up and running when the landing got busy. I learned how to
knock the dirt off a knot before bumping it to keep my chain sharp, how to
buck a log at the right length without getting it pinched, how to set chokers
on steep ground without catapulting any other logs further away from the
machine I was working under. I was drinking off a fire hydrant on a job
that doesn't often forgive mistakes.

A lot of people will read that story and just see a kid trying to figure
his way around the woods without breaking too many ribs. But it's also
a story about a kid gaining wisdom: figuring out how to achieve excellence in his small corner of the world, and learning something about
excellence in general.

Now, I know that sounds ridiculously highfalutin. But that's only
because we've made "wisdom" into something ethereal and abstract instead of something real and practical. The Greeks were smarter than
us. They'd see sixteen-year-old Zach Walker growing in what they
called *phronesis,* practical wisdom: the ability to figure out what to do
while at the same time knowing what is worth doing.

From Homer to Socrates, when the Greeks wanted to talk about wisdom, they often started by talking about it practically: a carpenter who
knows how wood warps over time, a horse trainer who knows when to
chasten and when to reward, a ship's captain who knows how to ride
the winds.

That's where good reflection takes you—it takes you to practical
wisdom. And whether that's wisdom about running a chainsaw, paving
a street, sustaining a marriage, flanking an enemy, or coaching your
kid's team, it all makes you better.

— 7 —

If we reflect on what we do, and part of what we do is to reflect, then
how do we reflect on our reflection?

OK, I made that sound convoluted on purpose, because you can tie yourself in a knot thinking about this, and you can make this more complicated than it is. But the question is straightforward: How do you know if you're reflecting well? How do you know if the reflection that you are doing is going to make you better?

The gold standard for good reflection is simply that it allows you to plan well. And planning leads to thoughtful action. It works like this: You act. You reflect on your action. You plan based on your reflection. Then you do it again. Act. Reflect. Plan.

This process of acting, reflecting, and planning sometimes takes place in the course of seconds and sometimes takes place over the course of years. But if we want to build resilience, it's critical that we engage in this process on a regular basis. If we build a habit of quality reflection into our lives, we will be able to consistently respond to hardship, error, pain, difficulty, and disorder in a way that makes us stronger.

— 8 —

Reflecting well also means recognizing the mindsets that stand in the way of insight.

A closed mind is sealed against new information, new training, and new growth. It filters out facts, leaving them unseen and unconsidered. Sometimes a closed mind is a product of arrogance: a conviction that someone is already in possession of a perfect, all-purpose ideology. Some people believe that they already know everything worth knowing.

More often, a closed mind is a product of fear. Certain beliefs are as central to our thinking as the pillars that support a cathedral. We use these beliefs to hold up our own conception of ourselves and to justify our place in the world. We're afraid that if we question their strength, the world around us might collapse.

A closed mind protects the ego, but at the cost of weakening and degrading our thinking. When we close our minds in fear or arrogance we lock ourselves away, just as we might lock a healthy person in a dark, solitary cell. The prisoner is safe from the outside world — nothing can hurt him. At the same time, the prisoner is also deprived of everything he needs to grow strong. Without sunlight, exercise, good food, and relationships, he grows weak and sickly. The same is true of a core belief that is never exposed to debate and conversation, never nourished with fresh insight.

Just as a person locked in isolation loses touch with reality, ideas that never have meaningful interaction with other ideas become erratic and fragile. As their ideas deteriorate in strength, many people lock them up all the more tightly and react all the more angrily when they are challenged. In this way, people who were once vibrant, interesting, and productive become stale, boorish, and self-destructive.

It's for this reason that, of all the vices, self-righteousness is often the most self-blinding.

— 9 —

When we reflect well on an event, we reflect not only on what happened, but on why it happened. When we begin to understand why something happened, we are not just revisiting a memory. We are creating understanding.

Done well, reflection is more than replaying memories; it is the process of making sense of those memories in the larger story of our lives.

Everyone can call back a memory. Not everyone can reflect on it. If our reflection is thorough, we move from having had an experience to having an understanding of what we've experienced. And if that understanding is then applied to how we live, we move from *having* an understanding to *living with* understanding.

In other words, with the right reflection we learn to turn our experience into wisdom that shapes how we live. The difference between a life that is happening to you and a life that you shape is often reflection.

Socrates talked about living an examined life. You put the words "Socrates" and "examined life" on paper and all of a sudden this can seem like something abstract, complicated, and daunting.

But the examined life is straightforward. Not easy, but straightforward.

You reflect on your purpose. You reflect on what you've done and you think about what you might do next. When you do this often enough, reflection becomes a part of who you are.

That's it. That's the examined life.

— 10 —

Will Guild, our command master chief when we went through BUD/S, was a Tier One operator who had thirty-some years in the Teams. He became the head mentor for all of the guys going through training.

Guild was about six foot four, 250 pounds. Guys who operated with him called him Big Will. Will had joined the Teams when he was nineteen, and after doing everything he could in the Navy — he'd been an assault team crew leader, a pilot, a free-fall jump master, a combat diver, Special Forces–qualified — he went to college at William and Mary. He studied English. Acted in plays. Came to love Shakespeare. Read the classics. Later he went to a program at Harvard Divinity School to study Greek, and he became the first enlisted person ever to teach ethics and a class in philosophy at the Naval Academy.

The first time Will taught a class to the junior officers at BUD/S, he started with that famous first line in *Hamlet:* "Who's there?" The point Will was making that day was not only that things were topsy-turvy in Hamlet's world, but that they were in ours as well. He explained how the role of the military in society was changing, and how after 9/11 we, as leaders, had to find ways to lead lives of service both in and out of uniform.

Will's an incredibly thoughtful guy. He was a good mentor and he's become a great friend. Will lives an examined life. In fact, he's done such a good job of living an examined life that he's built some wisdom about how to reflect well.

Will taught us that resilient people adapt well to what is happening around them. To do that, though, they have to understand clearly what is happening, without self-deception, too much optimism, or too much pessimism. They have to see the world around them as it actually is.

A lot of military definitions and methodologies get way too complicated. Have you ever seen a military visual for the OODA loop — Observe, Orient, Decide, Act? It's a perfect example of how a once-valuable concept can be complicated to the point of irrelevance. But Will has a straightforward way of thinking about situational awareness that's very easy to apply.

Will's idea allows for deep thinking and clear thinking at the same time. He says that there are four questions you have to answer to be situationally aware.

First, why am I here? The answer might be: to conduct a reconnaissance mission of a suspected terrorist target.

Second, what's going on around me? Headlights whipped around the corner and are barreling down the street toward the target house.

Third, what am I going to do about it? Watch the car until it pulls up in front of the house, take photographs of the people who step out of the car, and send those photographs back to the boss.

Fourth, how will my actions affect others? My commander will build a clearer picture of who is in the target house and what their pattern of movement is.

These four questions apply to almost any situation. For example:

First, why am I here? To have a productive conversation with my wife, and to show her that I love her.

Second, what's going on around me? She's mad at me because I've screwed up again: I was tired after training, was short with her, and I'm also home late again.

Third, what am I going to do about it? Apologize. Tell her that I was wrong. Give her a hug and let her know that I love her, respect her time, and want to be a good husband.

Four, how will my actions affect others? If I apologize sincerely, she may forgive me, and we can have a good night together. Next time, I can pause before I snap.

The model begins with you. To understand your surroundings, you need to start by understanding why you are there and how you fit in the picture. Next, you need to understand what is happening around you. But that's not enough, because you aren't a passive observer — you are part of what is happening around you. So you need to reflect on what you should do and on how what you do will shape your environment. If you can effectively answer all four questions, you have real situational awareness.

Each question allows for a quick answer or for deep and extended analysis. The depth to which you pursue each answer depends on what the situation calls for.

Why am I here? To strengthen my upper body.

Why am I here? To pave this driveway.

Why am I here? To celebrate my daughter's birthday.

It's important to remember that the model works best if you ask and answer the questions in the right order. You don't start recording everything that's happening around you without first thinking about your purpose in the moment — because your purpose makes some facts crucial and others trivial. You don't plunge into action without observing the world around you. You don't make a decision to act until you've taken stock of your effect on others. Each answer becomes stronger and makes more sense when you have a good answer to the previous question.

Try it. Think about a situation. Answer the four questions. Why am I here? What's going on around me? What am I going to do about it? How will my actions affect others? It's amazing to see the kind of clarity that this exercise can bring you. Sometimes your own course of action becomes clear immediately. Other times you realize that you don't fully understand what's happening around you, or you don't fully understand how your actions will affect others. That knowledge in and of itself can help you to learn more and to act better.

When you do this enough times, this way of thinking can itself become a habit. And that habit of thinking, over time, leads to greater situational awareness, which allows you to better adapt to and shape circumstances successfully — a skill at the heart of resilience.

— 11 —

If the word "wisdom" is sometimes thought of as ethereal and highfalutin, then "enlightenment" has an even worse connotation. People often think of it as arrogance that smells like aromatherapy. And that's a shame, because the basic idea of enlightenment is pretty simple: you see clearly what you couldn't see before.

In building your own insights, you might choose an example, a model, or a teaching to follow, but no one can do your reflecting for you, any more than someone can do your exercising for you.

Someone else can put a thought in your head. But an insight is something you have to earn on your own.

That was one of the Buddha's key teachings. When his students asked him where they could find enlightenment, he replied by telling them all the places they *couldn't* find it:

Do not go by revelation;
Do not go by tradition;
Do not go by hearsay;
Do not go on the authority of sacred texts;
Do not go on the grounds of pure logic;
Do not go by a view that seems rational;
Do not go by reflecting on mere appearances;
Do not go along with a considered view because you agree with it;
Do not go along on the grounds that the person is competent;
Do not go along because "the monk is our teacher" . . .
But when you know for yourselves, "These things are good; these
things are blameless; these things are praised by the wise; these things,
when adopted and carried out, lead to benefit and happiness," then you
should enter and remain in them.

The Buddha taught his students that they must know for themselves.
The work of reflection is something you have to do for yourself. No one
else can make you wise. Unreflective adherence to tradition, to sacred
texts, or to authority won't make you wise. It is not that the examples
of our teachers or the writings of earlier generations don't contain wisdom. It's just that they contain *someone else's* wisdom.

What matters to me and to you is not how wise Aristotle or the Buddha were, but how wise you can be. To be wise is to know *for yourself.*

Montaigne, too, put this well: "We can be knowledgeable with other
men's knowledge, but we cannot be wise with other men's wisdom."
Some things, Walker, you have to learn for yourself.

— 12 —

In most religious traditions, insight comes after a journey of some
kind. Moses and Jesus and Muhammad all walked the desert. All spent
time in solitude and reflection before they returned to their work in
the world. Their stories remind us that insight rarely comes without
effort.

People who see things differently usually do so because they have
trained their eyes and their spirits in a particular way. In Buddhist and
Christian monasteries, people dedicate themselves to living by disci-

plined habits and consistent choices. These choices can radically change how they see the world. In a documentary about life in a Carthusian monastery, *Into Great Silence,* an elderly monk reflects on the loss of his sight: "I often thank God that he let me be blinded. I am sure that he let this happen for the good of my soul."

You may or may not see the world as he does. My point is only that the way you see the world is shaped by the reflection you are willing to do.

--- 13 ---

Much of the compelling evidence that we have about elite performance suggests that practice helps people, sometimes literally, to see the world differently.

Great hitters in baseball aren't always blessed with incredibly fast reaction times. Instead — through practice — they've come to read a pitcher's delivery so well that they can reliably predict the pitch that's coming in a fraction of a second. Great boxers aren't so fast that they avoid flying punches. Instead — through practice — they are able to anticipate when and where a dangerous fist might fly.

In each case, practice makes the world look different. But it's also true — and this should help to keep us humble — that practice can help us to see very specific things while we remain blind to others that seem similar. The other day, I read about what happened to one of the greatest baseball players of our time when he tried to get a hit off of an Olympic softball pitcher: he whiffed three times. "I never want to experience that again," the player said.

You'd think a slugger like that would destroy a softball. A softball is bigger than a baseball and travels more slowly. But here's the problem: for most of his life the All-Star hitter had trained himself in the art of looking at pitchers throwing baseballs. So when he saw a softball delivered underhand and with an entirely different motion than he's used to seeing from baseball pitchers, he was like a hapless Little Leaguer all over again.

Why does this matter? First, insights come through practice. When we work at something, we come to see it differently. This is true of seeing a baseball differently. It's also true of seeing hardship differently.

Second, we all have limited insights. Because some insights are built only through practice, and because the amount of time we have to practice anything is limited, we can master only a limited amount in our lives. Part of wise reflection is reminding ourselves of the bounds of our mastery and the limits of our vision. And part of a wise life is having friends who can help us to see beyond our limited experience.

Friends

What is a friend? A single soul dwelling in two bodies.

— ARISTOTLE

When a young person asks me for advice about *what* he should do, I often ask him: Who do you want to be with?

Few things in life shape you more than the people around you, and few choices are more important than deciding who you'll be with. This is true for all of us, and it's true for all of our lives. Unfortunately, many people treat this idea as if it had an expiration date: the day you become an adult.

You know your kids are impressionable, Walker, and I bet you spend your fair share of time worrying about their choice of friends. But *we* are impressionable too, and whether or not we acknowledge it, we are all social animals. Every day we are shaped by the people we spend time with.

Be with people who are the way you want to be. If you want to be excellent, be around people who pursue excellence. If you want to be happy, be around people who are happy. If you are around resilient people, you're far more likely to be resilient yourself.

— 2 —

Who you should spend time with is a question for adults, and it has inspired some profound adult thinking.

Cicero took friendship seriously: a true friend, he said, is "a second self."

Seneca took friendship seriously in his letters to Lucilius: "Ponder for a long time whether you shall admit a given person to your friendship; but when you have decided to admit him, welcome him with all your heart and soul. Speak as boldly with him as with yourself."

Confucius took friendship seriously. At the very beginning of his collected teachings, we read, "Is it not a joy to have friends come from afar?"

You could make the case that Aristotle treated friendship as the single most important ingredient for a good life. His book on character and the pursuit of happiness, the *Nicomachean Ethics,* has ten chapters, each on a separate subject. Only one topic gets two chapters: friendship. No other subject in the book is discussed at greater length.

Aristotle viewed friendship as an essential requirement of both happiness and excellence. And as with almost everything he examined, Aristotle tried to break his subject down into manageable and measurable pieces. He believed that friendship could be based on one of three things: utility, pleasure, or virtue.

Friendships of utility bring together people who are useful to each other. Think of business partners, coworkers, teammates. Ideally you treat each other with respect and kindness. Over time, you may grow to like each other. But you're initially drawn together because you're useful to one another. Such relationships are part of every human life and can be genuinely valuable. But such friendships can also be fleeting: they are prone to disappear as soon as you stop being mutually useful.

Then there are friendships of pleasure. There are some people we just like being around. They make us happy. Every person should have friends like these; we have a blast with them. It's also true that you can enjoy being around such friends for years and then reach a point when you no longer find each other amusing, and the relationship may die.

A friendship based in virtue and excellence is different. Remember when we talked about the word *arête* — how it is usually translated as "virtue" but means something a bit closer to "excellence" in English.

This is important, because when people read Aristotle today and see that he thinks that the ultimate friendship is one based in "virtue," it can read as if Aristotle is giving a long, boring Sunday school lecture. (Walker, I once got so bored as a kid in Sunday school that I climbed out one of the classroom windows, jumped into the courtyard, and ran away.) But if you see that Aristotle is talking about friends who enrich one another's lives, who help one another live their best possible lives, then what he's saying starts to make sense.

Aristotle points out that your deep and true friends—sometimes he calls them your "perfect" friends—can also be pleasant and useful, but they don't have to constantly work at it. And neither do you. You aren't fearful that your true friends will lose interest. With your closest friends, it's often enough to simply be together.

Aristotle argues that such friendships are an end in themselves. It's not that we pursue them because they will help us to live an excellent life; we make time to create such friendships because they are *part* of an excellent life. In fact, Aristotle suggests—and I also believe—that we can't live our best lives or become our best selves without these kinds of friendships. The best friends support us, challenge us, inspire us. And we do the same for them.

It's been said that the deepest relationships are formed not when two people are looking at each other, but when two people are looking in the same direction. That's a very Aristotelian thought.

These true friendships are rare. Aristotle said that "it is natural that such friendships should be infrequent . . . such friendship requires time and familiarity." This isn't a shock to anyone who has built a real friendship. "A wish for friendship may arise quickly, but friendship does not."

I'm very fortunate to have a few friends I've known since I was a little kid. In fact, tonight I'm going to a surprise birthday party for a friend, Steve, who's turning forty. We started our friendship playing with toy cars in the dirt when we were six years old. Several other friends at the party are people I've also known for over thirty years.

It's hard to write about such a friend without drifting into clichés: "We've been there for each other in the best times and the worst times," et cetera, et cetera. But it's true. We spent hours and hours in buses and cars, traveling across Missouri to play baseball and soccer games. Steve—we called him "Bob"; never mind why—was always the best athlete. In baseball he played catcher and batted cleanup. In soccer he was the goalie and probably the only decent player on our team. We'd get murdered most every game, with the opposing team ripping shots at the goal, and Steve would be diving and grabbing and tipping and saving nearly every shot. Sometimes it seemed as if Steve were playing eleven-on-one. It was always: "Good job, Bob!" And then, thirty seconds later: "Great save, Steve-O!" Eventually the other team would get one by him, and we'd ride the bus home having lost 1–0. All the while Steve would be berating himself, as if he should have been able to save a hundred shots *and* score for us.

I remember, a decade later, shortly after I got divorced, three of these old friends flew out to visit me. I had only one bed and one couch, so two guys slept on the floor. We went out for Mexican food, and sometime later Steve fell ill with food poisoning and spent the whole night puking bad burrito into the toilet. I know that's not a pretty picture, but those are the kinds of stories you have when you have a friend for over thirty years. That's not something you can replace, buy, or borrow. It's precious. Rare. Worth protecting.

And you know what's fun for me about writing to you, Walker? It's fun because writing to you makes me reflect on my own life. In fact, just writing this letter about friendship makes me appreciate my own friends that much more, including you.

— 3 —

In my work with veterans, I ask people to come together as "fellows." Fellowship is different from friendship, but they're two ideas that have a lot in common. And it's in fellowship that friendship often has its roots.

We might begin as strangers, but in fellowship we make a decision to purposefully experience life together. We are not just in the same place, inhabiting the same space. In fellowship we are making a conscious effort to walk and work in the world with others. We are purposefully sharing, studying, serving, and — when necessary — suffering together.

I made a conscious choice to root my work with veterans in the idea and practice of fellowship. For veterans, the loss of a sense of camaraderie is often the most painful casualty in the transition from soldier to civilian. As soldiers, they walked the roads of a hostile land together. On the frontlines they forged friendships of a lifetime. Veterans move from a world in which they are surrounded by friends who risk their lives for one another to a world of strangers who might not care much for each other.

By beginning in the spirit of fellowship, we enable veterans to build new bonds as they experience life together here at home.

Friends help us flourish. They lighten our burdens, enlighten our thinking, enrich our lives. When we lose sight of our commitments, they remind us of them. When we falter, they help us stand. And we grow in resilience when we do the same for them, because the need to be strong for others often reveals untapped reserves of strength in ourselves.

— 4 —

We often turn to friends when we make life's biggest decisions, not because they will support us unquestioningly, but because they will not. It's easy for an acquaintance to brush off a dumb idea with "Sounds good to me." It's irresponsible for a real friend to do that.

Friends challenge the flaws in our thinking and the flaws in our character. When they do that, they make us better. Good friends hold us to a higher standard when we are ready to make an excuse for ourselves. Friends sympathize with our pain, but they stop us from wallowing in it. Friends point out our blind spots, and they do so not with vindictiveness or cruelty, but out of honesty, love, and a desire that we live the fullest and best life possible.

That's why, in the ancient world, philosophers stressed the importance of distinguishing true friendships from false ones — learning to tell apart the people who appeal to your best self and the people who flatter what's worst in you. Here's how Plutarch put it: "A true friend will not rashly commend nor imitate every thing, but only what really deserves it." On the other hand, "the flatterer claws and tickles the irrational part of the man only."

And remember, this was advice for adults, not children — there's never a point in your life when friendship ceases to matter. In fact, the older and (hopefully) wiser you get, the more you realize that true friendships aren't always easy.

You probably know this line from Lord Acton: "Power tends to corrupt, and absolute power corrupts absolutely."

I don't agree with that. I've known many people who were powerful and exceedingly honest, and I've known many people with little or no power who were conniving and vindictive and mean. But I do think that Lord Acton was right to notice that people go wrong more often the more powerful they become. I don't think that's because power corrupts, but because power so often fails to correct.

As you become more powerful, you have to work harder to make sure that people correct you. People no longer tell you what you did wrong. More and more, you have to ask yourself, "How can I become better?" When the powerful are surrounded by people who always say yes — by subordinates moved by fear or sycophants looking for the next reward or promotion — they gradually lose the good sense that helped make them powerful in the first place. Sometimes, they lose themselves.

There's a powerful story about this in the Bible. There, leaders like Moses are recognized as blessed, as chosen by God, but are still flesh-and-blood people who make grave mistakes. Think of David. He was the brave shepherd who defeated Goliath, but he also became the sometimes cruel and greedy king who ordered a man to his death just so he could sleep with Bathsheba, the man's wife.

One of David's closest advisers was the prophet Nathan. When Nathan discovered David's abuse of power, he requested an audience with the king. Nathan was wise enough to know that if he criticized the king directly, David might shut his ears. So instead, Nathan said that he came with news: there was a rich man in a nearby town who had terrorized and robbed his poorer neighbor. Lately, he had stolen and slaughtered the poor man's pet lamb.

> David burned with anger against the man and said to Nathan, "As surely as the Lord lives, the man who did this must die! He must pay for that lamb four times over, because he did such a thing and had no pity." Then Nathan said to David, "You are the man!"

Every powerful person needs friends and counselors like Nathan. Far too few have them. Who is your Nathan, Walker?

— 5 —

To be wise, we have to recognize that we know only a small fraction of what is worth knowing. To be resilient, we also have to recognize that we know only a small fraction of what is worth knowing *about ourselves.*

So much of the tragic tradition is about people who fail to know themselves until it's too late. Think of the story of Oedipus, who receives the terrible prophecy that he's fated to kill his father and sleep with his mother. Oedipus runs away, and only many years later — after he has killed men, married a queen, and become king of the city of Thebes — does he discover that he has returned to the home of the parents who abandoned him at birth and has fulfilled the prophecy.

The tragedy of Oedipus reminds us that even the most powerful and accomplished people can fail to know who they are. What makes life tragic is not only that we have limited time to live and limited strength to live with; it's also that we all have limited vision. None of us can see or understand everything about anything, and that includes ourselves. But if there's a hope of understanding ourselves better, it comes through real friendship.

Resilience takes awareness: awareness of yourself and of the world around you. And you aren't really aware of either without good friends. Your friends help to expand your stock of experience. Learning from a friend's hard experience can save us the pain of learning the same hard lesson.

Think of a community of friendship as a pool of experience that multiplies each member's wisdom. No one person, no matter how wise or experienced, can match the combined experience of a community. As long as we are imperfect, we will always find that the voice of a friend offers perspective and insight.

At the same time, friends also bring us perspective about ourselves. Have you ever stood on a table and realized that the room you are in looks different? Or lain down on the floor and seen what a baby sees? Or flown in a plane and watched your hometown pass below? In each case, you're looking at the familiar from a different angle — and you realize that you didn't know it as well as you thought.

We think that we see ourselves well. We do not. Good-quality, mass-produced mirrors (which have been around for less than two hundred years) are everywhere in our lives, and perhaps they give us a particularly false sense that we are able to see ourselves as others see us. But every time we take a look at ourselves — whether we examine our reflection in a mirror or examine our actions in memory — we see ourselves from only one perspective: our own. Of course, we can work to see ourselves from other angles. But we have to fight the powerful human tendencies to cover up or magnify our imperfections, to ignore or overly focus on our weak spots, to look at our every feature and every action in the softest or harshest possible light.

Because we have such trouble taking an objective look at ourselves, we will always be blind to at least some of our faults. This blindness weakens us.

In BUD/S training, Will Guild taught me a simple idea about what we know in relation to other people. He said there are four kinds of knowledge:

> THINGS THAT *we know and that others know as well; these things are known.*
> THINGS THAT *no one knows; these are unknown.*
> THINGS THAT *we know and others do not; these things are hidden.*
> THINGS THAT *others know that we don't know; these things we are blind to.*

Without help from others, we can be blind to a lot of what we need to know, including knowledge about ourselves.

Will made this point in the context of talking about elite performers and elite units. In Will's experience, he said, most truly elite performers are accessible, friendly, and humble. He found that these elite performers found ways to make connections between themselves and others, in part because they wanted to learn from other people and to lessen their own blindness as much as possible.

Of course, there are artists, athletes, and other exceptional performers who are arrogant. Most of them, however, are usually exceptional in only one area of endeavor. They may be great athletes but fail at coaching. Great entrepreneurs but bad fathers. Arrogance leads to blindness — and both blindness and arrogance, in time, exact a cost if we are trying to live a flourishing life.

I've written to you a bit about Homer, Walker. If you pick up one of Homer's epics, you'll probably notice a special habit of his. He almost always attaches a unique word or descriptive phrase to each character, a tag line that comes up every time that hero or god is mentioned. That's why you'll read about "fleet-footed Achilles," "bright-eyed Athena," "earthshaking Poseidon," and Hector, "breaker of horses."

This practice probably started as a handy memory tool. The first epic poets recited everything from memory (or made it up as they went along), and these tags were a way of holding their place while they were figuring out what to say next. But here's the important thing for us: these tag lines tell us what Homer considered the most descriptive traits for every character in his world.

What word did Homer use to introduce Odysseus, the hero who survived ten years of shipwreck and wandering before returning home from war? Wily. "*Wily* Odysseus."

When you first look at it, "wily" does not seem to be a word fit for a hero. But we should understand that the word can also be translated as something like "crafty," "clever," or "capable." "Wily" suggests a combination of awareness and ability. A wily hero can see what's happening clearly and act on it quickly.

Odysseus is a man who is aware of his surroundings, aware of his enemies, aware of himself. He has to be — it is the only way he makes it through those long years of war and exile. He knows that he cannot fight with the prowess of an Achilles, but he can devise the Trojan Horse, the strategy that wins the war.

He knows that he cannot stand toe to toe with a Cyclops, as Heracles did, but he is aware enough of the Cyclops's weaknesses to blind him and escape his clutches. Odysseus, a king, has learned to speak with everyone. He knows how to talk to the stable boy who tends his horse, to his fellow warriors, to the wife of a fallen comrade, to an ally, to a potential enemy.

Achilles is blinded by rage. Agamemnon is blinded by arrogance. Paris is blinded by lust. But Odysseus is wily, and he becomes aware and able because, of all of Homer's characters, he works the hardest to reduce his own blindness.

When you read the story of Odysseus, you realize that awareness *is* a heroic virtue, a quality fit for a king. And it is Odysseus's wiliness, his awareness and ability, that enables him to live through the greatest war of his age and return to his home long after he should have been given up for dead.

Odysseus is resilient because he is aware. For most of us, awareness comes when we have good friends.

— 6 —

We would never willingly drag a friend into our hardship. But having friends by our side during a difficult test can give us incredible strength. We wouldn't say, "I'm glad you're suffering too." But we do say, "I'm glad that you're here with me."

Friends are people to lean on, and they're people to be strong for. When servicemen and -women talk about the extraordinary camaraderie of serving and the tight-knit teams they served with, they know that such closeness, while punctuated by times of great fun and even joy, was also forged in the fires of difficulty. They drew strength from knowing that they were together when lives were on the line.

I don't know if I've ever told you about this, but my most challenging moment in BUD/S came during what should have been the easiest part of Hell Week. We were about seventy-two hours in, and the instructors were about to let us sleep for the first time. Now, as you'll remember, Walker, by the time we were seventy-two hours in, some of us were so tired that, when we were running down the beach, we'd stop, fall asleep standing up, and collapse to the ground. We were exhausted. Truly exhausted.

The instructors told us that before we could sleep, we had to compete in a dip contest on the parallel bars. Well, my crew lost, so I was the last person to run into the tents. When I got there, everyone else was already asleep.

I lay down . . . and I couldn't sleep. The last time I'd been through Medical, they'd wrapped my right foot too tightly, and with every beat of my heart I could feel the blood pulsing in my foot, so I got up, untied my boot, tore off the bandage, threw it on the ground, put my boot back on, and lay down again.

And still I couldn't fall asleep. I started to panic a bit then, thinking: We only get two to five hours of sleep over the course of the whole week. What's going to happen if I can't sleep?

I knew that I was going a little crazy, because the next thought that ran through my mind was: Well, maybe, maybe if I can't sleep, maybe they'll let me take a nap later. And then what happened is that the tent flap was open and there was a beam of light coming down on my cot and the cots of the guys next to me, and it was getting oppressively hot in the tent packed with bodies, and I started thinking: "This is not fair.

It's not fair that I ran into the tents last. It's not fair that they wrapped my foot the wrong way the last time I went through Medical. It's not fair that I got the worst cot." The more I let my own fear get to me, and the more I thought "this isn't fair," the weaker I became.

So I got up, went outside, and walked over to the wall where we had those faucets at about shoulder height. I turned one on, ducked my head underneath, and let the water wash over my head. And as I turned back to the tent I was, for one beautiful moment, thankful. Here I was in the middle of BUD/S, and I had a moment of peace absolutely to myself.

That's when I thought, This test isn't about you. The test was about my ability to be of service to the people who were asleep in that tent. And then all of that fear and self-pity left me, and I walked into the tent and fell asleep.

Now, it's not as if the instructors came in and gently shook us awake. They were setting off artillery simulators and smoke grenades and shouting on bullhorns, and as they started to run us down to the ocean to get us cold again, I remember that I had this huge smile on my face, because I realized that I'd just passed through my hardest moment.

When all I thought about was my own pain and how the world had dealt me an unfair hand, I became weaker. When I thought of the needs of my team, my friends, I became stronger.

We often think that our friends help us when we are weak. And they do. But it's also true that we become strong when we have friends to be strong for.

And Walker, one last word before I finish this letter. These letters are — as I promised they would be — imperfect and incomplete. You'll see most of the shortcomings on your own. But as we think about relationships, I do want to point out that one of the big flaws here is that there is no letter about marriage, or family, or faith.

Sheena and I have a wonderful marriage, and now we have a beautiful little boy at home. Perhaps, a few decades from now, I might feel that I can write a letter about friendship in marriage, or the role of the family in resilience. But right now I know only enough to know that I don't know enough.

I do know that there is an overwhelming power in boundless compassion and unconditional love. I know that I received from my own parents an unending love that gave me the confidence to take risks, and

I hope to provide the same love to my children. I also know that in my life and in the lives of many people I admire, a faith rooted in the love of God and the knowledge of God's love makes people resilient in the face of hardship.

But, Walker, there are millions of people who know more about this than I do. They have more experience, more wisdom, more insight than I can offer. You, for one, have more experience of marriage and of fatherhood than I do. Maybe in your next letter back you can tell me what you think, what you've learned. All I'll say here is that the subjects of marriage, family, and faith are important, they're missing from these letters, and a lot of people who know far more can probably help us both.

Mentors

My tae kwon do instructor once told all of his students that only five substances were allowed on the dojang floor: water, sweat, tears, blood, and puke.

Like any art, the martial art of tae kwon do offers infinite possibilities for complications and combinations. But becoming proficient in any art is usually not that complicated.

It takes hard work. Years of it. And few of us can get there without good coaches and mentors to guide us. They put before us the hard, unglamorous, and sometimes tedious reality of the work that leads to mastery, all while stoking the passion and wonder that set us on the path to mastery in the first place.

Walker, you know what it's like to be a mentor. A few years after you got the hang of logging, you were training kids who had brand-new workboots and little sense for the woods.

"As the years went by," you wrote, "greenhorns would show up and you'd have to teach them the ropes. You'd tell a guy not to stand where he was because the tree above him could be ripped over and end up in his lap. The greenhorn would scoff, and two minutes later he'd be trapped under the very tree you just warned him about."

A good mentor has *been there*. You knew where that tree was going to land because you'd watched felled trees come down many times. And so when you talked about it, you spoke with authority, even if the greenhorn didn't listen the first time.

As long as you keep growing and keep pushing into new endeavors, you'll need a mentor: someone who's been where you're going. Unfortunately, just like the models we talked about a few letters ago, people often stop seeking out mentors when they become adults.

I've had many mentors in my life, Walker. We've talked about some of them: Anne and Roger Richardson, Earl Blair. I'm in my late thirties, and I still need and benefit from mentors. About two years after I'd come back from Iraq, I met Anne Marie Burgoyne, an experienced executive who worked with many social entrepreneurs before me. She became a member of my board, and her guidance on team building, fundraising, and program design helped me grow a mission that had served a few dozen veterans to one that has served thousands.

I have editors who shape my writing. (One of them, Barbara Osburg, has been reading my work since I was sixteen years old.) And I have others — like my dad and my boxing coach, Earl Blair — who still offer advice that helps to give focus to my life.

This is pretty straightforward: I know that there are a lot of people who know much more than I do. So I try to find them, listen to them, and learn from them.

There's a lot to say about the difference mentors can make in your life. But even if you're with me on that, maybe you're starting with a more basic question. Why would someone put in the work to be a mentor in the first place? Why would she take time away from her own projects, her own ambitions, and her own accomplishments to build a connection with someone who *hasn't* been there and who knows only a fraction of what she knows?

Well, why did you put in the work to show new loggers the ropes? I'm sure you had plenty of reasons. Maybe it was part of your job description. Maybe it was a bit of an ego trip. But, knowing you, I think there was also something else, something more simple and powerful: you loved the work. You'd been pretending to be a logger since you could walk, and now that you had finally made it into the woods, you wanted to make sure that the kids who came up after you respected the work as much as you did.

Mastering a machine powerful enough to cut through a redwood, putting up with aches and pains without whining, clocking in for work even when your hands were curled into fists from handling a chainsaw all day — when you write about logging in your letters, you're describing not just a job, but a way of life. And part of respecting a way of life is passing it on, doing what you can to make sure it doesn't die with you. That goes for everyone from loggers to sportswriters to sculptors.

How do you explain the dad who spends three or four nights a week to get his Little League team ready to play in front of a handful of parents in the bleachers? How do you explain the teacher who's still in the classroom after a full day of work, going over the Pythagorean theorem with a sixth-grader one more time?

I don't think you can explain such actions without taking seriously mentors' love of what they do. And that's what you're looking for in a mentor, Walker: someone who respects whatever it is — gardening, parenting, or the concrete business — as much as you respected logging.

— 2 —

You can spend a lifetime reading books about painting without ever learning how to paint a tree. You can spend a lifetime watching videos of the great tae kwon do masters without ever learning how to throw a single kick.

You can pursue any practice you like without a mentor, and you can build knowledge, but it's unlikely that you'll ever build mastery. A mentor teaches you everything you can't learn from a book.

One of the people who has helped me think more clearly about the value of mentors is the British philosopher Michael Oakeshott. He taught that every activity relies on two kinds of knowledge: technical and practical. Technical knowledge can be captured in writing, rules, and mechanical practice. You grow in technical knowledge by absorbing information, not by doing.

Practical knowledge, on the other hand, "exists only in use . . . and (unlike technique) cannot be formulated in rules." It's passed on by experience, through communities. It's the kind of knowledge that we learn directly from others — as coaches teach players and masters teach their apprentices.

I like to think of this as the difference between "knowing that" and "knowing how." You can learn facts on your own. But if you want to know *how* to do something — from baking a cake to writing a story to disciplining a child — you usually have to be shown. The best mentors show us how.

* * *

Different disciplines create different kinds of knowledge. If you consider the sum total of what humans know about physics, you'll find that nearly all of it exists as technical knowledge scattered among books, journals, and articles.

If you consider the sum total of what humans know about tae kwon do, however, you'll find that only a small fraction of this knowledge has been captured and written down. So where is the rest of it? It's in the practice of the greatest masters, and it continues to exist because it's passed down to their students. If the masters disappeared tomorrow, the art of tae kwon do would likely disappear too.

The practice of every discipline requires both kinds of knowledge. Just as you can learn something about tae kwon do from books, there's a part of being a good physicist that you can't learn from books. My point is that you'll waste your time and energy unless you think clearly about the kind of knowledge you're after. Sometimes you'll need to be sure you find the right books. But if you're involved in a discipline like tae kwon do or parenting or leadership, you'll need to find the right mentors.

People will often scour the earth searching for the right book, but take whatever coach, teacher, trainer, or mentor who comes along.

It's not that one kind of knowledge is more important than the other. We only run into a problem if we convince ourselves that the only knowledge that matters is the kind that can be easily packaged.

Our mastery of the practices that matter — including the practice of living a good life — comes from people and through relationships. It comes from coaches, teachers, trainers, and mentors.

— 3 —

It's easy to find people willing to give you advice. It's hard to find people with advice worth giving.

Ideas are cheap. Advice is easy. And too often, "giving advice" is something that people do to reinforce their own deflated sense of self. It's worth pausing, then, to consider a few of the people who will *not* be able to help you.

Some people love to make their lessons overly complicated. If a mentor becomes lost in his lesson, you can usually assume one of several things. One, the mentor hasn't mastered the material. Two, the mentor is trying to make himself seem important. Or three, the mentor can't remember what it was like to learn the material himself.

I'm not suggesting that there's no such thing as complex material, or that you can expect your mentors to dumb things down for you. Instead, I'm suggesting that it's much easier to make information complex than it is to make it simple. A good mentor will focus on a simple thing that you can learn in order to get better.

There's a great line on this from the mathematician Blaise Pascal. He once wrote at the end of a letter to a friend, "I have made this longer than usual, because I have not had time to make it shorter."

The worst mentors are often the ones who say, about any complex subject, "Now, young man/woman, let me tell you how things *really* work."

There is no one way that the world works. In some fields, there are definite rights and wrongs. In many arts and activities, however, we leave the realm of right and wrong and enter the realm of better and worse, more or less.

How do you greet your students on the first day of class? How do you start a speech? How do you build a fence? How do you tend a garden? How do you paint a painting? We rely on mentors for the kind of knowledge that can't be captured in rules and certainties. We go to mentors for stories, experience, practice, and perspective. And good mentors will have the kind of humility that the truly excellent tend to possess. They'll understand that their own experience is a small piece of a much larger body of knowledge.

A good mentor will aim first not to give advice or instruct — activities that stress the mentor's superiority to the student — but to achieve understanding and then to share it.

We can't always achieve simplicity. Sometimes complex things must be appreciated in their complexity. But we can always seek clarity. Clear advice. Clear direction.

The master has mastery over her whole craft. She instructs with simple instructions: Relax. Breathe deeply. Stand tall. And in this way she gradually pushes her student, one step at a time, past the edge of her previous understanding.

Good mentors respect complexity. But because they've learned to separate essentials from distractions, they can offer clarity.

— 4 —

The best mentors must know two things: the challenge that's being faced and the person facing it. A mentor who knows one but not the other may be good, but is rarely great.

What does it mean for someone to know your challenge? To know your challenge means to have experience of the central question before you. (Unfortunately, a lot of bad advice is given, and taken, because people fail to identify the central question they face before acting.)

Imagine someone who has to make a choice between staying in school and leaving school to pursue a career as a professional dancer. There is a question here about dancing, but it's likely that the central question is about taking risks. So whose advice is worth seeking? Maybe not just a mentor with experience as a dancer, but a mentor with experience as a risk taker.

But even having experience of the challenge isn't enough. Advice that may be right for most people may not be right for you. Your mentor may understand how important risk-taking is to a well-lived life. But if she knows you, knows your father is very ill, and knows the history of your relationship with him, she may well advise you to keep other things steady while you spend what's likely to be a last loving year with your dad.

A mediocre running coach may know that most leading long-distance runners average a certain number of practice miles per week. But a better coach — having taught runners with your body type, your running cadence, and your personality — may decide to put you on a different program that's right for you.

Good teachers care less about proving they have a great system than about finding the best way to make each student grow. "This one needs a spur," said Plato, one of history's great teachers, about a student who seemed a little too lazy and self-satisfied. "That other one needs a brake," he said about a know-it-all too eager to rush ahead in his lessons (who happened to be Aristotle). Extraordinary coaches also know that sometimes the same person who needed a spur last week needs a brake this week.

Mentors who understand both the challenge and the person in front of them are extraordinarily valuable. They're also quite rare. (They're rare for the same reason that true friends are rare: the best relationships are only built over time.)

— 5 —

I've got a buddy who's a firefighter. The other day, he told me about a study on what separates an excellent firefighter from a novice. Here's how a journalist summed it up:

> Two groups of fire fighters, novices and experts, were shown scenes of fires and asked what they saw. The novices saw what was obvious — the intensity and color of the flames. But the experts saw a story; they used their mental models to infer what must have led to the current state of the fire and to predict what was likeliest to happen next. Note that these inferences and predictions are more than just interesting. They are evidence that the experts are far better prepared than the novices to fight the fire.

We'd expect experts to fight fires with more skill than beginners. This study helps us to see *why* experts are better. Where novices see surface details (the color of the flames), experts perceive patterns (where the fire is likely to go next). They see patterns not because they have a better understanding of the chemistry of fires, but because they have seen more fires. Their experience shapes what they see.

In a mentor, you're looking for someone who can look at you and your challenges and see more than surface details. You're looking for someone whose experience can help you to see where to go and what to do next.

A similar study helped to identify differences between expert pilots and novice pilots:

> Top-performing pilots and apprentices listened to recordings of air-traffic control radio communications, and then were asked to recall what they heard. The apprentices actually recalled more of the "filler" words that had no practical significance than the top pilots did.
>
> But the expert pilots recalled far more of the important concept words. Because they heard the communications as part of a rich mental model, they could focus their brainpower on what counted.

The best mentors have a sense for what matters. And if they don't see or can't hear an important detail, they'll ask you about it. Good mentors (and coaches and teachers) have learned to look at and hear the right things.

Standing on a pool deck, I can watch an entire swim race and have no idea why the winner won. The best I can do is say, "Um, because she swam faster?"

I have friends, though, who, standing on the same pool deck and watching the same race right by my side, can see imperfections in a stroke, differences in body position, alterations in the way a hand cuts into the water. I'll have watched the whole thing, but missed the details that made a difference. They'll have seen what mattered. And for that reason, they'd be much, much better swim coaches than I could ever be.

Good coaches cut through clutter and chaos. They direct your attention to the details that make a difference.

— 6 —

Not all experts are created equal.

Philip Tetlock, a political psychologist, proved it by putting together a massive study of expert judgment. Over twenty years, he asked 284 experts — academics, reporters, political officials, and others — to make predictions about world events. The experts made 28,000 predictions in all. Then Tetlock went back to check the results.

It wasn't professors who made the best predictions, or politicians. It wasn't liberals or conservatives. The biggest difference was between "foxes" and "hedgehogs."

Those terms come from the Greek poet Archilochus, whom we talked about a few letters back. He said, "The fox knows many things . . . the hedgehog knows one big thing."

When it came to the accuracy of his subjects' predictions, Tetlock found that foxes routinely outdid hedgehogs.

"The fox — the thinker who knows many little things, draws from an eclectic array of traditions, and is better able to improvise in response to changing events — is more successful in predicting the future than the hedgehog, who knows one big thing, toils devotedly within one tradition, and imposes formulaic solutions on ill-defined problems."

The best experts and the best mentors have flexible minds. The best experts and the best mentors won't claim to have one big idea about how the world works. Instead, they will constantly evaluate and reevaluate. They learn. They update their view of the world. In the face of changing facts, they stay humble.

Walker, I'd recommend that you avoid the hedgehog who claims to have "the answer." Find instead a mentor who is always willing to learn, someone willing to examine everything — including themselves. (And another thing about foxes, Walker: people who've built a habit of getting to know many things are much more likely to want to get to know you. And that, as we've said, will be critical to being a good mentor.)

— 7 —

Resilience is the virtue of growing through suffering and struggle. Most mentors have earned their wisdom only because they have struggled themselves.

So keep in mind that in great mentors, you'll find more than expertise in their field. It's likely that you'll also find expertise in the practice of resilience.

— 8 —

In Greek mythology, Chiron was a centaur — half horse and half man — and a great teacher. Many of the greatest Greek heroes were sent to study with him: he taught medicine to Asclepius, the first doctor, and navigation to Jason, who led a great sea voyage. Chiron was also a great warrior, and he taught Achilles to wield a sword and spear.

Machiavelli wrote about the myth of Chiron and what it tells us about teaching: "Achilles, and many other ancient princes, were given to Chiron the centaur to be raised, so that he would look after them with his discipline. To have as teacher a half-beast, half-man means nothing other than that a prince needs to know how to use both natures."

It wasn't just what Chiron taught that mattered. It was who he *was*. The very fact that he was half beast and half man showed his students that to learn a discipline they also had to master themselves. Sometimes the life of the teacher is more than half the lesson.

* * *

In a lot of what we have to learn, the messenger matters. That's especially true when it comes to teaching about how to live well. I've already written some about Will Guild, aka Big Will. He was a Navy SEAL for over thirty years, served in the nation's most elite units, and accomplished just about everything you could ever hope to accomplish in a military career.

When Will stands in front of a class of SEAL candidates and talks about ethics in combat, they *listen*. His words resonate not just because of the quality of his thinking, but because of the quality of his life. A very capable professor of ethics from Harvard could stand in front of the very same class. He could speak the very same words. And yet they'd have a fraction of the effect of Will's words on that audience.

The more complex an endeavor, the more the performance of the student will be tied to the ability of the master instructor. That's why a good PhD student seeks out a particular thesis adviser, and why dancers seek to train with particular dance teachers. In martial arts, people will often say, "She is a black belt under . . . ," meaning that she earned her belt from a particular instructor.

If all you need to know are the basics, Walker, your coach or mentor won't matter as much. But if you want to become great, you'll need a great coach.

— 9 —

The authority of trainers, teachers, and coaches comes from only one place: their willingness to take responsibility for results.

The root of the word "authority" is the Latin word *augere*, which means "grow," "increase," or "enrich." (This is also the root of the words "augment" and "author.") In its root, we see that the idea of authority was once tied to someone's ability to "author" a result.

Coaches, trainers, and teachers often have great power. Bad teachers and trainers believe that they have their power because of the position they hold. Good teachers and trainers know that the exercise of power is a responsibility: they are responsible for creating good results in the lives of those subject to their power and influence. Those results are what make their power legitimate.

— 10 —

Just as there are master painters of canvases, there are master painters of souls. Like paint, pain has to be applied with care to do its work well.

Pain can lead to beauty, and pain can lead to strength, but applying pain recklessly or stupidly creates nothing but mess and ugliness.

The philosopher asks a tough question and his fellow citizens have to confront their own ignorance. The boxing coach runs a tough drill and his students have to confront their own weakness.

It's easy to make people hurt. It's easy to make a kid do one hundred pushups with a hose in his face. It's easy to put a set of problems in front of a student without giving her any idea how to attack them. There are many bad teachers and brutal trainers who excel at making people uncomfortable.

Good teachers are comfortable with their students being uncomfortable, yet they understand that a confrontation with weakness, with ignorance, with pain, is not an end but a beginning. Awareness of our weakness opens a gateway to insight.

Bad and brutal trainers can inflict pain, but they have no idea how to tie the hardship they have created to the excellence their students aim to achieve. They have brought the trainee to the palace of insight, but they can't unlock the gate. Embarrassed and confused by their own inability, they usually just keep shouting.

A coach who is always shouting usually communicates one thing: I'm out of control.

— 11 —

Applying pain in the lives of others puts one in a position of great power and responsibility. Abusive coaches and undisciplined sergeants can gravely harm students and trainees. And maybe worst of all, their reliance on fear can curdle a student's love for a practice into a passionate hatred.

I once gave a talk on SEAL team training to a college fraternity. After my talk, a fraternity member asked, "If SEAL trainers can do that ["that" being make recruits suffer], why can't we do it to pledges?"

Part of the answer: You cannot do that because you want to do it for the wrong reasons. You want to do it to feel powerful and to satisfy your ego. And part of the answer is that you have not earned the privilege of training someone else. You don't know what you are doing. You are very liable to hurt someone, and if some good result is produced, it will come by accident rather than intention.

Any coach or mentor — any fool, for that matter — can apply hardship.

To be capable, mentors and coaches must have the right character and the right knowledge. Earlier I wrote that they must understand you and the challenges you're facing. They also have to understand the environment you're working in.

Understanding and shaping the environment is essential because, depending on conditions, the same elements can combine to produce completely different results. Consider this analogy:

In very hot conditions: 2 hydrogen + 1 oxygen = steam.

In normal conditions: 2 hydrogen + 1 oxygen = water.

In very cold conditions: 2 hydrogen + 1 oxygen = ice.

Steam, water, and ice are made up of the same building blocks, combined in almost the same way, but the environment around them profoundly shapes the form they take. In the same way, the elements of learning are often made up of the same building blocks and are combined in almost the same way. Pain is a part of learning. So is reflection.

In some conditions: pain + reflection = progress.

We struggle. We reflect. We try again and grow stronger.

But at other times: pain + reflection = whining.

We think of how frustrated we are, and we complain rather than grow.

In still other conditions: pain + reflection = drinking.

We're overwhelmed by the difficulty in front of us, and we turn to self-destructive activities.

It's important to recognize this, Walker, because the practice of resilience is about finding strategies for living, not formulaic, one-size-fits-all answers. You have to live your answers, and you have to do so in *your* world. You have to live your answers in your time, in your environment, facing all of the obstacles and using all of the assets you have at hand.

Good teachers or coaches know that what worked for the last student may not work for you. And they know that what worked for you yesterday may not work for you today.

— 12 —

The anthropologist Sir James Frazer reported that in some Aboriginal tribes of central Australia, elders at teenagers' initiation rites swung the bull-roarer, an ancient instrument that makes an eerie, droning sound when it is whirled through the air: "The bull-roarers are swung when a boy is being circumcised, and the women and children believe that the roaring noise is the voice of the great spirit Twanyrika, who has come to take the boy away. Twanyrika enters the body of the boy and carries him off into the bush until his wound is healed, when the spirit goes away and the boy returns an initiated man."

On the Indonesian island of Seram, each village had a long wooden house for the initiation of young men:

> Thither the boys who are to be initiated are conducted blindfolded, followed by their parents and relations . . . When all are assembled before the shed, the high priest calls aloud upon the devils. Immediately a hideous uproar is heard to proceed from the shed. It is made by men with bamboo trumpets, who have been secretly introduced into the building . . . Then the priests enter the shed, followed by the boys, one at a time. As soon as each boy has disappeared within the precincts, a dull chopping sound is heard, a fearful cry rings out, and a sword or spear, dripping with blood, is thrust through the roof of the shed. This is a token that the boy's head has been cut off, and that the devil has carried him away to the other world, there to regenerate and transform him . . .
>
> The boys remain in the shed for five or nine days. Sitting in the dark, they hear the blast of the bamboo trumpets . . . As they sit in a row cross-legged, with their hands stretched out, the chief takes his trumpet, and placing the mouth of it on the hands of each lad, speaks through it in strange tones, imitating the voice of the spirits . . .
>
> [Finally,] the high priest takes them to a lonely place in the forest, and cuts off a lock of hair from the crown of each of their heads. After these initiatory rites the lads are deemed men, and may marry.

For thousands of years, people all over the world have applied pain in ceremonies called rites of passage. In a rite of passage, a person transitions from one chapter of life to another. Such ceremonies often mark puberty, the time when a teenager is just acquiring the physical strength and capacities of an adult, but still has the mind of a child.

Often in these rites, the young man is taken from the community and isolated in the bush, the desert, or the woods. Over several days he will endure painful tests under the guidance of a cadre of men who have been through the process before. Often, as in the dozens of examples Frazer mentioned in *The Golden Bough,* the child undergoes a symbolic death and rebirth. His childhood is over, and he is reborn as a man.

The intention of this pain is not to punish. The intention is to demonstrate the teenager's maturity. Children don't respond well to stress: they panic and scream and squeal. By passing through pain, the teenager is introduced to the depths of his physical powers and strength as an adult.

More important, the child also comes to understand the purposes toward which he can turn his power. The mark of a mature man — one who can be strong enough to protect his community and his family — is his ability to excel under hardship. Through hardship, a boy is taught that a man is community-oriented rather than self-oriented.

(And here again, Walker, it's good to acknowledge how limited and imperfect these letters are. You and I were both Navy SEALs. Before we joined the SEAL teams, you spent years logging and I spent years boxing. I'm writing to you as my friend, and because of our shared experience some of these thoughts will work for us in a way that they may not work for others. You are also the father of a daughter, and it'll make sense at some point to think about rites of passage for girls, and how women find good mentors and models. When it comes to that, some of the thoughts in this letter may be helpful, others may not, and I'm sure there's a ton that's missing. I'm not writing about how girls move through rites of passage not because it's unimportant, but because I know that I don't know enough. It's another place where you and I have to have the humility to look for help from others.)

Young men, especially, seek pain. They seek pain because they know that they need to grow, and they sense that growth comes through risk-taking, through fear-seeking, through difficulty.

When I first read about the Indonesian rite of passage, it sounded odd to me. It's hard to imagine going through that or putting a son through it. You can imagine an American teenager saying, "That's f——d up."

Well, it certainly seems strange to us. Stranger still, however, is the way that many young men come of age in America today.

If Shane and Keith didn't have you for a father, it's possible that they'd grow up in a culture that would rarely test them. But they'd find ways to test themselves. What are fraternities doing when they haze new members? What are gangs doing when they invent their own initiation rituals? They're creating rites of passage. Other boys drive too fast and drink too much. They're responding to the desire, particularly among young men, to pass through trials, to treat adulthood as something earned.

When we read about an Aboriginal initiation ritual, it sounds a bit dangerous. But compared to American highways, where thousands of boys die every year — most of them speeding or drinking or both, and many of them killing their fellow passengers and other motorists along with themselves — the Aboriginal ritual sounds positively peaceful.

Modern rites of passage in fraternities and gangs can be brutal, undisciplined, uncontrolled. They're often driven by young men barely older than the ones they initiate — young men who have stumbled into powers and responsibilities they barely understand. This is what happens when rites of passage are organized without the cultural scaffolding that once held them up and gave them meaning.

In a traditional society, the most respected members — priests, chiefs, and elders — presided over the rite of passage. There is some wisdom in this: the trials that change us for the better, rather than scar us, should be overseen by mentors whose authority we respect, who are worthy of our trust.

In traditional societies, the rite of passage often marked a young man's transition from child to potential warrior: from one who had to be protected to one who could protect his people when times demanded. And while few of us go to war today, the transition from child to warrior, from dependence to responsibility, still captures something about what it means to attain adulthood.

Part of the allure and power of BUD/S in our time, Walker, is that it represents America's greatest initiation ritual. Military training promises the prospective service member a transformation — from civilian to United States Marine, for example. From "puke" to Ranger. From "reject" to Recon.

Why is SEAL team training, the most difficult military training in the world, a source of fascination for so many people? It's not because people are captivated by underwater knot-tying. In large part it's because SEAL training embodies the possibility of transformation: it's about turning a young man focused on himself into a warrior built to protect society.

One of my commanding officers once asked me to put together some thoughts on training in Naval Special Warfare. I came up with a plan called "The Complete Warrior." In it, I wrote about a few of the distinctions between the child and the warrior.

When the child is skillful, he boasts.
When the warrior has a skill, he teaches.

When the child is strong, he attacks the weak.
When the warrior is strong, he protects the weak.

The child criticizes others to make himself feel better.
The warrior is his own most demanding critic.

The child brandishes symbols as a substitute for substance.
The warrior knows that it is not his position, his rank, his education,
    or his warfare pin that makes him a man, but his honor.

The child serves himself.
The warrior serves others.

The child relishes gossip.
The warrior speaks through action.

The child never makes mistakes.
The warrior admits his mistakes and corrects them.

The child's character is cloudy.
The warrior's character is clear.

If the child can recognize that he needs teaching, he may one day
    become a warrior.
When the warrior meets the child, he seeks to teach him.

— 13 —

Maybe you're completely on board with all of this, Walker. But maybe you look around and see that there's no one in your life like the kind of mentor I'm describing.

In that case, the question isn't "Why do I need a mentor?" It's "How do I find a mentor?" There are no guarantees. But I'll tell you what I learned about finding a mentor from kung fu films.

I'm a sucker for cheap martial arts movies. And when I first started tae kwon do, I rented a bunch of 'em. In *Forbidden Kingdom,* the kung fu master is on a long journey with a new student. The student thinks he knows more than he does.

Jackie Chan, playing the master, starts pouring the student a cup of tea. The cup fills and Jackie continues to pour. The cup overflows and hot tea begins to run down the student's arm. When the student protests, Jackie says, "How can you fill your cup when it's full?"

It was a simple, classic kung fu movie lesson: no matter how wise the master, he can teach nothing until the student is ready to learn. If you think you know everything, you can't learn anything. The first thing we have to learn is that our cup is empty.

There's a saying: When the student is ready, the teacher will appear.

As with a lot of popular sayings and quotations, it's unclear exactly who first said this or when. I don't know that it matters. No one can promise you that your mentor will materialize out of nowhere.

But the idea stands on its merits: learning does not happen to you because you want it to. Learning is something you must prepare for.

If you want to learn, make yourself ready to learn.

This is the first task in any training, and it's the most important, because it is the prerequisite for all other learning.

It may take you time to find the right coach or the right mentor. You'll have to ask for advice, do some research, meet people, travel. It all takes time, it's all pretty simple, but there is a real danger in doing it: you might succumb to frustration.

Wonder, Plato said, is where all wisdom begins. That's true. But what Plato didn't tell us is that wonder is often weak. It comes — and then we have to make dinner. We feel it — and then the baby needs to be bathed.

It touches us — and then we have another ready excuse to let it float out of our lives.

Eric Hoffer once wrote, "That which is unique and worthwhile in us makes itself felt only in flashes. If we do not know how to catch and savor the flashes we are without growth and exhilaration."

Wonder is the sense of our smallness in the presence of something greater. But it is not fear: we don't want to run from the object of our wonder, but to come closer to it. We want to learn more about it. And that takes effort. It also takes patience.

It's hard to stay curious. It's hard to keep wonder alive. But you've always been willing to do hard things, Walker. So do it again now. Savor the flashes of wonder that light your life, keep your curiosity alive, and soon enough you'll find the right mentor.

Teams

Walker,

I don't know about you, but log PT was, for me, the most searingly painful evolution during BUD/S. Log PT is such an innocuous name for making seven shivering-cold and salt-soaked trainees pick up a 150-pound log, run it over a fifteen-foot-high sand berm, drop it in the sand, immediately pick it up and press it over their heads, run the log into the ocean, and then carry the soaked, slippery log back through the soft sand to start all over again.

And that's the easy part. The physical portion of the training is horrible, but bearable. What makes you really hurt is that you don't know how long it's going to last. Are we almost done? Have we barely started? What's next? You run the log up and down the beach. You cross the finish line in first place, but then you get punished for cheating when you thought that you ran the course the right way. Next time, you run the log up and down the beach, come in second place, and get punished for losing.

Then you change positions on the log, the weight shifts, and you feel as if you're holding the whole log yourself. Are the other guys slacking? Everybody's in pain. If it's early in the training and you still have a clown in your crew, everybody starts to wonder if the clown is pulling his weight. Everyone's thinking that somebody else is slacking, their own will deflates a bit, the log gets heavier, and then — wham — log's on the ground and the instructors pile on.

You think: We have how many more hours of this, how many more weeks of BUD/S? You reach a point of exhaustion at which you seem to be able to express yourself only in prayer or profanity. Most guys combine the two in very creative ways. You bend down to pick up the log, but you and your crew are all a little less certain. You manage to lift it over your head, but it's a struggle and a fight this time, and as you waste your energy and spend your strength, you stoke your anger.

Here, one of two things happen. One, a crew breaks down completely. Men start to snipe at each other, each person believing that somebody else is slacking. Or two, a crew comes together. The trainees figure out a way to slow down, breathe, lift on a single clear command, and win the next race. Two hours later in the chow hall, everybody's laughing and a few of the guys on the log are going to be friends for the rest of their lives.

One moment in log PT, I came to a realization. We were carrying the log at the low carry, so that our arms extended in front of our bodies. We collectively had the log cradled in the crook of our elbows, and my biceps and shoulders and back were burning, and I remember thinking: If these guys weren't here right now, I'd probably stop. I wouldn't believe I could go on, but these guys are keeping on right beside me, so I guess I can go on too.

We've already talked about the importance of friends, Walker. Friends you have. It's also likely that soon—in your work, in your coaching, or in your service—you're going to be part of a team again. The strength of others can make us stronger. So let's think a bit about how teams are formed, and what makes people come together.

— 2 —

At the most basic level, people form bonds when they share things. Breaking bread brings people together. In my office, we stop every day at three o'clock for tea time. It's something I picked up from the Brits. For fifteen minutes everyone has a cup of tea or coffee, maybe some popcorn, or a piece of carrot cake that our number one volunteer, Nancy, brings from home. It's a time to slow down, to be together. It's not magic, but in a hard-charging office where people can go a whole day without seeing each other, it helps.

People also become connected through common study and shared discovery. When I say "study" here, I mean much more than sitting in a classroom. I also mean someone, wrench in hand, learning to fix a leak.

If you ask most people whom they're closest to besides their family, they'll often tell you about a friend they explored the world with, a friend they went to school with, a buddy from boot camp, a partner from their first business, or a friend from their first job. We become close to the people with whom we discover the world.

People form even deeper bonds when they serve together. "Serve" is not quite the right word, but it's better than "work." People can work with others and not feel any sense of common cause. Being in the same place, working for the same boss, and even doing the same tasks can breed resentment, alienation, competition, and distrust just as easily as they can bring people together.

Serving together is different. When we share a purpose with others, our work creates a shared connection. When the work matters, we're more often able to overcome personal differences in service of a shared goal. Before I joined the military, if you'd asked me how important it was to like the people I worked with, I would have told you it was very important. When I was a student, it was.

Later, practicing combat diving at fifteen feet deep and kicking for half a mile underwater through a pitch-black night in a pitch-black bay, I didn't really care about how much I liked the guy swimming beside me. My life and our mission depended on one thing: his competence.

If I were going to suggest a general rule for understanding this, I'd say that the extent to which personal differences disrupt a team is inversely proportional to the importance people place on the mission. In other words, the more vital people consider a mission, the more they'll learn to deal with people who rub them the wrong way. The less the mission matters, the more people care about being around those they like.

That's helpful to remember if you're ever on a team that's starting to tear itself apart in the face of hardship. Often people react to these breakdowns by trying to ensure that there's more "understanding," or that people's "feelings are respected." Sometimes that's essential. But much of the time, when animosities and jealousies rule the day, it's because the work simply isn't important enough for people to put their differences aside. We're often told that work that's too intense can break a team. Maybe — but intense work that matters can just as often save a team.

Clarity of purpose creates perspective. When people have a shared commitment, differences and disagreements don't disappear, but they can be seen in a new light.

Shared success can also help form teams.

"Magnanimity" means "greatness of soul," and Aristotle thought it was a suitable virtue for a successful and honorable person. The magnanimous person is not grasping, insecure, or jealous, not small or mean. The magnanimous person does not bear grudges or seek revenge. Rather, the magnanimous person is generous, eager to do a favor, quick to forget an insult, independent-minded, brave in the face of danger. The magnanimous move and speak with well-earned confidence. They are — the word sounds old-fashioned now — noble. People on successful teams can often find ways to be generous and kind with each other.

Of course, shared success can lead to rivalry and jealousy, to back-stabbing and broken promises. But it doesn't have to. On a team with magnanimous people, shared success brings everyone together more tightly.

Real success is usually a product of struggle. And it's important to understand how shared struggle brings people together.

In college I studied a number of struggles. One of them was the American civil rights movement, particularly the Freedom Riders, the teams of black and white citizens who endured beatings, firebombs, and arrests in their work to desegregate interstate buses in the South. Listen to the historian Taylor Branch writing about the remarkable solidarity of forty-five Freedom Riders packed into the maximum security wing of the Mississippi State Penitentiary:

> Their hymns, spirituals, and freedom songs once again became the principal issue of contention with the jail authorities, who, to regain control of the prison atmosphere, threatened to remove all the mattresses from the cells if the Freedom Riders did not fall silent. Hank Thomas soon exploded with zeal, rattling the bars as he shouted for the guards. "Come get my mattress!" he cried. "I'll keep my soul!" The outburst inspired the entire cell block to sing "We Shall Overcome," and one prisoner after another flung his mattress against the cell door for the guards to collect.

Yes, arguments and shoving matches broke out from time to time over their weeks of confinement. But in general,

the Freedom Riders maintained an astonishing esprit as their number swelled in Parchman Penitentiary. Only a few asked to have their mattresses back. They lay on the steel springs at night, and they sang steadfastly through all the punishments devised to break them. When normal prison intimidations failed to work, frustrated authorities tried dousing them with fire hoses and then chilling them at night with giant fans. They also tried closing all the windows to bake them in the Mississippi summer heat. None of these sanctions had the desired effect, and many of them backfired. When the original group of Freedom Riders bailed out for appeal on July 7, they nearly floated out of the cells in the knowledge that they had gone into the heart of the beast and survived.

We need teams to face pain. It's also often true that we need pain to build teams. Fractures and fissures can lead teams to crack and crumble under pressure. But teams that are moved by great purpose become tighter still when things are tough. Great teams are formed only when they experience this pain — when they sweat together, bleed together, cry together, struggle together.

— 3 —

Having said all that, Walker, let's talk again about what really makes a team.

Originally, "team" just meant a pair of animals yoked side by side. They had to pull a heavy load together. Sometimes that's what human teams feel like. We're yoked to other people for no purpose other than to pull a burden that has no meaning to us.

Real teams work with and for one another. They share a purpose that is larger than any one person.

But human motivation is rarely simple. The philosopher Søren Kierkegaard wrote that "purity of heart is to will one thing." How many people do you know who are completely pure of heart? It's rare that anyone wills only one thing.

And what's true for us as individuals is magnified when we form teams. One person has many motivations. Bring a few people together and you have a multiplicity of motivations.

Some teams are tight like families. Other teams work more like allies. But all resilient teams share one thing: an ability to manage many interests while serving a purpose that is larger than the interests of any one person.

This is — to put it mildly — very hard to do. But I've found that it's worth the effort. A resilient team is rare. Most beautiful and excellent things are.

Leadership

Don't *say* things. What you *are* . . . thunders so that I cannot
hear what you say to the contrary.

— RALPH WALDO EMERSON

Walker,

I'm really happy for you. Over the course of the past several months
you've made many good things happen. Your son Keith came into the
world, you started a new job, you've stayed sober seven months, you
are serving your community again, playing a role in your church. It's all
solid and strong.

And you've started to lead again. You were always a leader in our
class, a leader in the SEAL teams, and when you first came home you
were a leader in your community. So let's spend a little time thinking
about leadership.

Resilient leadership is rooted in resilient living. Winston Churchill was
a resilient leader. But to me it's more accurate to think of him as a resilient man who led. Same with Lincoln. Same with Harriet Tubman.
Same with Clara Barton. They lived resilient lives. *And* they led.

Let's always remember that resilient living is the foundation for resilient leadership. Let's also remember that, just as there are many ways
to live a good and resilient life, there are many ways to lead effectively.

In reading any set of essential traits of leaders, you're likely to run
into one of two things. One, you'll see that there are often as many ex-

ceptions to the rules as there are examples. Or two, you'll find that the categories are defined so broadly as to be meaningless.

A similar thing happens when people create a list of rules for leadership or living. I've found that life operates not by a series of rules, but by a set of consequences. What is true about how we live and lead is usually true only most of the time. Part of wisdom is knowing the exceptions to the rules. What is always true is that what you do will have consequences. With that in mind, there are still a few things worth special attention as we think about your resilient leadership.

I remember reading *Henry V* in school. As far as Shakespeare goes, it doesn't get any better for a high school boy — action, adventure, battles, sword fighting. Of course, the really famous part — the part that people recognize even if they've never heard of the play — is the great speech that comes before the battle of Agincourt. The phrase "band of brothers" comes from *Henry V*.

Let me set the scene for you. And keep in mind that while this is a play, it's based on an actual battle. The English army — starving, soaked, exhausted — stands across the field from the army of France on the morning of a clash that will determine the fate of both nations. The English are outnumbered — and this part's a historical fact — by as much as six to one.

King Henry calls his army together, gets up on a tree stump, and tries to say something that will inspire his men.

Remember, we're in the Middle Ages here. Everyone in that army believes that the king gets his power directly from God. When the king speaks, they are listening to God's representative on earth. So what does Henry say? "Fight for your king, so I can conquer France"? "You should all be honored to die for your king"? "Your king commands you to run across that field"?

No. Here, according to Shakespeare, is what he says:

He today that sheds his blood with me
Shall be my brother; be he ne'er so vile,
This day shall gentle his condition.

In other words, even if you are a fifteen-year-old peasant kid who'd never left the farm until the army came through, stuck a bow in your hands, and marched you to France, you can become royalty today. You can be the king's brother, a gentleman, a prince.

And, Henry promises, no matter how vile, how sinful, how tortured your life has been, this day can make you great.

Henry and his army won.

Of course, Shakespeare made all of that up a couple of hundred years after the fact. But a historian at the time of the battle reported what King Henry actually said to inspire his men. The gist was: If we lose today, I don't plan on being captured. I plan on being killed.

To know what that meant to the people who heard it, you have to understand that in the Middle Ages nobles were often captured in battle and held for ransom. Captured nobles weren't thrown in prison; they got to enjoy what amounted to a vacation at the enemy's court while their country scraped together the money to bail them out.

As you can probably guess, common foot soldiers in a losing army didn't have that privilege. If they lost a battle, they usually lost their lives.

So what King Henry actually said wasn't far from the words Shakespeare put in his mouth. The point was the same: I'm going to fight beside you and share your fate.

If you think of the most inspiring, effective leaders you've worked with, I bet you'll find they have a lot in common with Henry V. Their devotion to their cause and to their team was greater than their devotion to perks and privilege. They worked and fought and struggled beside you. They endured what you endured. Think of officers sleeping on the same cold ground as their men, or employers working longer hours, traveling away from home more, shouldering responsibility, and taking blame. The idea is the same. *Don't do this for me — do this with me.* A leader earns devotion by showing devotion.

Walker, set the example. Endure more than those you lead. Demonstrate your devotion through action. That's how you'll lead with strength.

There are no ironclad laws here, and most great leaders are people of contradictions. For many in my grandparents' generation, Franklin Roosevelt was an icon of breezy confidence and effortless strength. They knew him as a smiling face on newsreels, as a confiding voice issuing from their radios for a fireside chat. But beneath the self-assured image was what the historian Garry Wills called "a consummate actor." Just to appear to walk in public, Roosevelt, with his polio-stricken legs, would have to shift his weight from a cane on one side to the son who held him up on the other side. "The strain always left his suit soaked with sweat, the hand on the cane shaking violently from the effort, the son's arm bruised where his fingers had dug in. And all this while he would be smiling, keeping up pleasant banter, pretending to enjoy himself. It was an excruciating ordeal turned into a pleasant stroll."

The unflappable politician and the struggling polio survivor were the same person.

Or take his wartime ally Winston Churchill. Churchill was a man of immense physical courage; as a young man he escaped from a POW camp in South Africa and made a three-hundred-mile journey to safety. But he was no Spartan: he loved to eat breakfast and work in bed. He had his servants check the temperature of his hot baths with a thermometer, and he dictated much of his memoirs from the tub. Once he showed up at a friend's villa on the French Riviera — without a servant — and bragged about how easy it was to travel on his own. The friend's wry response: "Winston, how brave of you." The effete aristocrat and the courageous adventurer were the same person.

So there is no one list of a leader's qualities. There is no one formula for leadership. But most of the time you'll find that what we learned about leading in the SEAL teams still holds. Officers eat last. Leaders lead from the front. Never ask someone to endure more than you are willing to endure yourself.

— 2 —

It's possible to read King Henry's speech and come to the wrong conclusion: "Leaders provide motivation."

Sometimes. There's no question that after I get off the phone with you I feel more energized to write well — talking with you motivates me. And the other day you wrote to me, "Thank you for challenging me, G."

That's what friends do for each other. And seeing the effect that one person can have on another, some people falsely conclude that a leader's job is to supply someone else's motivation. This is the cheerleader school of leadership thought. I chant for you and cheer for you, and then you are inspired to do hard work.

There's a place for chanting and a place for cheering. But nothing truly valuable — from painting a portrait to raising a child to preparing for a game — is accomplished without persistent work. And people who can perform only when they have someone chanting slogans beside them are rarely capable of such work.

The reason I'm sharing this with you, Walker, is that as you work with people — veterans who are struggling, your partners in AA, families in your church — you have to understand what you can and cannot do.

You can listen and counsel. You can lend ideas and hard work and home-cooked meals. You can be a friend and a fan. You can share your favorite books and fix a flat tire. You can inspire people and encourage them. You can sweat beside them and support them. But you cannot make their choices for them. You cannot take their excuses from them. You cannot make them resilient.

You know the old saying, "You can lead a horse to water, but you can't make it drink"? It sounds like something you might have heard from your mom or dad. In fact, it's something kids have been hearing from their moms and dads for more than eight hundred years. In fact, it has a claim to being the oldest proverb in the English language. Here's a version from as early as 1175: *Hwa is thet mei thet hors wettrien the him self nule drinken?* ("Who can give water to the horse that will not drink of its own accord?")

It's simple. It's true. And yet, when you really, really want to help someone else, it's easy to ignore. You want to *make* that person drink the water. You have to remember that it's as impossible now as it has always been. As a friend, as a leader, you have to have the humility to understand that your power is limited.

And just one hint about using that limited power effectively, Walker. As a young leader, I often made the mistake of trying to solve problems. If I saw something I thought was wrong, I tried to fix it. A lot of leaders do this. It makes them feel that they are serious (tackling tough problems) and needed (doing the hard work). What I learned after knocking my head against the wall a hundred times is that some problems will never be fixed.

Someone once asked what could be done to "fix" a "broken" community in Cambodia. Families there lived on less than a dollar per day. The disabled were often viewed as a burden. Medical care was nearly nonexistent; schools were unattended or too expensive; a lot of the men drank too much. And on and on.

A lot of leaders begin with a mechanical mindset: find what's missing or broken and replace or repair it. But in many social systems, the trick isn't to repair what's broken, but to multiply what's working. Who has well-fed children? Who's been injured and is still working? Who lost friends and is still serving? Be a model yourself. Then promote other people who can serve as models. Through emulation and multiplication, communities can begin to heal themselves.

If you can fix something that needs to be fixed, go ahead and fix it. But real leadership is most often needed where simple solutions have already been tried and have failed. When things are hard, sometimes the best thing you can do is to drown what's wrong in a sea of what's right.

— 3 —

To inspire is to put the spirit, the breath of life, into something. To inspire is to help someone answer a simple question: why?

When courses in leadership are designed, people often begin by assembling the tools and techniques that they think will lead to better organization, better communication, better collaboration. And it's true that those tools and techniques can make a difference on the margins.

Too often, however, we are quick to jump to the *how* — instruction in the tools of management — without asking if the leader in training has the right *why*.

Too often we put good students into leadership training because, as good students, they've demonstrated that they learn quickly. But do they have the right *why?* What do they want to lead *for?*

We talked about this before in terms of your own life, Walker. If you're going to lead, it's essential that you ask it of yourself again: why? What are you leading *for?* What are you willing to sacrifice for?

Some of the most common (and nauseating) leadership slogans — "Think outside the box," "Big, hairy, audacious goal" — obscure the importance of belief and sacrifice. Do you want to lead and expect some other sucker to do the hard work? Or do you want to lead because you believe enough in something to put your comfort, your ease, even your life on the line for it?

Dreams become reality through work and sacrifice. People who stoke fantasies about the way of the world often stumble and fall on first contact with reality. Other times, they confuse thinking or talking about what they want to accomplish with actually doing the work. And just as this is true of individuals, it's also true of teams, groups, communities, and countries. That's why one of the recurring themes in Marcus Aurelius's writings is, "Leadership's responsibility is to work intelligently with what is given and not waste time fantasizing about a world of flawless people and perfect choices." Walker, you'll be able to lead others not because you promote a fantasy about the way the world will be, but because of what you are willing to do.

— 4 —

We are almost always better led by men and women who have been hardworking, resilient failures early in life than by those who, by dint of privilege, luck, or circumstance, rise through life without ever having put their souls into a task that tries them. We are almost always better led by those who have pushed themselves up to and past their limits than by those who don't know where their limits are.

Walker, you've failed plenty. That doesn't automatically make you qualified to lead. But having failed doesn't disqualify you either.

Wise people look for a history of success *and* failure in a leader. Find in your failures resources for your own leadership. Let them be proof that you've pushed yourself. Let them be a constant reminder of how hard it is to fight well, and of how hard you must fight when you are down. Let them be a reminder of how and where you've earned your wisdom.

Beware the person who seeks to lead and has not suffered, who claims responsibility on the grounds of a spotless record.

We can only be well led by those who have learned well the habits of resilience. Those habits take work, pain, and time. Resilience is a leader's defining trait — not only because the leader of any worthwhile effort will have to confront hardship and suffering, but because the character of a true leader can only be forged in the fire where resilience does its work.

— 5 —

You speak through your actions. The vast majority of training is modeling. The vast majority of inspiration comes by example. Henry V didn't merely speak some nice words and then hide. He spoke some true words and then fought. Leadership isn't a set of techniques or tricks. Like resilience, it's a way of being.

If you want to inspire devotion, be devoted.

If you want to inspire belief, believe.

If you want to motivate, be motivated.

You can't fake any of it. If you want to lead, get yourself right first.

I believe in you, friend. And I'm happy for those who will have the opportunity to follow you.

Freedom

Walker,

Two of your kids are already in elementary school, and if their time in school is anything like yours or mine, I bet they'll be told—many times—to "be creative," to "think for yourself," to "make your own rules."

Creativity—ours and others'—makes life beautiful. We have to learn to think for ourselves, to question authority, and to disregard the rules at the right time. It's often a fun experiment or a helpful technique to paint without a canvas, to write without editing, to photograph without looking.

All of this is good when we understand it in the context of what really creates creativity.

What can be destructive is the idea that being creative is our natural state, that we'd all be Mozarts or Shakespeares if we weren't repressed by rules. What's worse is the thought that we'd all be more creative if only we were more free—free from constraints, from requirements. That confuses the relationship between discipline and creativity. The two may seem like opposites in theory, but in practice you usually need one to have the other.

Let's think about freedom for a second. In the United States we spend most of our time thinking about freedom *from*. The Bill of Rights is based on the idea that no government, not even a democratic government of our fellow citizens, can interfere with our basic, God-given rights. Some philosophers call this idea negative liberty, because it's rooted in a belief about what other people *cannot* do to you. It's fundamental to the American conception of the proper and limited role of government.

Because most Americans think about freedom *from* in the context of rights and government, we often forget—in the context of our own lives—to think about freedom *to:* the freedom to accomplish what we want.

When it comes to creativity, people often focus on freedom *from.* They think they'd be more creative if they were only free from constraints, from interference, from obligations. We'd do better to spend as much time thinking about freedom *to.* You can be free from rules and obligations, but that doesn't make you free to create.

You can, for example, be free from rules and still not have mastery over yourself. You have freedom *to* when you can say, "I am my own master."

Imagine that you've decided to lose ten pounds. But despite your decision, despite your best intentions, you cannot stop yourself from having the extra chocolate donut every morning. You're free from tyranny. No one's forcing you to eat the donut. But are you free? I'd say that you're not. You're still a slave to your craving.

And if we're honest with ourselves, we'll realize that there are moments almost every day when we are ruled by something other than what's best in us. "Show me a man who is not a slave!" said Seneca. "One is a slave to lust, another to greed, another to ambition, and all men are slaves to fear."

Some of our freedom can only be won through self-mastery.

Now let's come back to creativity. Say that your daughter decides she wants to play the violin. You go together to a music store, you rent her a violin, and you tell her that she can get started. She is free from interference. No one's stopping her.

But is she really free to play the violin? Not yet. As much as she wants to, there's a barrier more stubborn than barbed wire between her and creating music: she doesn't know how.

If she wants to play the violin—not in a screech, but with some measure of beauty—she'll have to be disciplined. She'll have to learn musical scales and how to read a score. She'll have to sacrifice many after-school hours to practice. She'll have to listen to her music teacher, and she'll have to practice even when practice is hard, or boring, or the last thing she feels like doing that day.

At the end of all that, and only then, will she be *free* to play the violin. After years of practice she might move beyond the basics and bring her own personality and artistry to her playing, to create something beautiful that no one has ever heard before. You achieve that kind of creativity, and that kind of freedom, only through devotion. The freedom to create is often the result of resilient practice.

St. Louis, my hometown, prides itself on its blues and jazz traditions. Even our hockey team, as you know, is called the Blues. Downtown, there's a great place not far from my office called BB's Jazz, Blues, and Soups. It is what it says it is: a place to listen to jazz and blues while you eat soup. When you come to St. Louis, I'll take you there.

"Jazz is a purely democratic music," said the great drummer Max Roach. Now Walker, I know nothing about jazz except that I like it. But when I remember the great jazz sets I've heard in St. Louis or New Orleans — the music ebbing and flowing, each player contributing in turn — what Roach said sounds right to me.

In jazz clubs you often hear musicians who place the perfection of their craft above all other tasks. The inventive man on the trumpet is someone who *earned* the freedom to play his horn with genius.

It's likely he spent years shut in small rooms, practicing and playing and practicing some more. There's a word for that among jazz musicians: woodshedding. Originally, it meant that you went out back, locked yourself in a shed, and spent hours at a time honing your technique in private. The saxophonist Paul Klemperer explained it this way: "You have to dig deep into yourself, discipline yourself, become focused on the music and your instrument, before you can unlock the treasure chest. At the same time, woodshedding is a process of demystifying the music. The amazing solo, the intricate bebop melody, the complex rhythmic pattern, can be learned, if one is patient. It is a humbling but necessary chore, like chopping wood before you can start the fire."

And it's not as if you submit to the discipline once and never have to do it again. Excellence is renewed through deliberate practice, day in and day out.

At the end of all that practice, the musician will have deft fingers and a trained ear. Put that together with other practiced professionals and you have a team of musicians who have learned, together, how to make the world beautiful.

— 2 —

We're fortunate, Walker: we don't have to worry about someone snatching us from our bed in the middle of the night and carting us off to prison. Throughout most of history, people had no appeal to the rule of law. They were subject to the desires of kings, warlords, chieftains, dictators.

In the book of Samuel, the prophet warns the people of Israel what will happen if they turn over their freedom to a single ruler: "He will take your sons and make them serve with his chariots and horses, and they will run in front of his chariots . . . He will take your daughters to be perfumers and cooks and bakers . . . He will take a tenth of your flocks, and you yourselves will become his slaves. When that day comes you will cry out for relief from the king you have chosen, but the Lord will not answer you in that day."

Today, dictators oppress millions of people around the world. But freedom from oppression is not the only kind of freedom that matters. For many people in the Western world, freedom is limited not so much by what others do to us, but by what we cannot do for ourselves.

Walker, imagine that you have something important to do one morning, but before you can get out of bed, someone comes into your house and holds you down — not all day, but for a crucial hour or two. Or, imagine someone forces you, day after day, to go into your backyard and waste two hours walking in a circle. Imagine what you'd do to someone who made you waste a part of your life every day.

You'd probably kick that person's ass. But that person, Walker, is you. And for me, it's me. It's all of us who rail against the way the world is designed, but who don't muster the effort to master ourselves. Most of us can make ourselves more free through self-mastery.

— 3 —

Walker, your life is full of commitments right now. You're committed to volunteer on the sidelines of football games each weekend. You're committed to your job. You're committed to your wife and to raising three children to be as strong and wise and compassionate as they can be.

Maybe there are times when you think of these obligations as constraining your freedom, just as a painter might feel constrained by a canvas. Beauty comes, though, not when the painter is able to rid himself of his canvas, but when he concentrates on it. Your commitments are the same.

The object in life is not to have as few commitments as possible, but to have the right kinds of commitments. When you make a commitment that's in keeping with what you value most, you've made a decision to be your best self. And when you keep that commitment — when you get up at three in the morning to answer Keith's cries, when you stand in the rain to help those kids learn football, when you show up at church and volunteer — you're making yourself into the man you want to be.

Your commitments will sometimes feel heavy to you. And though this won't make them any lighter, it might help to remember that it's a bigger burden to live without commitments. A life with nothing to care for and no one to care about is one of the hardest things for a human being to bear.

— 4 —

When it comes to commitments, some things — like providing daily care for a dying and disoriented parent — can be hard just because they're so heavy. But most of the time, we struggle not so much with the weight of what we have to bear, but with the effort to balance it all.

So what's the best way to think about bringing our lives into balance?

Remember the log run on the O course?

Either end of the log rested on a wooden beam, and as you ran down the length of the log, it rolled. We quickly learned that if you jumped up on the log and tried to set yourself, the log would likely roll and you'd fall. Even if you did manage to set yourself, when you tried to step forward the log would turn with each footfall and eventually you'd drop. We both fell plenty of times.

I'm sure you also remember what we learned about crossing to the other side. Your best bet was to have a friend at the end stick his boot on the log and hold it in place for you. When the instructors weren't looking, that worked pretty well. But most of the time they were watching, so your next best bet was to focus your eyes on the end of the log and just run. Amazingly enough, your feet found their balance.

Many people try to find balance in their lives first, and then run.

Sometimes that works. But a lot of times it's in the running itself that you find your balance.

A better analogy might be to learning to ride a bike. Kids don't find their balance by sitting on a bike standing still but by riding one that's rolling. In either case, the result is the same: if you plan and calculate and obsess over finding your balance before you begin to run, you'll often wind up flat on your face. The balance comes in the running.

— 5 —

When people use the phrase "work-life balance," most of them imagine a seesaw or a scale. On one end is "work," and on the other end is "life." The two are linked in such a way that everything is a tradeoff. If work is up, life is down. If life is up, work is down.

More of one means less of the other.

This is insane.

"Work-life balance" implies that work is separate from living a life, or that it's something to be balanced against your life. That's strange, given that most people spend more time working every day than they do in any other activity. If all of those hours are not part of life, then something is deeply wrong.

Life and work are not two enemies battling for our limited attention. In fact, the opposite tends to be the case. When we have meaningful, fulfilling, purposeful work, it radiates through our lives. And when we have happy, secure, loving relationships, they, too, radiate through our lives.

The balance we seek is not that of a seesaw, but of a symphony. Every element of a symphony has a role to play: sometimes loud, sometimes quiet, sometimes silent, sometimes solo. The balance we seek is not for every instrument to be played in moderation at every moment — that's just a long, boring honk — but for a complementary relationship where each instrument is played at the right pitch and the right intensity, with the right phrasing and the right tempo.

At certain times, particular aspects of our lives come to the fore, while others fall into the background. As new harmonies emerge, we can create something beautiful.

"To everything there is a season, and a time to every purpose under the heaven."

* * *

Of course you have to make choices. You can't be in two places at once.

Life demands that we make hard decisions. I've just found that people who think about balance in that seesaw way end up driving themselves crazy, making themselves miserable, or both. If you feel that every moment of life is a moment of slacking from work, or that every moment at work is a moment that you're, say, stealing time from your daughter, I don't know how you'd stay sane.

Some people aim to solve this problem by half committing to everything they do. And, of course, everything ends up mediocre. When you half-ass it at work and with your family, when you always worry about being somewhere other than the place you are, nothing feels exceptional.

You don't need that, Walker. You need intensity tempered by intensity. Work hard. Pray powerfully. Exercise intensely. Laugh raucously. Love completely. And then . . . sleep deeply.

I'm not the first one to say this, Walker. You've probably heard it enough that it can sound like a cliché. As you think about balance, I just want you to recognize that your balance will be that of the adult artist who brings sound or color together into a harmonizing whole, not the balance of a four-year-old on the playground.

And that means that, yes, sometimes you'll work through the weekend. Sometimes your family won't see you. Other times your family will be first and your work will lie fallow. Sometimes you'll live a solo, focusing on just one thing. Other days everything will work together.

Give yourself the freedom to live a life that's balanced — not like a seesaw but like a beautiful work of art.

One final note about this, Walker. It's fashionable to imagine that work-life balance is a recent problem or phenomenon. I think that's mostly a way of flattering ourselves. We imagine that our generation is so special that no one has ever been as overwhelmed as we are today. But this tension about how and where to spend our energy has existed as long as work and life have existed. And the best solution has always been essentially the same.

An English minister summed up a great answer in the 1930s. This quotation greets me every day in the lobby of my building:

A master in the art of living draws no sharp distinction
between his work and his play; his labor and his leisure; his
mind and his body; his education and his recreation. He
hardly knows which is which. He simply pursues his vision
of excellence through whatever he is doing, and leaves
others to determine whether he is working or playing. To
himself, he always appears to be doing both.

Story

All sorrows can be borne if you put them into a story.

— BORIS CYRULNIK

Walker,

If there have been a lot of stories and memories in these letters, there's a reason for that. We often think in stories.

Of course we think in many other ways as well. We think in terms of rules, definitions, associations, calculations, and proofs, to name a few. But the human mind is narrative and always has been. When humans first figured out how to turn sounds and ideas into pictures, and how to put those pictures onto a clay tablet — how to write — we started with basic recordkeeping: *Sargon owes me ten sheep.* But soon enough we were writing down chronicles, poems, epics — stories.

We know almost nothing about the Greeks of Homer's time, but we know the stories they told each other — the *Iliad* and the *Odyssey*. Stories are at the heart of religions and philosophies the world over, from the sayings of Confucius to the *Bhagavad Gita* to the parables taught by Jesus. When we come home at the end of the day and turn on the TV or pick up a book, what do we use to entertain ourselves? Mostly stories.

What all of this means, I think, is that stories play a larger role in our lives than we may recognize.

Remember my college professor Alasdair MacIntyre? He wrote, "Man is in his actions and practice, as well as in his fictions, essentially a story-telling animal." We learn who we are and where we come

from, what is right and what is wrong, from hearing and telling stories
— something that begins in infancy and lasts as long as we're alive:

> It is through hearing stories about wicked stepmothers, lost children,
> good but misguided kings, wolves that suckle twin boys, youngest sons
> who receive no inheritance but must make their own way in the world
> and eldest sons who waste their inheritance on riotous living and go into
> exile to live with the swine, that children learn or mislearn both what
> a child and what a parent is, what the cast of characters may be in the
> drama into which they have been born and what the ways of the world
> are. Deprive children of stories and you leave them unscripted, anxious
> stutterers in their actions as in their words.

Your life, Walker, isn't just *one* kind of story. It's not simply a romance
or a tragedy or a comedy. Your story will have elements of death and
rebirth, rivalry and revenge, temptation and sacrifice, discovery and
deliverance, envy and love; and it will have all of these things not just
one time, but many times over.

This might not be right for everyone, Walker, but I think it makes
sense to think of your life in terms of a quest. What's a quest? It's a
journey with meaning. It's not a treasure hunt, where X marks the spot
and reaching that spot is what matters. On a quest we discover the true
nature of what we're after only *by going on the journey.*

Here's how MacIntyre put it: "It is in the course of the quest and only
through encountering and coping with the various particular harms,
dangers, temptations and distractions which provide any quest with its
episodes and incidents that the goal of the quest is finally to be understood."

You figure out the purpose of your life by living your life. You give
meaning to your quest by what you do and say and suffer. The challenges you face and the choices you make create the meaning of your
story. The harms, dangers, temptations, and distractions that confront
you are obstacles, yes, but it's only by wrestling with those obstacles that
your purpose can be understood.

Here again, sitting at the center of a well-lived life, we find resilience.

Rilke put this well: "Be patient toward all that is unsolved in your
heart and try to love the questions themselves, like locked rooms and
like books that are written in a very foreign tongue. Do not now seek

the answers, which cannot be given you because you would not be able to live them. And the point is, to live everything. Live the questions now. Perhaps you will then gradually, without noticing it, live along some distant day into the answer."

— 2 —

Without knowledge of the past, we become lost in the present and fearful of the future.

Knowing our history can make us more resilient, especially when we understand our connection to the people who went before us. I recently read about a study on kids' mental toughness. The more kids knew about their family history, the more resilient they turned out to be.

> Do you know where your grandparents grew up? . . . Do you know where your parents met? Do you know an illness or something really terrible that happened in your family? Do you know the story of your birth?
>
> The more of these stories kids know — the more they feel their own lives as part of a story that spans generations — the happier and emotionally stronger they are.

I wouldn't be surprised to see that the same thing is true for teams, for communities, and for countries — that people with a strong sense of the past are often better able to deal with the hardships of the present.

Why? Because as long as we're part of a story, we're not alone. Because we know that others have done what we now have to do. Others have suffered and survived; others have been beaten and still, ultimately, thrived. Those who don't know history become lost in the desert of the present.

Every family, every community, every culture, every country has found ways to weather hardship. But what happens when people don't know this?

Often, it seems to me, they think the hardship they face is their own fault. Children, especially, tend to be self-centered, and it's natural for them to ask the question, "Why me?" If kids don't know that everyone has struggled, that everyone has suffered, they are more likely to conclude that *they* are what's wrong. (Of course, this is as unhelpful for adults as it is for children.)

It's equally problematic when people lost in the desert of the present believe that their suffering is so special that it deserves everyone's sustained attention. Yes, your life is hard. Yes, you have suffered. And if you are hurting and I can help, then I am here for you. But your hardship makes you human; it does not make you unique. An absence of historical awareness often leads to an abundance of self-fascination.

Worst of all, perhaps, is that people with no sense of the past often have no well-founded hope for the future. Overwhelmed by the present and desperate for solutions, they begin to believe in miracle products, magic formulas, easy tricks, and insider secrets. This can lead to an ever-deeper fascination with novelty and new beginnings. Thus people toss away their money, their votes, their time, and their energy on the false promises of others rather than see in themselves the same potential that so many others have realized in the past.

— 3 —

Walker, I've already mentioned that I worked in Rwanda in 1995, shortly after the genocide there.

I remember one young man who had studied English in Kigali and hid with his sister and two young neighbor girls during the violence. He told me that during the killings he thought of Elie Wiesel, the Holocaust survivor, and he asked me if I'd read Wiesel's memoir, *Night*.

A kid in Rwanda read the story of a Romanian-born Jew who, as a teenager, had lived through horror over fifty years before. He said that when he most needed it, that story gave him a measure of comfort. It gave him a model: someone who had survived a genocide and found meaning in bearing witness.

And this probably goes without saying, but I'll say it anyway: just as it'll do limited good for a boxer to train only on the day of a fight, you can't decide to cast about for models at the climactic moment of your suffering. The young man read Wiesel's story *before* the genocide. Not during. We need to teach our children and ourselves the stories and histories that matter *now*, not in the moment of crisis.

Before we deployed in 2004, I shared with the guys in my unit a story about the three hundred Spartans who died at Thermopylae. After the battle, the invading Persians desecrated the corpse of the Spartans' leader: they cut off his head and impaled it on a spear. A year later, the Spartans won a decisive victory of their own — and many of them demanded that their king defile the body of the Persian general in the same way.

The Spartan king refused: "Such actions are more fit for barbarians than Greeks, and even in them we find it a matter of offense. For conduct such as this, God forbid that I should find favor! . . . It is enough for me to please the men of Sparta by decent action and decent words."

I wanted my men to know that no matter how vile, how barbaric their enemies, warriors are expected to combine courage and ferocity in battle with decency and humanity in victory. I told them a story because I wanted us to have models to aspire to, and because I wanted to show that what I was asking wasn't impossible.

— 4 —

If you want to understand why storytelling is so essential to resilience, you have to understand this:

Stories are not an endless stream of "this happened, and then this happened, and then *this* happened." Out of the raw material of events, some details are cut (we don't need to know what Odysseus has for breakfast every day). Some events are explained (Odysseus is trapped in the Cyclops's cave). And some events become the story's climax (Odysseus makes it home to his family after ten years at sea).

Your life is no different. The events of your life are raw material, and they take on the meaning you give them. Your mind isn't a camera. You don't just record; you select, you recall, you reinterpret the events of your life. All of this is part of storytelling.

And so you must remember this, Walker: storytelling is not just a way to remember what happened; it's a way to *understand* what happened. When you tell a story, you give an event meaning.

In storytelling we bring past, present, and future together in a way that helps us to make sense of events and make sense of our lives.

Not every event has a moral. Not every moment is meaningful. Some things are best forgotten. But especially when dramatic and unforgettable things happen to us, we have to recognize that over time we will react to, recall, and reflect on these events by weaving them into a story.

Different people put the same raw material to vastly different uses. "I messed up again." Or, "I was brave and I tried. But I failed to prepare and I failed. Now I'm going to practice." A different story doesn't change the fact of what happened, but it does change the meaning of what happened.

In moments of crisis, the right stories provide sustenance. And that's true on the scale of your own life and on the scale of history.

On June 18, 1940, two weeks after the rescue of British troops from Dunkirk, the United Kingdom stood virtually alone against the triumphant Nazi regime. Four days earlier, Hitler's troops had marched into Paris; almost all of Western Europe, from Norway to France, was under their sway.

Winston Churchill's words to the British people couldn't change what had happened. And they certainly didn't turn the tide of war on their own. But they did inspire people to keep resisting at a time when surrender seemed, by far, the more prudent choice. Here's what he said to move a nation that was staring defeat in the face: "Let us therefore brace ourselves to our duties, and so bear ourselves, that if the British Empire and its Commonwealth last for a thousand years, men will still say, This was their finest hour."

Remember, Churchill was saying, that you are part of a story that is larger than yourself. It did not begin with you. It will not end with you. But think, now, in this moment of danger, how you have been called upon and what you are capable of.

That is how resilient people tell stories. Failure and pain and hardship have the meaning we choose to give them.

— 5 —

When I first went to do humanitarian work overseas, I traveled with a professor who specialized in working with children in war zones. I don't need to tell you about the things such children have seen — homes destroyed, friends abused, parents killed, sisters and brothers tortured in front of them. But the professor I worked with and others had found that two interventions were especially good at helping those children deal with trauma. Sometimes he'd ask them to draw about what they'd lived through. Later, some of the kids might put on a play about what they had endured.

Now, nothing horrific in life ever heals quickly. I don't want to give you the impression that drawing a picture or putting on a play made things OK in some way. The simple point is that the act of drawing a picture and then explaining it, or designing a play and then acting it, helped kids begin to make sense of what had happened to them.

My mom found that one of the best ways to help her preschoolers who were having a hard time coping with something was to read them stories — stories about problems not that far removed from their own.

There's a reason why shelves in the children's section of bookstores are lined with stories about dogs who are mad at their siblings, bears who don't want to share their toys, pigs who need to prepare, little kids looking to find what will fit them just right, and a reindeer named Rudolph, born with a funny nose. When children listen to these stories, they may learn how to make stories of their own that help them to create meaning in their young lives.

— 6 —

You've already lived through a wealth of stories, Walker. You've known more triumph and tragedy, more fear and excitement, more love and loss in your life than a lot of people. And so I can almost hear you saying: *All this about writing my story, living my story, beginning my story — this is advice for a kid, not a grown man. I'm reading this letter twenty years too late.*

But think of the first page of most of the stories that our culture treasures. What's on that first page? A lot of the time, the best stories don't start at the beginning, but at the point at which things become interesting.

Achilles' story doesn't start when the Greek army sails to Troy for war. It starts after a ten-year siege when his decisions finally begin to bring the war to its end.

Odysseus's story doesn't start when he leaves Troy for home. It starts when, after he has wandered for ten years, his son comes of age and sets out to track him down.

Hamlet's story doesn't start when his father dies. It starts when his father's ghost appears to announce that he was murdered.

In *Paradise Lost,* Satan's story doesn't start when he declares war on God. It starts after the battle is lost, after his long fall from heaven, when he hits bottom and discovers that he's landed in hell.

Centuries ago, in fact, writers recognized that the best stories often start *in medias res,* in the middle of things. They realized that time in stories doesn't run like time on clocks. In a story, the real beginning comes when things start to matter in a different way.

So you're in the middle of things. Who's to say the real story, the story that will have mattered all along, doesn't start right now? Maybe your story starts today.

—7—

As with everything in these letters, Walker, there's no free lunch here. It's worth pausing to point out that "telling yourself a story" doesn't change what happened, and it won't change what you do or who you become, unless you are also willing to make hard choices. Telling stories can devolve into delusion and fantasy just as often as it helps you to dig deep and push through.

In the letter on mastering pain, we made clear that self-talk does not work alone. It works only when it is accompanied by resilient practice. Likewise, it's not enough to *tell* yourself a better story. You have to *live* your better story. It's not enough to make meaning out of what has already happened. In light of that meaning, you have to live the next moment, the next chapter, the next scene.

Walker, you can be the town drunk if you choose. You'd upset your family and you'd hurt your kids, but truth be told, a lot of other people wouldn't mind so much. You'd make it easy for them to understand you: nice local kid, became a Navy SEAL, went to war, came back a hero, had a stress disorder, started drinking, ended up a disappointment. That's a simple story, easy to understand.

The real Walker is a hell of a lot more complicated and a hell of a lot more capable. You're going to live a real life. It's not going to be perfect; it won't always be pretty. But you can decide what the themes of your story are going to be.

There's the theme of hard work: a story about a kid who started working about the same time he learned how to spell, who went from logging to the SEAL teams to owning his own business. There's your wrestle with alcoholism: how it pinned you down once or twice, but you never stopped fighting and found a way to win. There's the theme of fighting: a story about a warrior who learned the discipline to serve justice, not vengeance; serve his country, not himself. There's the story about all the times you've been called on to teach others—as a SEAL instructor, a coach, a father.

These are the themes you've chosen for yourself. You are the author of your own story. What are you going to write today?

You and I, Walker, we're both going to be dead someday. I hope it won't be soon. We both love living, and we'll take every moment we can get.

But it seems as if we showed up at BUD/S just a blink ago. That was a dozen years ago, mate. How many blinks have we got left?

There will come a day when the lights go out one last time, a day when the work and the living and the loving is all done. No one knows for certain what lies beyond that day. But if you've lived well, you can hope to become part of a story that others are proud to tell.

Death

There are people who do not live their present life; it is as if
they were preparing themselves, with all their zeal, to live
some other life, but not this one. And while they do this,
time goes by and is lost.

— ANTIPHON (FIFTH CENTURY BC)

You are going to die, Walker.

That's a strange way to start a letter, isn't it? I can hear you saying,
"Jeez, G, thanks for the reminder."

But why are you reading these letters at all? Why worry about building resilience and creating happiness now? Why not put it off until tomorrow, or next week, or next year?

You know why: because your time is limited. It's precious because it's
finite. You don't know how much you'll get, so you know to appreciate
what you've got.

And it's in this way that death — the source of our greatest fears, the
fear behind all fears — provides the urgency behind our greatest efforts.

None of this is news, Walker. We know we're going to die. But we're pretty
darned good at forgetting it. Forget too long and you can spend a lifetime
postponing and procrastinating. You can put off the life you want to live
until you wake up to find that it's too late. You study but never act. You
plan but never travel. You think it, but never tell anyone you love them.

As Antiphon said, there are people (and we're all like this sometimes) who simply forget to live their present life. Antiphon died two

thousand five hundred years ago. People have been procrastinating for a while, Walker. But you don't have to.

— 2 —

If it's important that we don't forget the fact of our death, it's also important that we don't fixate on it.

The best analogy I've ever heard about this says that death is like the sun. It infuses every part of our lives, but it doesn't make sense to stare at it.

The urgency that comes from the limited span of our lives pushes us to find meaning in the time we have. But fearing death, obsessing over it, staring directly at it, blinds us to the possibilities of living.

The resilient person learns to live with the knowledge of death without being overcome by it.

How do you do that? Remember how, in the letter on practice, I said that you can practice anything? That includes death.

— 3 —

How many guys do you know who said this about combat: "I don't know if I'll ever feel that alive again"?

Any honest account of the experience of combat has to make room for the experience — even the joy — of absolute engagement, the electric sensation of knowing that everything matters.

A lot of ancient philosophers recognized that through disciplined reflection on death, we bring urgency and vividness and meaning to the days that we live.

They didn't "practice for death" because they were gloomy, or morbid, or because they wanted everyone to appreciate how "deep" they were. They did it because they wanted to live more fully.

As usual, Seneca captured the idea clearly: "At the moment we go to sleep, let us say, in joy and gaiety: 'I have lived. I have traveled the path which Fortune assigned to me.' If a god gives us the next day as a bonus, let us receive it with joy . . . Whoever has said to himself 'I have lived' can arise each day to an unexpected gift. Hurry up and live, and consider each day as a completed life."

I love that. Hurry up and live!

Keep in mind that in Seneca's time, if your healthy thirty-five-year-old friend got a cold, he might well die. If his toothache worsened and his mouth swelled, he might well die. If he had a cut that got infected, he might well die.

So: hurry up and live!

My boxing coach Earl Blair used to do this. If at the end of practice I said to Earl, "See you tomorrow," he'd say, "See you tomorrow, if the Lord spares me." If I dropped him off at his house and said, "I'll see you Monday," he'd say, "See you Monday, if the Lord spares me."

Every time a plan was made, Earl would say, "If the Lord spares me." If you asked him about this, he'd tell you that it was, in part, a way of being respectful to God: "My Father owns every second, and he'll take me when he wants to."

It was also a way of practicing death — of reminding yourself and others around you that your time is limited.

Reflecting like this has a way of changing the way you see the world. Lucretius, a Roman poet who lived a bit before Seneca, wrote that all of the miracles of the natural world — everything we take for granted like spoiled children — would awe and stun us if we could see them again for the first time: "If all these objects suddenly surged forth to the eyes of mortals, what could be found that was more wonderful than this totality, whose existence the human mind could not have dared to imagine?"

Children sometimes see with eyes like this. And we can too, if we remember that our eyes will one day close for good.

Think about it. When do you see things most vividly and love things most intensely? Often it's when you first discover them — or when they're about to be taken away.

We talked before about mental rehearsal and visualization. Seneca, Epictetus, and Marcus Aurelius believed in the importance of mentally rehearsing their own deaths. They recognized the role of fortune enough to know that it was impossible to predict the exact time or place they would die. At the same time, they knew that we can prepare for death, as we can prepare for any fearful thing. For centuries, wise people have tried to follow their example.

* * *

In 1569, Michel de Montaigne was a local lord in western France. He'd read the classics deeply, but his political responsibilities kept him too busy to pursue his passion for study. That winter, he was out for a ride when another horse smashed into his. He was thrown high into the air and then crashed down onto the road.

To the servants who tried to carry his broken body back home, Montaigne seemed to be a man in unbearable pain, moaning and coughing up blood. But from the inside, it all felt remarkably pain-less. He later wrote, "It seemed to me that my life was hanging only by the tip of my lips; I closed my eyes in order, it seemed to me, to help push [life] out, and took pleasure in growing languid and letting myself go." At what looked to be the end of his life, he discovered (in the words of his recent biographer, Sarah Bakewell) that "death could have a friendly face."

But Montaigne recovered, and went on to live twenty-three more years. He retired from his political work and spent much of the rest of his days in his library, a tower room lined with a thousand books, where he wrote the essays that made him one of the most revolution-ary writers to ever live. And it might not surprise you that he spent a lot of that time thinking about death — how it was that coming so close to death had cured him of his fear, and how the rest of us might cure ourselves in a similar way.

"To begin to strip [death] of its greatest advantage against us," he wrote, "let us take an entirely different way from the usual one. Let us rid it of its strangeness, come to know it, get used to it . . . At the stum-bling of a horse, the fall of a tile, the slightest pin prick, let us promptly chew on this: Well, what if it were death itself?"

Does that sound morbid to you? Montaigne didn't think so: "Pre-meditation of death is premeditation of freedom. He who has learned how to die has unlearned how to be a slave."

In accepting that we are going to die, we gain a tremendous power over ourselves.

Like all fears, the fear of death does its worst work when it knocks around in our mind. Fear likes to lurk in shadow. When Montaigne thinks "What if it were death itself?" and Earl says "If the Lord spares me," they put the bright prospect of death right in front of their eyes. Over time, they become comfortable with the idea that they too will one day do the one thing we all have to do.

— 4 —

And while we're thinking about death, Walker, let's take a moment to think and talk about how we remember those who have died.

Pericles was Greece's greatest statesman, and one of his responsibilities was to speak in memory of those who died in battle. His speech over the Athenian dead is still read and admired to this day. One line in particular stands out to me: "Heroes have the whole earth for their tomb . . . There is enshrined in every breast a record unwritten with no tablet to preserve it, except that of the heart."

What lives on is not what is engraved in stone monuments, but what we have woven into the lives of others. Those who have lived with us become a part of us.

We honor the dead by living their values. Through our efforts, we ensure that the good things they stood for continue to stand even when they are gone. Our actions become a living memorial to their memory.

Your life carries forward the story of all those who shaped it for the good and who are now gone. And you can live in such a way that those after you will be proud to weave your life into their own.

Sabbath

Six days a week we wrestle with the world, wringing profit
from the earth; on the Sabbath we especially care for the
seed of eternity planted in the soul.

— ABRAHAM JOSHUA HESCHEL

Walker,

This'll be my last letter for now. You don't need a big, emotional conclusion to understand the work you have ahead of you, or my help to
reflect back — with pride, I hope — on all the work you've already done.
You're a man of incredible strength, more than a match for the work
ahead.

But there is one thing missing before we go.

These letters are full of work: striving, overcoming, sweating, pushing through, bearing down. Making ourselves more resilient is necessary and can be joyful, but it's not easy. And if I've stressed the difficulty
of the path ahead of you, it's partly because I've wanted to set these letters against the message our culture too often sends: that you can have
happiness and fulfillment effortlessly and instantly.

These have been letters about the work of your life. But now I want
to add: not all of life is work. Not all of life is overcoming. Not all of life
requires resilience.

There are Roman roads, laid down two thousand years ago, that you
can drive a car on today. Roman temples and stadiums still stand. Roman aqueducts still carry water.

The Romans were some of the great makers and builders and work-men of the ancient world. They were masters of *things:* of digging things out of the ground, of moving things from one end of the Con-tinent to the other, of building towering forts and long walls, stacking thing upon thing.

Our word "reality" comes from *res,* the Latin word for "thing."

But there's a danger in thinking of reality this way. There is more to our lives than making, getting, buying, building, owning, doing, work-ing.

When the Romans came into contact with the Jews, their first reac-tion was shock: they had never met a people so lazy. Every seventh day, the Jews stopped all their work. Fields went unplowed, tools collected dust, businesses went silent. From the high priest to the lowest servant, everyone — even the horses and the oxen — spent an entire day at rest.

This was the Sabbath. And for the Romans, who were masters of things and activity, it looked as if an entire people spent one-seventh of their lives doing nothing.

For all their accomplishments, there were parts of reality the Ro-mans simply couldn't see.

The most meaningful book I've read on the idea of the Sabbath was written by Rabbi Abraham Joshua Heschel. Rabbi Heschel was resilient in his own right. His father died when he was nine. He was arrested by the Gestapo when he was twenty-one and deported to Poland. He made it to England a few weeks before the Germans invaded Poland, but one sister was killed in a German bombing, his mother was mur-dered by the Nazis, and two other sisters died in concentration camps. In America, Heschel later marched for civil rights with Dr. Martin Luther King Jr. and became one of the most profound religious think-ers of the twentieth century.

Heschel didn't have it easy and he didn't take it easy. But he reminds us that there's more to reality than the world of things and objects. There is also *time.*

We're even more skilled than the Romans at dominating nature and controlling space. We spend the bulk of our lives doing things. And yet some of the most meaningful parts of our lives come when we simply choose to *be,* when we let time carry us, when we "face sacred moments." Space is something we strive to control and conquer; you can grab things with your hands. You can't grab time. You can't slow it down or speed it up. Time is beyond your control. Yet you have to live meaningfully in time as well as in space.

The Romans built magnificent palaces in space. But the Jews built "a palace in time"—the Sabbath. "Remember the Sabbath day: to keep it holy." One day set apart from all the others, "a realm of time where the goal is not to have but to be, not to own but to give, not to control but to share, not to subdue but to be in accord."

There are all sorts of rituals to help us leave the ordinary world and enter this realm. Jews may light Sabbath candles, say a blessing over wine and bread, and enjoy a family meal. Christians may go to church to worship, pray, praise, and enjoy the fellowship of their community of faith. Other religions and practices emphasize meditation, silence, stillness.

The point, I think, is less about which rituals we follow and more about whether we can change our frame of mind to find the holy space in time that God has created and commanded humankind to keep. As Heschel says: "He who wants to enter the holiness of the day must first lay down the profanity of clattering commerce, of being yoked to toil. He must go away from the screech of dissonant days, from the nervousness and fury of acquisitiveness and the betrayal in embezzling his own life. He must say farewell to manual work and learn to understand that the world has already been created and will survive without the help of man."

We *should* move through fear to courage. We *should* move through suffering to strength. We *should* move through pain to wisdom. But sometimes we don't have to move at all. We simply have to be, and to practice the virtue of restful joy in a world that is not at rest.

So, Zach, whether you use a religious tradition to sanctify time or you find your own way of setting time apart, what matters most is that you find time to stop. Stop striving, stop struggling, stop thinking about how to be resilient. Find joy and rest in a world that never stops moving.

Take a long walk. Eat a slow meal. Pick up a book. Daydream. Spend time with people you love.

And this is important: don't think of this quiet as a way to "recharge" for the work in front of you. That may well be what happens, but to treat your Sabbath as a way to prepare for work is just another way of making the Sabbath work by another name.

The Sabbath doesn't exist for work. In the Jewish tradition, the Sabbath comes every Friday at sunset—whether or not your work has been successful, whether you've been resilient or weak, whether you're flourishing or floundering. The Sabbath comes without your help. And when it comes, your only duty is to celebrate it. The Sabbath is an end in itself. Rest and enjoy—simply because.

You don't celebrate the Sabbath to become more resilient. The Sabbath is the counterbalance to resilience. Excellence and enjoyment, resilience and rest; with the Sabbath we make our lives whole.

We fill our lives just as I've filled these pages.

If we're resilient, we fill them with purpose, with meaning, with wisdom, and with work. And then on the Sabbath—whether it comes once a week at sunset or when you catch your breath looking in your new child's eyes—we turn the crowded page, just as you can turn to the last page I'll send you for now, and we rest.

Till soon, my friend.

Acknowledgments

The writing of this book was generously supported by a grant from the Templeton Foundation's Character and Virtue Development program. I thank the team there, and hope that this work reflects the twin virtues of humility and curiosity exemplified in their motto, "How little we know, how eager to learn." My literary agent, E. J. McCarthy, is a wise counselor and enthusiastic reader who encouraged this project every step of the way. Bruce Nichols has been a great ally for many years. As an editor he made these letters tighter and stronger, and as a publisher he brought the entire team at Houghton Mifflin Harcourt together to bring this book into the world. At HMH I also want to thank Patrick Barry, Larry Cooper, Lori Glazer, Ben Hyman, Katrina Kruse, and Megan Wilson for their creative and capable work.

Tim Ly spent many hours over the course of many years taking notes as I talked through a thousand thoughts about resilience, character, virtue, and leadership. He claims that he is still sane. He is, at least, now in law school, and I thank him for helping me to arrange a lot of these initial ideas. Rob Goodman served as an exceptional editorial assistant on this project. He brought an incisive mind, a way with words, a love of Cato, and a deep appreciation for Thai food and fish tacos to this work. Thanks for making this both excellent and fun, Rob. Krystal Taylor, a trusted colleague for many years, did an exceptional job of running the effort to launch this book.

Leading The Mission Continues has been some of the most meaningful work of my life, and I thank the staff, the veterans we work with, and the volunteers and investors who supported us over the past seven years. I've learned a lot from all of you. This book benefited from the insights of many readers—family and friends—who made it stronger. Thank you, Catherine Chestnut, Janet Chestnut, Tim Chestnut, Gregg Favre, Marc Greitens, Rob Greitens, Warren Lockette, Barbara Osburg, and Jesse Sullivan. Any reader will see that Will Guild's thoughts have shaped mine deeply. He's known me since I first showed up to BUD/S with a shaved head, and if to be a philosopher means to live an examined life of courage and service, Will is one of our generation's greatest philosophers.

Sheena remains the love of my life, and in the course of writing this book we brought Joshua into the world. You both are a daily reminder that no words I write can ever do justice to the depth of my happiness.

And finally, though we've talked a lot since then, I don't know that I ever said to you, "Thanks for calling, Zach." I love you.

St. Louis, Missouri, 2014

Notes

LETTER 1: *Your Frontline*

5 *"awful grace of God"*: Edith Hamilton, *The Greek Way* (New York: W. W. Norton, 1993), 194.
"killed the birds in the air": Aeschylus, *Agamemnon*, in *An Oresteia*, trans. Anne Carson (New York: Faber and Faber, 2009), 30.

LETTER 2: *Why Resilience?*

8 *"into an enjoyable challenge"*: Mihaly Csikszentmihalyi, *Flow: The Psychology of Optimal Experience* (New York: Harper Perennial, 1990), 200.
9 *"as our legitimate property"*: Quoted in Pierre Hadot, *What Is Ancient Philosophy?*, trans. Michael Chase (Cambridge: Harvard University Press, 2002), 277. Friedrich Nietzsche, "Posthumous Fragments," in Nietzsche, *Werke*, ed. Giorgio Colli and Mazzino Montinari, trans. Pierre Hadot (Berlin: De Gruyter, 1973), 5.2.552–53. When people quote Nietzsche, they often feel the need to apologize for some reason. Let's acknowledge this about Nietzsche: he was a bit nuts, a bit destructive, and just as I wouldn't recommend his life to anyone, I wouldn't recommend that anyone swallow his whole philosophy unexamined. Still, some of what he wrote is brilliant. And we should learn from it. Let's not throw away diamonds of genius because they were produced by imperfect people.
10 *"Culture" was originally a word*: Of course, this way of thinking about culture has ancient roots in Eastern as well as Western thought. Two and a half millennia ago, for instance, Confucius was asked which of his disciples loved learning the most. He answered, "There was one Yen Hui who was eager to learn. He did not vent his anger upon an innocent person, nor did he make the same mistake twice." The student who loved learning the most was not the one who had mastered the most facts; he was the one whose character had been shaped

most deeply by what he'd learned. Confucius, *The Analects*, VI.3, trans. D. C. Lau (New York: Penguin, 1979), 81.

"culture is innate": Jacques Barzun, *The Culture We Deserve* (Middletown, CT: Wesleyan University Press, 1989), 22.

"fighting done by fools": This quotation is often attributed to Thucydides. Its real source seems to be a nineteenth-century British general, William Francis Butler. The original line reads: "The nation that will insist upon drawing a broad line of demarcation between the fighting man and the thinking man is liable to find its fighting done by fools and its thinking done by cowards." Butler, *Charles George Gordon* (London: Macmillan, 1892), 85.

11 *"nature of the subject allows"*: Aristotle, *Nicomachean Ethics*, trans. Terence Irwin (Indianapolis: Hackett, 1985), 1094b19-26 (emphasis added).

13 *"we bring them back"*: Hamilton, *The Greek Way*, 9–10.

"people love old truths": Luc de Clapiers, Marquis de Vauvenargues, *Réflexions et Maximes*, trans. F. G. Stevens (London: Humphrey Milford, 1940), $400.

14 *"set before our eyes"*: Lucius Annaeus Seneca, Epistle XCIV, in *Moral Epistles*, vol. 3, trans. Richard M. Gummere (Cambridge: Harvard University Press, 1917–1925), 27–29.

15 *"and tolerate other people"*: Epictetus, *Discourses*, 3, 21, 4–6. See Pierre Hadot, *Philosophy as a Way of Life*, trans. Michael Chase (Malden, MA: Blackwell, 1995), 267.

16 *"magnanimity, and trust"*: Henry Thoreau, *Walden* (Philadelphia: Courage, 1990), 13.

"face of the void": Boris Cyrulnik, *Resilience: How Your Inner Strength Can Set You Free from the Past*, trans. David Macey (New York: Penguin, 2009), 47.

LETTER 3: *What Is Resilience?*

19 *"heavily for their acquiring"*: Ernest Hemingway, *Death in the Afternoon* (New York: Charles Scribner's Sons, 1932), 192.

20 *"through these labors"*: Sophocles, *Philoktetes*, trans. Seth L. Schein (Newburyport, MA: Focus, 2003), 85.

21 *"The wounded man knows something"*: Robert Bly, *Iron John* (New York: Vintage Books, 1992), 32.

"the road through suffering": Quoted in Fred Jerome and Rodger Taylor, *Einstein on Race and Racism* (New Brunswick, NJ: Rutgers University Press, 2006), 147.

22 *"What's done cannot be undone"*: William Shakespeare, *Macbeth*, V.1.71, ed. Sylvan Barnet (New York: Signet, 1998), 83.

24 *"strong at the broken places"*: Ernest Hemingway, *A Farewell to Arms* (New York: Charles Scribner's Sons, 1957), 249.

26 *"free from freedom"*: Eric Hoffer, *The True Believer: Thoughts on the Nature of Mass Movements* (New York: HarperCollins, 2002), 31.

27 *"or rather, all the difference"*: Aristotle, *Nicomachean Ethics*, in *The Basic Works of Aristotle*, trans. W. D. Ross, ed. Richard McKeon (New York: Random House, 1941), 1103b25–26.

29 *"who botch the business"*: Terry Eagleton, "The Nature of Evil," *Tikkun,* Winter 2011, 80.

30 *"whatever they might be"*: Quoted in James C. Collins, *Good to Great* (New York: Harper Business, 2001), 85.

31 *"Give no ground"*: In Richmond Lattimore, trans., *Greek Lyrics,* 2nd ed. (Chicago: University of Chicago Press, 1960), 3.

"Exactly like it, just as round": In Guy Davenport, trans., *Archilochus, Sappho, Alkman: Three Lyric Poets of the Late Greek Bronze Age* (Berkeley: University of California Press, 1980), 38.

LETTER 4: *Beginning*

32 *"don't let me f*** up"*: Quoted in Tom Wolfe, *The Right Stuff* (New York: Macmillan, 2008), 198 (and still known as "Shepard's Prayer"). However, Shepard himself later reported the quotation as, "Don't f*** up, Shepard."

34 *"beginning of philosophy"*: Plato, *Theatetus,* in *Plato in Twelve Volumes,* vol. 12, trans. Harold N. Fowler (Cambridge: Harvard University Press, 1921), 155d.

35 *"one cannot feel tamely"*: Hamilton, *The Greek Way,* 141.

36 *"able to find those words"*: Rainer Maria Rilke, *Letters to a Young Poet* (New York: Norton, 1934), 27.

37 *"wisdom to know the difference"*: Deborah Galasso, *Living Serenity* (Cicero, NY: 5 Fold Media, 2014), 12.

"reconciled to the uncontrollable": Solomon ibn Gabirol, *A Choice of Pearls,* XVII, trans. Benjamin Henry Ascher (London: Trübner and Co., 1859), 41.

38 *"saying no to that situation"*: Joseph Campbell with Bill Moyers, *The Power of Myth* (New York: Anchor Books, 1991), 83.

40 *"purification of the motive"*: T. S. Eliot, "Little Gidding," in *Four Quartets* (New York: Harcourt, 1943), 57. See also Ignatius of Loyola, *The Spiritual Exercises of St. Ignatius: A New Translation,* trans. Louis J. Puhl (Westminster, MD: Newman Press, 1951), 76.

41 *"chastity . . . but not yet"*: Augustine, *Confessions,* 2nd ed., trans. F. J. Sheed, ed. Michael J. Foley (Indianapolis: Hackett, 2006), 152.

"loved you so late": Augustine, *Confessions,* X, 27, 38.

42 *"evidence of a man's own"*: Michel de Montaigne, "That the Taste for Good Depends in Good Part upon the Opinion We Have of Them," in *Essays of Montaigne,* vol. 2, trans. Charles Cotton, ed. William Carew Hazlitt (London: Reeves & Turner, 1902), 46.

43 *"great joy and light"*: Eric Greitens, *The Heart and the Fist* (Boston: Houghton Mifflin Harcourt, 2011), 119–20.

not caring for their own poor: Navin Chawla, *Mother Teresa* (New Delhi: Penguin, 1993), 39, 57.

44 *"light must have gnats"*: Victor Hugo, "Villemain," in *The Works of Victor Hugo in Twenty Volumes,* vol. 14 (New York: Jenson Society, 1907), 67.

"which have never happened": Thomas Jefferson, letter to John Adams, April 8, 1816, in *The Adams-Jefferson Letters: The Complete Correspondence Between*

Thomas Jefferson and Abigail and John Adams, ed. Lester J. Cappon (Chapel Hill: University of North Carolina Press, 1988), 467.

45 *"gentle and kind people"*: Quoted in Joyce Carol Oates, *On Boxing* (Garden City, NY: Dolphin/Doubleday, 1987), 28.

46 *"desperate and diseased on it?"*: January 7, 1851. Quoted in Lynn McDonald, ed., *Florence Nightingale: An Introduction to Her Life and Family* (Waterloo, ON: Wilfrid Laurier University Press, 2001), 99.

"his relation to the cosmos": John F. Nash Jr., "Autobiographical Essay," in Tore Frängsmyr, ed., *Les Prix Nobel 1994* (Stockholm: Norstedts Tryckeri, 1995).

48 *"power and magic in it!"*: William Hutchison Murray, *The Scottish Himalayan Expedition* (London: J. M. Dent & Sons, 1951), 6–7.

LETTER 5: *Happiness*

50 *"a life affording them scope"*: Hamilton, *The Greek Way*, 24.

51 *"way of perfect excellence"*: Aristotle, *Nicomachean Ethics*, trans. D. P. Chase (Mineola, NY: Dover, 2012), 1102a5–6.

53 *"laws of sun, ice, and water"*: Quoted in Jefferson Humphries, ed., *Conversations with Reynolds Price* (Jackson, MS: University Press of Mississippi, 1991), 276.

56 *"own side of the question"*: John Stuart Mill, *Utilitarianism* (London: Longmans, Green, and Co., 1879), 14.

57 *"happen without a reason"*: Seneca, "To Lucilius on Providence," in *Moral Essays*, vol. 1, trans. John Basore (Cambridge: Harvard University Press, 1928), 3–5.

59 *"increasingly extraordinary individual"*: Csikszentmihalyi, *Flow*, 6.

"something difficult and worthwhile": Ibid., 3.

60 *"needed in this world"*: Hannah Senesh, *Hannah Senesh: Her Life and Diary, The First Complete Edition* (Woodstock, VT: Jewish Lights, 2007), 67.

62 *only way out is through*: Robert Frost's line, in "A Servant to Servants," is "the best way out is always through." Robert Frost, *Early Poems*, ed. Robert Faggen (New York: Penguin, 1998), 87.

63 *"the way it started"*: Quoted in Mark Will-Weber, ed., *The Quotable Runner* (Halcottsville, NY: Breakaway, 2001), 18.

"and run and run": "He Ran and Ran and Ran," *The Times of India*, August 8, 2004.

64 *"constitutes our abundance"*: This quotation is widely attributed to Epicurus, including by Klein, in *Travels with Epicurus*.

LETTER 6: *Models*

66 *"but from a human soul"*: Jacques Barzun, *Teacher in America*, rev. ed. (Indianapolis: Liberty Press, 1981), 12.

68 *"but a way of living"*: Greitens, *The Heart and the Fist*, 32.

"is valuable and pleasant": Aristotle, *Nicomachean Ethics*, trans. Martin Ostwald (Indianapolis: Bobbs-Merrill, 1962), 1176b, 25 (emphasis added).

69 *"the mistakes of others"*: Karl Marlantes, *What It Is Like to Go to War* (New York: Atlantic Monthly Press, 2011), v.

72 *"you will find yourself"*: Quoted in Austin Kleon, *Steal Like an Artist: 10 Things Nobody Told You about Being Creative* (New York: Workman Publishing, 2012), 33.

"imitate anything, produce nothing": Salvador Dalí, *Dalí by Dalí*, trans. Eleanor R. Morse (New York: Harry N. Abrams, 1970), 137.

74 *Hunter S. Thompson once set out*: Louis Menand, "Believer," *The New Yorker*, May 7, 2005.

75 *"to find a similar case"*: Quoted in Maynard Solomon, *Beethoven*, 2nd ed. (New York: Schirmer, 1998), 153.

LETTER 7: *Identity*

79 *"as rational as possible"*: Plato, *Apology*, 36c, trans. Hadot and Chase, in Hadot, *What Is Ancient Philosophy?*, 29.

81 *"low opinion of other things"*: Plutarch, "Cato the Younger," in *Plutarch's Lives*, vol. 8, trans. Bernadotte Perrin (Cambridge: Harvard University Press, 1919), 249, 251.

82 *"more . . . we'll deserve it"*: Joseph Addison, *Cato: A Tragedy*, in *Eighteenth-Century Plays*, ed. Ricardo Quintana (New York: Random House, 1952), 11.

"perhaps the word 'empathy'": Confucius, *The Analects*, XV.24, 135. Confucius uses the word *shu*, which some render as "empathy" and D. C. Lau translates as "using oneself as a measure in gauging the wishes of others."

"winged horses and a charioteer": Plato, *Phaedrus*, in *The Dialogues of Plato*, 3rd ed., vol. 1, trans. Benjamin Jowett (London: Oxford University Press, 1892), 246a.

83 *"which can move the world"*: Mahatma Gandhi, *Young India*, September 15, 1929. See *The Essential Gandhi: An Anthology of His Writings on His Life, Work, and Ideas*, 2nd ed., ed. Louis Fischer (New York: Vintage, 2002), 210.

85 *"that was 20 years ago"*: Robert L. Strauss, "Mind Over Misery," *Stanford*, September/October 2013, 47.

88 *you'll feel better*: Melinda Wenner, "Smile! It Could Make You Happier," *Scientific American Mind*, September/October 2009, 14–15.

89 *"would like to seem"*: This is frequently attributed to Socrates, though it does not appear in Plato's dialogues. See Mary Renault, *The Last of the Wine* (New York: Vintage, 2001), 77.

92 *"with regard to London?"*: Clare Sargent, "Radley Hall School, 1819–1844," *The Victorian Web*, www.victorianweb.org/history/education/radley/rhs.html.

LETTER 8: *Habits*

96 *"chiseling your own statue"*: Plotinus, *Enneads*, 2nd ed., trans. Stephen MacKenna (New York: Pantheon, 1957), 63.

98 *"courage makes a majority"*: Attributed, most likely incorrectly, to Andrew Jack-

son. See Robert F. Kennedy, foreword to *Profiles in Courage* by John F. Kennedy (New York: HarperCollins, 2003), xv.

100 *"the muscles of figures"*: Leonardo da Vinci, *The Notebooks of Leonardo da Vinci*, trans. Jean Paul Richter (Mineola, NY: Dover, 1970), 245.

101 *"when we are growing"*: J. B. *Yeats Letters to His Son, W. B. Yeats, and Others, 1869–1922* (New York: E. P. Dutton & Co., 1946), 121.

LETTER 9: *Responsibility*

107 *"the world of Epictetus"*: James Bond Stockdale, *Courage Under Fire: Testing Epictetus's Doctrines in a Laboratory of Human Behavior* (Stanford, CA: Hoover Institution Press, 1993), 7.

"that you'd break it?": Origen, *Contra Celsum*, trans. Henry Chadwick (Cambridge, Eng.: Cambridge University Press, 1980), 54.

108 *"bring to bear upon things"*: Epictetus, *Enchiridion*, 5, trans. Hadot and Chase, in Hadot, *What Is Ancient Philosophy?*, 131.

"I would not trade": Quoted in Collins, *Good to Great*, 85.

110 *"so to speak, for life"*: Hoffer, *The Passionate State of Mind and Other Aphorisms* (New York: Harper & Row, 1955), 111.

114 *"obstacle in the path"*: Or, as rendered by Elaine Pagels, "one who throws something across one's path." Pagels, *The Origin of Satan* (New York: Vintage Books, 1996), 39.

LETTER 10: *Vocation*

118 *could he maintain hope?*: Greitens, *The Heart and the Fist*, 288–89.

119 *"the world's great need"*: Peter J. Gomes, Spring Commencement Address, University of North Carolina, May 15, 2005, alumni.unc.edu/article.aspx?SID=2608.

120 *"external goods" and "internal goods"*: Alasdair C. MacIntyre, *After Virtue: A Study in Moral Theory*, 2nd ed. (Notre Dame, IN: University of Notre Dame Press, 1984), 188–91.

121 *buy a single book*: Aidan Conti, "The Price of a Book in the Middle Ages," *Nugatorius Scriptor: Scribblings on Textual Culture*, September 16, 2010, scribalculture.org/weblog/2010/09/16/the-price-of-a-book-in-the-middle-ages.

"he spent his time": John Bunyan, *The Pilgrim's Progress* (Mineola, NY: Dover, 2003), 14.

122 *"nothing is interesting"*: Daniel Klein, *Travels with Epicurus: A Journey to a Greek Island in Search of a Fulfilled Life* (New York: Penguin, 2012), 47.

123 *"heart is turned toward heaven"*: Talmud Bavli: Berakhot, 17, in Chaim Stern, ed., *Gates of Repentance*, rev. ed. (New York: CCAR Press, 2004), 10.

125 *"bear almost any how"*: Nietzsche, "Maxims and Arrows," Maxim 12, in *Twilight of the Idols*; quoted in Viktor E. Frankl, *Man's Search for Meaning*, 4th ed. (Boston: Beacon Press, 1992), 109.

126 *"boons on his fellow man"*: Joseph Campbell, *The Hero with a Thousand Faces* (Princeton, NJ: Princeton University Press, 1949), 23.

"power to serve others": Campbell and Moyers, *The Power of Myth*, xiv.

128 *"significant contributions to humankind"*: Csikszentmihalyi, *Flow*, 42.

LETTER 11: *Philosophy*

129 *"opportunity to do philosophy"*: Plutarch, *Whether a Man Should Engage in Politics When He Is Old*, XXVI.796d, trans. Hadot and Chase, in Hadot, *What Is Ancient Philosophy?*, 38.

130 *the philosopher Hypatia*: Maria Dzielska, *Hypatia of Alexandria*, trans. F. Lyra (Cambridge: Harvard University Press, 1995), 25, 55.

131 *"I contain multitudes"*: Walt Whitman, "Song of Myself," in *The Complete Poems* (New York: Penguin, 1996), 123.

"every thing you said to-day": Ralph Waldo Emerson, *The Complete Works of Ralph Waldo Emerson*, vol. 2, ed. Edward Waldo Emerson (Cambridge: Riverside Press, 1904), 391–92.

132 *in his private diary*: Hadot, *What is Ancient Philosophy?*, 173.

"What's the use?": Marcus Aurelius, *The Emperor's Handbook: A New Translation of the Meditations*, trans. C. Scot Hicks and David V. Hicks (New York: Scribner, 2002), 61.

"the ability to function": F. Scott Fitzgerald, *The Crack-Up* (New York: New Directions, 2009), 69.

133 *"Hard cases make bad law"*: *Northern Securities Co. v. United States*, 193 U.S. 197, 400 (1904) (Justice Holmes dissenting). The saying appears to have been proverbial before Holmes cited it.

134 *performed aloud, like plays*: See Nikos G. Charalabopoulos, *Platonic Drama and Its Ancient Reception* (New York: Cambridge University Press, 2002).

135 *"not knowledge but action"*: Aristotle, *Nicomachean Ethics*, in *The Basic Works of Aristotle*, 1095a4–5.

"warned against and avoid?": J. A. Leo Lemay, *The Life of Benjamin Franklin* (Philadelphia: University of Pennsylvania Press, 2006–2009), 340–41.

136 *"will be dead in the morning"*: Epictetus, *Discourses*, 3.24.88. Also quoted in Marcus Aurelius, *Meditations*, trans. Gregory Hays (New York: Modern Library, 2003), 157.

died before their tenth: Peter Garnsey, "Child Rearing in Ancient Italy," in David I. Kertzer and Richard P. Saller, eds., *The Family in Italy from Antiquity to the Present* (New Haven: Yale University Press, 1991), 52.

139 *"dawn of universal happiness"*: Maximilien Robespierre, speech to the National Convention, February 5, 1794. Quoted in Paul Harold Beik, ed., *The French Revolution* (New York: Macmillan, 1971), 279.

"private as well as public": James Madison, "Federalist 51," in Terence Ball, ed., *The Federalist with the Letters of "Brutus"* (New York: Cambridge University Press, 2003), 252.

140 *"to the advantage of others"*: Niccolò Machiavelli, *The Prince*, trans. George Bull (London: Penguin, 2003), 12.
"bend others to your will?": Thomas à Kempis, *The Imitation of Christ*, I.17 (Milwaukee: Bruce Publishing Co., 1940), 22–23.

141 *"a piece of his own heart?"*: Aleksandr Solzhenitsyn, *The Gulag Archipelago, 1918–1956: An Experiment in Literary Investigation*, parts 1–2 (New York: Harper & Row, 1973), 168.

142 *intentions and results:* On the "morality of results," see Robert D. Kaplan, *Warrior Politics: Why Leadership Demands a Pagan Ethos* (New York: Random House, 2002), 53.
was courageous action: Greitens, *The Heart and the Fist*, 58.

144 *helped to break families apart:* Eric Greitens, *Strength and Compassion* (Washington, DC: Leading Authorities Press, 2008), 10–11. Also see Greitens, *Children First: Ideas and the Dynamics of Aid in Western Voluntary Assistance Programs for War-Affected Children Abroad* (Oxford University DPhil dissertation, 2000), pp. 251–54.

145 *"There is no try"*: Greitens, *The Heart and the Fist*, 149.

146 *hammer by staring at it:* Martin Heidegger, *Being and Time: A Translation of Sein und Zeit*, trans. Joan Stambaugh (Albany: State University of New York Press, 1996), 65.

LETTER 12: *Practice*

147 *"dance under those lights"*: Quoted in Michael Gaffney, *The Champ: My Year with Muhammad Ali* (New York: Diversion Books, 2012), 14.

148 *"hide nothing from myself"*: Seneca, *On Anger*, III.36.1–3, trans. Hadot and Chase, in Hadot, *What Is Ancient Philosophy?*, 200.

153 *"be reminded than informed"*: C. Scot Hicks and David V. Hicks, introduction to *The Emperor's Handbook*, 2.

154 *"labours of a spasmodic Hercules"*: Anthony Trollope, *Autobiography of Anthony Trollope* (New York: Dodd, Mead & Co., 1905), 105.

155 *"but I do what I hate"*: Romans 7:15 (Holman Christian Standard Bible).

LETTER 13: *Pain*

158 *"but drags the unwilling"*: Seneca, Epistle CVII (quoting the Greek Stoic Cleanthes), in *Moral Epistles*, vol. 3.

159 *"you will be happy"*: Epictetus, *Enchiridion*, 8, trans. Hadot and Chase, in Hadot, *What Is Ancient Philosophy?*, 133.

160 *"not been built to hold her"*: Machiavelli, *The Prince*, trans. David Wootton (Indianapolis: Hackett, 1995), 74–75.

162 *episodes of depression:* Nassir Ghaemi, "Depression in Command," *Wall Street Journal*, July 30, 2011.
"fire of his great work": Joshua Wolf Shenk, "Lincoln's Great Depression," *The Atlantic*, October 2005, 53, 68.

165 *"to rouse a deaf world"*: C. S. Lewis, *The Problem of Pain* (New York: Macmillan, 1959), 81.

166 *"no evil ascends so high"*: Marcus Aurelius, *Meditations*, trans. George Long (Mineola, NY: Dover, 1997), 61.
"masochistic rather than heroic": Frankl, *Man's Search for Meaning*, 148.

167 *"a freely chosen task"*: Ibid., 109–10.

LETTER 14: *Mastering Pain*

173 *"without loss of manly vigor"*: Hamilton, *The Greek Way*, 66.
Thich Nhat Hanh writes: Thich Nhat Hanh, *Work: How to Find Joy and Meaning in Each Hour of the Day* (Berkeley, CA: Parallax Press, 2012), 85.

174 *Associated Press polled:* See Michael MacCambridge, ed., *ESPN Sports Century* (New York: Hyperion, 1995), 95.

175 *"roared their approval"*: Allen Barra, "'Dempsey and Firpo': The Greatest American Sports Painting," *The Atlantic*, April 24, 2012, www.theatlantic.com/entertainment/archive/2012/04/dempsey-and-firpo-the-greatest-american-sports-painting/256256.
"school had become a reality": Chawla, *Mother Teresa*, xv.

177 "Breathe. Stay tough.": James Hardy et al., "A Descriptive Study of Athlete Self-Talk," *The Sport Psychologist* 15 (2001): 312–13.

179 *watch the sun set?*: Greitens, *The Heart and the Fist*, 185–86.
"functioning of the imagination": Ernest Hemingway, ed., *Men at War: The Best War Stories of All Time* (New York: Crown, 1955), xxiv.

181 *"the smallest of things"*: Seneca, Epistle CVII, trans. Thomas V. Morris, in Morris, *The Stoic Art of Living: Inner Resilience and Outer Results* (Peru, IL: Carus Publishing, 2004), 32.

183 *"suffers what he fears"*: Montaigne, "Of Experience," in *Essays of Montaigne*, vol. 4, 255.

184 *"Keep yourself simple, good, pure"*: Marcus Aurelius, *The Emperor's Handbook*, 70.
"corpse or a heap of ash": Ibid., 51.
"not be afraid to lose him?": Marcus Aurelius, *Meditations*, IX.40. Quoted in Anthony R. Birley, *Marcus Aurelius: A Biography*, rev. ed. (New York: Routledge, 2004), 107.

185 *"had in it elements of fear"*: Tom Bethell, *Eric Hoffer: The Longshoreman Philosopher* (Stanford, CA: Hoover Institution Press, 2012), 64.
"upon the face of the waters": Genesis 1:2.

189 *"all the other virtues"*: Marcus Tullius Cicero, *Pro Plancio*, XXXIII, in *The Orations of Marcus Tullius Cicero*, trans. C. D. Yonge (London: George Bell & Sons, 1891), 80.

190 *who practice gratitude:* Michael McCullough et al., "The Grateful Disposition: A Conceptual and Empirical Topography," *Journal of Personality and Social Psychology* 82(1) (2002): 112–27; T. B. Kashdan et al., "Gratitude and Hedonic and Eudaimonic Well-Being in Vietnam War Veterans," *Behaviour Research and Therapy* 44(2) (2006): 177–99.

overwhelmed by bad fortune: A. M. Wood et al., "Coping Style as a Psychological Resource of Grateful People," *Journal of Social and Clinical Psychology* 26(9) (2007): 1076–93.

One finding stands out: A. M. Wood et al., "Gratitude Uniquely Predicts Satisfaction with Life: Incremental Validity above the Domains and Facets of the Five Factor Model," *Personality and Individual Differences* 45 (2008): 49–54.

"stabbing the other hand": Talmud Yerushalmi: Nedarim 9, in Joseph L. Baron, ed., *A Treasury of Jewish Quotations*, rev. ed. (Lanham, MD: Rowman & Littlefield, 2004), 529.

"hope for a better past": "The Necessity of Forgiveness: An Interview with Dr. Fred Luskin," PBS, www.pbs.org/kqed/onenight/stories/forgive.

191 *"regardless of how it turns out":* Václav Havel, *Disturbing the Peace* (New York: Vintage Books, 1991), 181.

"rebuild a weakened will": Chaim Stern, ed., *Gates of Prayer* (New York: CCAR Press, 1975), 325.

LETTER 15: *Reflection*

192 *perfecting the steam engine:* Matthew Crawford, *Shop Class as Soulcraft: An Inquiry into the Value of Work* (New York: Penguin, 2010), 22–23.

193 *"to the ground and died hastily":* Robert Lindsay of Pitscottie, *The History of Scotland from 1436 to 1565*, 2nd ed. (Glasgow: R. Urie, 1749), 120.

194 *"can never ripen into truth":* Ralph Waldo Emerson, *The Essential Writings of Ralph Waldo Emerson*, ed. Brooks Atkinson (New York: Random House, 2000), 49.

205 *"enter and remain in them":* Buddha, Kalama Sutta: Angutarra Nikaya 3:65; I.188–93. For a similar translation, see S. P. Talukdar, *The Sakyans of South-East Asia* (New Delhi: Gyan, 2006), 106.

"with other men's wisdom": Montaigne, "Of Pedantry." For a similar translation, see *The Complete Essays of Montaigne*, trans. Donald M. Frame (Stanford, CA: Stanford University Press, 1965), 101.

206 *"to experience that again":* David J. Epstein, *The Sports Gene: Inside the Science of Extraordinary Athletic Performance* (New York: Penguin, 2013), 3.

LETTER 16: *Friends*

208 *"soul dwelling in two bodies":* Quoted in Diogenes Laertius, *Lives of Eminent Philosophers*, trans. R. D. Hicks (Cambridge: Harvard University Press, 1925), V.1.20.

"a second self": Cicero, *On Friendship*, in *Letters of Marcus Tullius Cicero with His Treatises on Friendship and Old Age* (New York: P. F. Collier & Son, 1909), 36.

209 *"with him as with yourself":* Seneca, Epistle III, in *Moral Epistles*, vol. 1, 11.

"friends come from afar?": Confucius, *The Analects*, I.1, 3.

Only one topic gets two chapters: This book was assembled from Aristotle's lecture notes. So while we can't be sure he intended the chapters to sort out as they did, we can be sure that he spent a large chunk of his time talking to his students about friendship.

210 *"but friendship does not"*: Aristotle, *Nicomachean Ethics,* in *The Basic Works of Aristotle,* 1156b24–32.

212 *"irrational part of the man only"*: Plutarch, "How to Tell a Flatterer from a Friend," in *Plutarch's Morals,* vol. 2, trans. William Goodwin (Boston: Little, Brown & Co., 1871), 110, 128.

"absolute power corrupts absolutely": John Dalberg-Acton, Letter to Bishop Mandell Creighton, April 5, 1887, in *Historical Essays and Studies,* ed. John Neville Figgis and Reginald Vere Laurence (London: Macmillan, 1907), 504.

213 *"You are the man!"*: 2 Samuel 12:5–7 (New International Version).

215 *things we are blind to:* See Joseph Luft and Harrington Ingham, "The Johari Window, a Graphic Model of Interpersonal Awareness," *Proceedings of the Western Training Laboratory in Group Development* (Los Angeles: UCLA, 1955).

217 *most challenging moment in BUD/S:* Greitens, *The Heart and the Fist,* 193–94.

LETTER 17: *Mentors*

222 *"cannot be formulated in rules"*: Michael Oakeshott, "Rationalism in Politics," in *Rationalism in Politics and Other Essays* (New York: Basic Books, 1962), 8.

224 *"time to make it shorter"*: Blaise Pascal, Letter 16, *Lettres Provinciales* (Paris: Lefèvre et Brière, 1823), 29.

225 *"other one needs a brake"*: Diogenes Laertius, *Lives of Eminent Philosophers,* IV.2.6.

226 *"novices to fight the fire"*: Geoff Colvin, *Talent Is Overrated: What Really Separates World-Class Performers from Everybody Else* (New York: Penguin, 2010), 124.

"brainpower on what counted": Ibid., 123.

227 *"hedgehog knows one big thing"*: Archilochus, Fragment 201, in *Iambi et elegi graeci ante Alexandrum cantati,* vol. 1, ed. M. L. West (Oxford: Oxford University Press, 1971). See also Isaiah Berlin, *The Hedgehog and the Fox: An Essay on Tolstoy's View of History,* rev. ed. (Chicago: Elephant, 1993), 3.

"solutions on ill-defined problems": Philip E. Tetlock, *Expert Political Judgment: How Good Is It? How Can We Know?* (Princeton, NJ: Princeton University Press, 2005), 2.

228 *"how to use both natures"*: Machiavelli, *The Prince,* trans. Harvey C. Mansfield Jr. (Chicago: University of Chicago Press, 1985), 69.

231 *may not work for you today:* I'm using the terms interchangeably here, but there is often a difference between a coach and a mentor, and the difference can be worth considering. Broadly speaking, coaches focus on skills and tactics. They demonstrate, you repeat. They test, you practice. You ask, they answer. A good coach can teach you how to ascend without making bubbles, or how to swing a bat. A mentor, on the other hand, usually helps you to answer broader questions: How do I live a good life? What does it mean to be a good man? Because

we live our lives practically, we often learn about these broader questions not when we consider them abstractly, but when we practice them concretely. It's in this way that practice—how to kick a soccer ball, how to play the violin—provides the opportunities for modeling behavior, demonstrating values, and reinforcing character, which help us to answer even more important questions. The coaches that we tend to remember are those who taught more than a set of skills; they helped us to develop a way of living. The most memorable coaches are usually magnificent mentors.

232 *Sir James Frazer reported:* James Frazer, *The Golden Bough: A Study in Magic and Religion,* vol. 3 (London: Macmillan, 1900), 423–24.
"deemed men, and may marry": Ibid., 443–45.

237 *"without growth and exhilaration":* Eric Hoffer, *Reflections on the Human Condition* (New York: Harper & Row, 1973), 51.

LETTER 18: *Teams*

242 *"heart of the beast and survived":* Taylor Branch, *Parting the Waters: America in the King Years, 1954–63* (New York: Touchstone, 1988), 484–85.
"is to will one thing": Søren Kierkegaard, *Purity of Heart Is to Will One Thing: Spiritual Preparation for the Office of Confession,* trans. Douglas V. Steere (New York: Harper & Row, 1948).

LETTER 19: *Leadership*

244 *"what you say to the contrary":* Ralph Waldo Emerson, "Social Aims," in *Letters and Social Aims,* rev. ed. (Boston: James R. Osgood and Co., 1876), 80.

245 *"shall gentle his condition":* William Shakespeare, *Henry V,* IV.3.61–63, ed. John Russell Brown (New York: Signet, 1998), 89.

247 *"turned into a pleasant stroll":* Garry Wills, *Certain Trumpets: The Call of Leaders* (New York: Simon & Schuster, 1994), 27.
"how brave of you": William Manchester, *The Last Lion: Winston Spencer Churchill, Visions of Glory, 1874–1932* (Boston: Little, Brown, 1983), 27.

248 *"drink of its own accord?":* R. Morris, ed. and trans., *Old English Homilies* (London: Trübner and Co., 1868), 8–9.

250 *"flawless people and perfect choices":* Marcus Aurelius, *The Emperor's Handbook,* 7.

LETTER 20: *Freedom*

252 *Some philosophers call this:* Charles Taylor, "What's Wrong with Negative Liberty," in Alan Ryan, ed., *The Idea of Freedom* (Oxford: Oxford University Press, 1979), 175–93; Isaiah Berlin, "Two Concepts of Liberty," in *Four Essays on Liberty* (London: Oxford University Press, 1969), 128–30.

253 *"I am my own master":* Berlin, "Two Concepts of Liberty," 132.

"*all men are slaves to fear*": Seneca, Epistle XLVII, in *Moral Epistles*, vol. 1, 311.

254 "*purely democratic music*": Quoted in Richard Harrington, "The Drummer Who Beat a Path to the Height of Jazz Artistry," *Washington Post*, August 17, 2007.
"*you can start the fire*": Paul Klemperer, "Woodshedding and the Jazz Tradition," www.bigapplejazz.com/woodshedding.html.

255 "*not answer you in that day*": 1 Samuel 8:11–18 (New International Version).

257 "*every purpose under the heaven*": Ecclesiastes 3:1 (King James Version).

259 "*appears to be doing both*": Lawrence Pearsall Jacks, *Education Through Recreation* (London: University of London Press, 1931), 1–2.

LETTER 21: *Story*

260 "*put them into a story*": Cyrulnik, *Resilience*, 151.

261 "*actions as in their words*": MacIntyre, *After Virtue*, 216.
"*is finally to be understood*": Ibid., 219.

262 "*distant day into the answer*": Rilke, *Letters to a Young Poet*, 27.
"*emotionally stronger they are*": Marshall P. Duke et al., "Knowledge of Family History as a Clinically Useful Index of Psychological Well-Being and Prognosis: A Brief Report," *Psychotherapy: Theory, Research, Practice, Training* 45(2) (2008): 268–72.

263 *I remember one young man*: Greitens, *Strength and Compassion*, 12.

264 "*decent action and decent words*": Herodotus, *The History*, IX.79, trans. David Grene (Chicago: University of Chicago Press, 1987), 647. See also Robert D. Kaplan, "A Historian for Our Time," *The Atlantic*, January/February 2007.

265 "*their finest hour*": Winston Churchill, speech to the House of Commons, June 18, 1940.

LETTER 22: *Death*

269 "*time goes by and is lost*": Antiphon, B LIIIa, LII, trans. Hadot and Chase, in Hadot, *What Is Ancient Philosophy?*, 188.

270 "*each day as a completed life*": Seneca, *Epistles*, XII, CI, trans. Hadot and Chase, in Hadot, *What Is Ancient Philosophy?*, 194.

271 "*not have dared to imagine?*": Lucretius, *On the Nature of Things*, II.1023f., trans. Hadot and Chase, in Hadot, *What Is Ancient Philosophy?*, 230.

272 "*and letting myself go*": Montaigne, "Of Practice," in *The Complete Essays of Montaigne*, 269.
"*death could have a friendly face*": Sarah Bakewell, *How to Live: Or, A Life of Montaigne in One Question and Twenty Attempts at an Answer* (London: Chatto & Windus, 2010), 20.
"*how to be a slave*": Montaigne, "That to Philosophize Is to Learn to Die," in *The Complete Essays of Montaigne*, 60.

273 "*except that of the heart*": In Thucydides, *The Peloponnesian War*, rev. ed., trans. Richard Crawley (New York: Modern Library, 1982), II.43.

LETTER 23: *Sabbath*

274 *"eternity planted in the soul"*: Abraham Joshua Heschel, *The Sabbath: Its Meaning for Modern Man* (New York: Farrar, Straus and Young, 1951), 13.
275 *never met a people so lazy:* Ibid.
   "face sacred moments": Ibid., 6.
276 *"but to be in accord"*: Ibid., 12, 3.
   "survive without the help of man": Ibid., 13.

Bibliography

Addison, Joseph. *Cato: A Tragedy.* In *Eighteenth-Century Plays.* Ed. Ricardo Quintana. New York: Random House, 1952.

Aeschylus. *Agamemnon.* In *An Oresteia.* Trans. Anne Carson. New York: Faber and Faber, 2009.

Aristotle. *The Basic Works of Aristotle.* Trans. W. D. Ross. Ed. Richard McKeon. New York: Random House, 1941.

———. *Nicomachean Ethics.* Trans. Martin Ostwald. Indianapolis: Bobbs-Merrill, 1962.

———. *Nicomachean Ethics.* Trans. Terence Irwin. Indianapolis: Hackett Publishing Co., 1985.

———. *Nicomachean Ethics.* Trans. D. P. Chase. Mineola, NY: Dover, 2012.

Augustine. *Confessions.* 2nd ed. Trans. F. J. Sheed. Ed. Michael J. Foley. Indianapolis: Hackett Publishing Co., 2007.

Bakewell, Sarah. *How to Live: Or, A Life of Montaigne in One Question and Twenty Attempts at an Answer.* London: Chatto & Windus, 2010.

Baron, Joseph L., ed. *A Treasury of Jewish Quotations.* Rev. ed. Lanham, MD: Rowman & Littlefield, 2004.

Barra, Allen. " 'Dempsey and Firpo': The Greatest American Sports Painting." *The Atlantic,* April 24, 2012. www.theatlantic.com/entertainment/archive/2012/04/dempsey-and-firpo-the-greatest-american-sports-painting/256256.

Barzun, Jacques. *The Culture We Deserve.* Middletown, CT: Wesleyan University Press, 1989.

———. *Teacher in America.* Rev. ed. Indianapolis: Liberty Press, 1981.

Beik, Paul Harold, ed. *The French Revolution.* New York: Macmillan, 1971.

Berlin, Isaiah. *The Hedgehog and the Fox: An Essay on Tolstoy's View of History.* Rev. ed. Chicago: Elephant, 1993.

———. "Two Concepts of Liberty." In *Four Essays on Liberty.* London: Oxford University Press, 1969.

Bethell, Tom. *Eric Hoffer: The Longshoreman Philosopher.* Stanford, CA: Hoover Institution Press, 2012.

Birley, Anthony R. *Marcus Aurelius: A Biography.* Rev. ed. New York: Routledge, 2004.

Bly, Robert. *Iron John.* New York: Vintage Books, 1992.

Branch, Taylor. *Parting the Waters: America in the King Years, 1954–63.* New York: Touchstone, 1988.

Bunyan, John. *The Pilgrim's Progress.* Mineola, NY: Dover, 2003.

Burke, Daniel. "The Happiness Business." *Washington Post,* December 4, 2010.

Butler, William Francis. *Charles George Gordon.* London: Macmillan, 1892.

Campbell, Joseph. *The Hero with a Thousand Faces.* Princeton, NJ: Princeton University Press, 1949.

———, with Bill Moyers. *The Power of Myth.* New York: Anchor Books, 1991.

Charalabopoulos, Nikos G. *Platonic Drama and Its Ancient Reception.* New York: Cambridge University Press, 2002.

Chawla, Navin. *Mother Teresa.* New Delhi: Penguin, 1993.

Cicero, Marcus Tullius. *On Friendship.* In *Letters of Marcus Tullius Cicero with His Treatises on Friendship and Old Age.* New York: P. F. Collier & Son, 1909.

———. *Pro Plancio.* In *The Orations of Marcus Tullius Cicero.* Trans. C. D. Yonge. London: George Bell & Sons, 1891.

Clapiers, Luc de, Marquis de Vauvenargues. *Réflexions et Maximes.* Trans. F. G. Stevens. London: Humphrey Milford, 1940.

Collins, James C. *Good to Great.* New York: Harper Business, 2001.

Colvin, Geoff. *Talent Is Overrated: What Really Separates World-Class Performers from Everybody Else.* New York: Penguin, 2010.

Confucius. *The Analects.* Trans. D. C. Lau. New York: Penguin, 1979.

Conti, Aidan. "The Price of a Book in the Middle Ages." *Nugatorius Scriptor: Scribblings on Textual Culture.* September 16, 2010. scribalculture.org/weblog/2010/09/16/the-price-of-a-book-in-the-middle-ages.

Crawford, Matthew. *Shop Class as Soulcraft: An Inquiry into the Value of Work.* New York: Penguin, 2010.

Csikszentmihalyi, Mihaly. *Flow: The Psychology of Optimal Experience.* New York: Harper Perennial, 1990.

Cuda, Gretchen. "Just Breathe: Body Has a Built-In Stress Reliever." National Public Radio. December 6, 2010. www.npr.org/2010/12/06/131734718/just-breathe-body-has-a-built-in-stress-reliever.

Cyrulnik, Boris. *Resilience: How Your Inner Strength Can Set You Free from the Past.* Trans. David Macey. New York: Penguin, 2009.

Dalberg-Acton, John. Letter to Bishop Mandell Creighton, April 5, 1887. In *Historical Essays and Studies.* Ed. John Neville Figgis and Reginald Vere Laurence. London: Macmillan, 1907.

Dalí, Salvador. *Dalí by Dalí.* Trans. Eleanor R. Morse. New York: Harry N. Abrams, 1970.

Davenport, Guy, trans. *Archilochus, Sappho, Alkman: Three Lyric Poets of the Late Greek Bronze Age.* Berkeley: University of California Press, 1980.

Diogenes Laertius. *Lives of Eminent Philosophers.* Trans. R. D. Hicks. Cambridge: Harvard University Press, 1925.

Duke, Marshall P., et al. "Knowledge of Family History as a Clinically Useful Index of Psychological Well-Being and Prognosis: A Brief Report." *Psychotherapy: Theory, Research, Practice, Training* 45(2) (2008): 268–72.

Dzielska, Maria. *Hypatia of Alexandria*. Trans. F. Lyra. Cambridge: Harvard University Press, 1995.

Eagleton, Terry. "The Nature of Evil." *Tikkun*, Winter 2011.

Edmunds, R. David. *Always a People: Oral Histories of Contemporary Woodland Indians*. Bloomington: Indiana University Press, 1997.

Einstein, Albert. "On the Method of Theoretical Physics." *Philosophy of Science* 1(2) (1934): 163–69.

Eliot, T. S. *Four Quartets*. New York: Harcourt, 1943.

Emerson, Ralph Waldo. *The Complete Works of Ralph Waldo Emerson*. Vol. 2. Ed. Edward Waldo Emerson. Cambridge: Riverside Press, 1904.

——. *The Essential Writings of Ralph Waldo Emerson*. Ed. Brooks Atkinson. New York: Random House, 2000.

——. "Social Aims." In *Letters and Social Aims*. Rev. ed. Boston: James R. Osgood and Co., 1876.

Epictetus. *The Discourses of Epictetus with the Encheiridion and Fragments*. Trans. George Long. London: George Bell and Sons, 1909.

Epstein, David J. *The Sports Gene: Inside the Science of Extraordinary Athletic Performance*. New York: Penguin, 2013.

Fitzgerald, F. Scott. *The Crack-Up*. New York: New Directions, 2009.

Frankl, Viktor E. *Man's Search for Meaning*. 4th ed. Boston: Beacon Press, 1992.

Frazer, James. *The Golden Bough: A Study in Magic and Religion*. Vol. 3. London: Macmillan, 1900.

Frost, Robert. *Early Poems*. Ed. Robert Faggen. New York: Penguin, 1998.

Gaffney, Michael. *The Champ: My Year with Muhammad Ali*. New York: Diversion Books, 2012.

Galasso, Deborah. *Living Serenity*. Cicero, NY: 5 Fold Media, 2014.

Gandhi, Mahatma. *The Essential Gandhi: An Anthology of His Writings on His Life, Work, and Ideas*. 2nd ed. Ed. Louis Fischer. New York: Vintage, 2002.

Garnsey, Peter. "Child Rearing in Ancient Italy." In *The Family in Italy from Antiquity to the Present*. Ed. David I. Kertzer and Richard P. Saller. New Haven: Yale University Press, 1991.

Ghaemi, Nassir. "Depression in Command." *Wall Street Journal*, July 30, 2011.

Gomes, Peter J. Spring Commencement Address. University of North Carolina, May 15, 2005. alumni.unc.edu/article.aspx?SID=2608.

Greitens, Eric. *The Heart and the Fist*. Boston: Houghton Mifflin Harcourt, 2011.

——. *Strength and Compassion*. Washington, DC: Leading Authorities Press, 2008.

Hadot, Pierre. *Philosophy as a Way of Life*. Trans. Michael Chase. Malden, MA: Blackwell, 1995.

——. *What Is Ancient Philosophy?* Trans. Michael Chase. Cambridge: Harvard University Press, 2002.

Hamilton, Edith. *The Greek Way*. New York: W. W. Norton, 1993.

Hardy, James, et al. "A Descriptive Study of Athlete Self-Talk." *The Sport Psychologist* 15 (2001): 306–18.

Harrington, Richard. "The Drummer Who Beat a Path to the Height of Jazz Artistry." *Washington Post,* August 17, 2007.

Havel, Václav. *Disturbing the Peace.* New York: Vintage Books, 1991.

"He Ran and Ran and Ran." *The Times of India,* August 8, 2004.

Heidegger, Martin. *Being and Time: A Translation of* Sein und Zeit. Trans. Joan Stambaugh. Albany: State University of New York Press, 1996.

Hemingway, Ernest. *Death in the Afternoon.* New York: Charles Scribner's Sons, 1932.

——. *A Farewell to Arms.* New York: Charles Scribner's Sons, 1957.

——, ed. *Men at War: The Best War Stories of All Time.* New York: Crown, 1955.

Herodotus. *The History.* Trans. David Grene. Chicago: University of Chicago Press, 1987.

Heschel, Abraham Joshua. *The Sabbath: Its Meaning for Modern Man.* New York: Farrar, Straus and Young, 1951.

Hoffer, Eric. *The Passionate State of Mind and Other Aphorisms.* New York: Harper & Row, 1955.

——. *Reflections on the Human Condition.* New York: Harper & Row, 1973.

——. *The True Believer: Thoughts on the Nature of Mass Movements.* New York: HarperCollins, 2002.

Hugo, Victor. "Villemain." In *The Works of Victor Hugo in Twenty Volumes.* Vol. 14. New York: Jenson Society, 1907.

Humphries, Jefferson, ed. *Conversations with Reynolds Price.* Jackson, MS: University Press of Mississippi, 1991.

Ibn Gabirol, Solomon. *A Choice of Pearls.* Trans. Benjamin Henry Ascher. London: Trübner and Co., 1859.

Ignatius of Loyola. *The Spiritual Exercises of St. Ignatius: A New Translation.* Trans. Louis J. Puhl. Westminster, MD: Newman Press, 1951.

Jacks, Lawrence Pearsall. *Education Through Recreation.* London: University of London Press, 1931.

Jefferson, Thomas. Letter to John Adams, April 8, 1816. In *The Adams-Jefferson Letters: The Complete Correspondence Between Thomas Jefferson and Abigail and John Adams.* Ed. Lester J. Cappon. Chapel Hill: University of North Carolina Press, 1988.

Jerome, Fred, and Rodger Taylor. *Einstein on Race and Racism.* New Brunswick, NJ: Rutgers University Press, 2006.

Kaplan, Robert D. *Warrior Politics: Why Leadership Demands a Pagan Ethos.* New York: Random House, 2002.

——. "A Historian for Our Time." *The Atlantic,* January/February 2007.

Kashdan, T. B., et al. "Gratitude and Hedonic and Eudaimonic Well-Being in Vietnam War Veterans." *Behaviour Research and Therapy* 44(2) (2006): 177–99.

Kennedy, Robert F. Foreword to *Profiles in Courage* by John F. Kennedy. New York: HarperCollins, 2003.

Kierkegaard, Søren. *Purity of Heart Is to Will One Thing: Spiritual Preparation for the Office of Confession.* Trans. Douglas V. Steere. New York: Harper & Row, 1948.

Klein, Daniel. *Travels with Epicurus: A Journey to a Greek Island in Search of a Fulfilled Life.* New York: Penguin, 2012.

Klemperer, Paul. "Woodshedding and the Jazz Tradition." www.bigapplejazz.com /woodshedding.html.

Kleon, Austin. *Steal Like an Artist: 10 Things Nobody Told You about Being Creative.* New York: Workman Publishing, 2012.

Langworth, Richard, ed. *Churchill by Himself: The Definitive Collection of Quotations.* New York: Public Affairs, 2011.

Lattimore, Richmond, trans. *Greek Lyrics.* 2nd ed. Chicago: University of Chicago Press, 1960.

Lemay, J. A. Leo. *The Life of Benjamin Franklin.* Philadelphia: University of Pennsylvania Press, 2006–2009.

Leonardo da Vinci. *The Notebooks of Leonardo da Vinci.* Trans. Jean Paul Richter. Mineola, NY: Dover, 1970.

Lewis, C. S. *The Problem of Pain.* New York: Macmillan, 1959.

Lindsay of Pitscottie, Robert. *The History of Scotland from 1436 to 1565.* 2nd ed. Glasgow: R. Urie, 1749.

Luft, Joseph, and Harrington Ingham. "The Johari Window, a Graphic Model of Interpersonal Awareness." *Proceedings of the Western Training Laboratory in Group Development.* Los Angeles: UCLA, 1955.

MacCambridge, Michael, ed. *ESPN Sports Century.* New York: Hyperion, 1995.

Machiavelli, Niccolò. *The Prince.* Trans. Harvey C. Mansfield Jr. Chicago: University of Chicago Press, 1985.

——. *The Prince.* Trans. David Wootton. Indianapolis: Hackett Publishing Co., 1995.

——. *The Prince.* Trans. George Bull. London: Penguin, 2003.

MacIntyre, Alasdair C. *After Virtue: A Study in Moral Theory.* 2nd ed. Notre Dame, IN: University of Notre Dame Press, 1984.

Madison, James. "Federalist 51." In *The Federalist with the Letters of "Brutus."* Ed. Terence Ball. New York: Cambridge University Press, 2003.

Manchester, William. *The Last Lion: Winston Spencer Churchill, Visions of Glory, 1874–1932.* Boston: Little, Brown, 1983.

Marcus Aurelius. *The Emperor's Handbook: A New Translation of the Meditations.* Trans. C. Scot Hicks and David V. Hicks. New York: Scribner, 2002.

——. *Meditations.* Trans. George Long. Mineola, NY: Dover, 1997.

——. *Meditations.* Trans. Gregory Hays. New York: Modern Library, 2003.

——. *Meditations.* Trans. Martin Hammond. New York: Penguin, 2006.

Marlantes, Karl. *What It Is Like to Go to War.* New York: Atlantic Monthly Press, 2011.

McCullough, Michael, et al. "The Grateful Disposition: A Conceptual and Empirical Topography." *Journal of Personality and Social Psychology* 82(1) (2002): 112–27.

McDonald, Lynn, ed. *Florence Nightingale: An Introduction to Her Life and Family.* Waterloo, ON: Wilfrid Laurier University Press, 2001.

Menand, Louis. "Believer." *The New Yorker,* May 7, 2005.

Mill, John Stuart. *Utilitarianism.* London: Longmans, Green, and Co., 1879.

Montaigne, Michel de. *The Complete Essays of Montaigne.* Trans. Donald M. Frame. Stanford, CA: Stanford University Press, 1965.

———. *Essays of Montaigne.* Vols. 2, 4. Trans. Charles Cotton. Ed. William Carew Hazlitt. London: Reeves & Turner, 1902.

Morris, R., ed. and trans. *Old English Homilies.* London: Trübner and Co., 1868.

Morris, Thomas V. *The Stoic Art of Living: Inner Resilience and Outer Results.* Peru, IL: Carus Publishing, 2004.

Murray, William Hutchison. *The Scottish Himalayan Expedition.* London: J. M. Dent & Sons, 1951.

Nash, John F., Jr. "Autobiographical Essay." In *Les Prix Nobel 1994.* Ed. Tore Frängsmyr. Stockholm: Norstedts Tryckeri, 1995.

"The Necessity of Forgiveness: An Interview with Dr. Fred Luskin." PBS. www.pbs .org/kqed/onenight/stories/forgive.

Nhat Hanh, Thich. *Work: How to Find Joy and Meaning in Each Hour of the Day.* Berkeley, CA: Parallax Press, 2012.

Nietzsche, Friedrich. *Werke.* Trans. Pierre Hadot. Ed. Giorgio Colli and Mazzino Montinari. Berlin: De Gruyter, 1973.

Northern Securities Co. v. United States, 193 U.S. 197, 400 (1904), Justice Holmes dissenting.

Oakeshott, Michael. "Rationalism in Politics." In *Rationalism in Politics and Other Essays.* New York: Basic Books, 1962.

Oates, Joyce Carol. *On Boxing.* Garden City, NY: Dolphin/Doubleday, 1987.

Origen. *Contra Celsum.* Trans. Henry Chadwick. Cambridge, Eng.: Cambridge University Press, 1980.

Pagels, Elaine. *The Origin of Satan.* New York: Vintage Books, 1996.

Pascal, Blaise. *Lettres Provinciales.* Paris: Lefèvre et Brière, 1823.

Plato. *Phaedrus.* In *The Dialogues of Plato.* 3rd ed. Vol. 1. Trans. Benjamin Jowett. London: Oxford University Press, 1892.

———. *Theatetus.* In *Plato in Twelve Volumes.* Vol. 12. Trans. Harold N. Fowler. Cambridge: Harvard University Press, 1921.

Plotinus. *Enneads.* 2nd ed. Trans. Stephen MacKenna. New York: Pantheon, 1957.

Plutarch. "Cato the Younger." In *Plutarch's Lives.* Vol. 8. Trans. Bernadotte Perrin. Cambridge: Harvard University Press, 1919.

———. "How to Tell a Flatterer from a Friend." In *Plutarch's Morals.* Vol. 2. Trans. William Goodwin. Boston: Little, Brown, & Co., 1871.

Renault, Mary. *The Last of the Wine.* New York: Vintage, 2001.

Rilke, Rainer Maria. *Letters to a Young Poet.* New York: Norton, 1934.

Sargent, Clare. "Radley Hall School, 1819–1844." *The Victorian Web.* www.victorian web.org/history/education/radley/rhs.html.

Seneca, Lucius Annaeus. *Moral Epistles.* Vols. 1–3. Trans. Richard M. Gummere. Cambridge: Harvard University Press, 1917–1925.

———. *Moral Essays.* Vol. 1. Trans. John Basore. Cambridge: Harvard University Press, 1928.

Senesh, Hannah. *Hannah Senesh: Her Life and Diary, The First Complete Edition.* Woodstock, VT: Jewish Lights, 2007.

Shakespeare, William. *Henry V.* Ed. John Russell Brown. New York: Signet, 1998.

——. *Macbeth.* Ed. Sylvan Barnet. New York: Signet, 1998.

Shenk, Joshua Wolf. "Lincoln's Great Depression." *The Atlantic,* October 2005.

Solomon, Maynard. *Beethoven.* 2nd ed. New York: Schirmer, 1998.

Solzhenitsyn, Aleksandr. *The Gulag Archipelago, 1918–1956: An Experiment in Literary Investigation.* Parts 1–2. New York: Harper & Row, 1973.

Sophocles. *Philoktetes.* Trans. Seth L. Schein. Newburyport, MA: Focus, 2003.

Stern, Chaim, ed. *Gates of Prayer.* New York: CCAR Press, 1975.

——. *Gates of Repentance.* Rev. ed. New York: CCAR Press, 2004.

Stockdale, James Bond. *Courage Under Fire: Testing Epictetus's Doctrines in a Laboratory of Human Behavior.* Stanford, CA: Hoover Institution Press, 1993.

Strauss, Robert L. "Mind Over Misery." *Stanford,* September/October 2013.

Talukdar, S. P. *The Sakyans of South-East Asia.* New Delhi: Gyan, 2006.

Taylor, Charles. "What's Wrong with Negative Liberty." In *The Idea of Freedom.* Ed. Alan Ryan. Oxford: Oxford University Press, 1979.

Tetlock, Philip E. *Expert Political Judgment: How Good Is It? How Can We Know?* Princeton, NJ: Princeton University Press, 2005.

Thomas à Kempis. *The Imitation of Christ.* Milwaukee: Bruce Publishing Co., 1940.

Thoreau, Henry. *Walden.* Philadelphia: Courage, 1990.

Thucydides. *The Peloponnesian War.* Trans. Richard Crawley. Rev. ed. New York: Modern Library, 1982.

Trollope, Anthony. *Autobiography of Anthony Trollope.* New York: Dodd, Mead & Co., 1905.

Vardalos, Marianne, et al., eds. *Engaging Terror: A Critical and Interdisciplinary Approach.* Boca Raton, FL: Brown Walker, 2009.

Warren, Rick. *The Purpose-Driven Life: What on Earth Am I Here For?* Grand Rapids, MI: Zondervan, 2002.

Wenner, Melinda. "Smile! It Could Make You Happier." *Scientific American Mind,* September/October 2009.

West, M. L., ed. *Iambi et elegi graeci ante Alexandrum cantati.* Vol. 1. Oxford: Oxford University Press, 1971.

Whitman, Walt. "Song of Myself." In *The Complete Poems.* New York: Penguin, 1996.

Will-Weber, Mark, ed. *The Quotable Runner.* Halcottsville, NY: Breakaway, 2001.

Wills, Garry. *Certain Trumpets: The Call of Leaders.* New York: Simon & Schuster, 1994.

Wolfe, Tom. *The Right Stuff.* New York: Macmillan, 2008.

Wood, A. M., et al. "Coping Style as a Psychological Resource of Grateful People." *Journal of Social and Clinical Psychology* 26(9) (2007): 1076–93.

Wood, A. M., et al. "Gratitude Uniquely Predicts Satisfaction with Life: Incremental Validity above the Domains and Facets of the Five Factor Model." *Personality and Individual Differences* 45 (2008): 49–54.

Yeats, J. B. *Letters to His Son W. B. Yeats and Others, 1869–1922.* New York: E. P. Dutton & Co., 1946.